# NEED A LITTLE HELP?
# Call me.

### I'M HERE TO HELP

Stop banging your head against the wall! The LSAT and law school admissions aren't as mind-boggling as you might think. If there's a type of LSAT question that's bothering you, or you're really confused by the whole "sufficient vs. necessary" thing, or you want to know how to negotiate for law school scholarships... please let me help! I'm a nerd about this stuff, and I love to show students how easy it can be. Email me any time at **nathan@foxlsat.com**, or just pick up the phone. I'm generally available to talk between 9 am and 7 pm PST.

### ONLINE LSAT COURSE

If you like my books, I think you'll love my online LSAT class. It includes the exact same tests, quizzes, and lectures as my 12-week "Extended-Length" Class in San Francisco. Students pay $1495 for the 12-week classroom experience, but the class video is yours to watch and rewatch at your own pace from anywhere in the world for just $595. All materials included. And you're always encouraged to call or email me directly if you have any questions during the course. Like I said, I'm a nerd.

**www.foxlsat.com/online-lsat-course**

*No confusing jargon, no pulled punches, no bullshit.*
LSAT made simple.

---

 @nfox
 facebook.com/FoxTestPrep
 foxlsat.com/lsat-blog
 linkedin.com/in/foxlsat

# CALL NATHAN TODAY
# 415-518-0630

Copyright © 2012 by Nathan Fox

Design copyright © by Christopher
Imlay

Layout by Eric Uhlich

Published by Avocado Books, Los
Angeles, California

ISBN: 978-0-9838505-2-6

# Exposing The LSAT: The Fox Guide to a Real LSAT, Volume 3

**by Nathan Fox**

# TABLE OF **CONTENTS**

# Fox LSAT

www.foxlsat.com
372 West Portal Ave. #4
San Francisco, CA 94127
415-518-0630
nathan@foxlsat.com

**EXPOSING THE LSAT:
THE FOX GUIDE TO A
REAL LSAT, VOL. 3**

by Nathan Fox

# Welcome

## (or, "Exposing the LSAT")

The purpose of this book is to expose the LSAT's biggest secrets. Like the dirty old man in the trenchcoat, the LSAT can shock the unprepared. My goal with this book is to give you a peek beneath that trenchcoat, so that you can learn to see what's coming, long before it comes shuffling up the sidewalk. Once you've seen it, you really can't un-see it.

### Logic Games: Exposing the patterns
The LSAT isn't quite the one-trick pony that the flasher is, but it has far fewer tricks than most students imagine. As this book goes to press, the LSAC has released 65 LSATs—that's 260 different Logic Games available for you to study—but the overwhelming majority of these games fall into one of only two basic types: putting things in order, and putting things in groups. Those two operations simply aren't that hard, once you develop some basic techniques. Everyone struggles with Games at first, but this is actually the easiest, most learnable section of the test. You'll kick yourself when you see how easy it can be.

### Reading Comprehension: Exposing the big picture
The secret here is that there *is* no secret. Your goal is to read the passage and, um, comprehend it. Toss out whatever complicated strategies you may have learned somewhere else. Just read the passage and see if you can get the big picture. If you can just do that, you can answer at least half of the questions with relative ease. I'll show you how.

### Logical Reasoning: Exposing the bullshit
For me, this is the most fun section of the test. The arguments presented on the LSAT are almost always nonsense. Your first and most important task is simply to *argue*. If we can explain why the arguments are bullshit, then we can easily answer any question—frequently, we'll predict the answer to the question *before it's even been asked*.

# Meet Your Guide

I took the official LSAT in February 2007 and scored 179. Unfortunately, I then went to law school... I couldn't have hated it more. Extremely fortunately, I found LSAT teaching around the same time. It's a weird little niche–nobody grows up wanting to do what I do–but it's my niche. I'm good at it, I love it, and I get paid for it. Therefore, I never really work a single day in my life. I wish the same for you.

I like to write in bars. (Take heed, if you like the way I write and you need to crank out a law school personal statement.) Right now, I'm sitting in a bar on Clement Street. The 540 Club. It's 10:30 PM on a Monday, and I've never been here before. There's free wifi, and Speakeasy Prohibition on tap. It's a perfect spot for writing, provided you like rap music and you don't mind looking like a nerd. I definitely don't mind looking like a nerd. And I guess you don't either; after all, you're currently holding an LSAT book.

I'll be as honest as possible in the pages to come. So here are a few opening shots:

1) **This shit ain't for everybody.** Law school, and bar exams, and the legal profession, are hard. If you don't have strong English listening, speaking, reading, and writing skills, you should ask yourself whether this line of work—which is basically the modern-day Coliseum for English-language gladiators—is really the best fit for you.

2) **Grad school in the United States—especially law school— looks an awful lot like an economic bubble right now.** Tuitions and enrollments are both sky-high, and there are more grads than there are jobs waiting for them on the other side. If you know that your life won't be complete unless you become a lawyer, then law school is necessarily for you, and I will do my damndest to get you there. But if you don't know that law school is a part of your dream, then I will do my best to talk you out of it. If I succeed I will sleep soundly, knowing I have earned far more than what I charge.

3) **Thank you, from the bottom of my heart, for picking up this book.** If you've read this far, then I consider you my student. I am your humble servant, not only for the LSAT but also for the entire ordeal of application, and any career issues. My cell phone number is 415-518-0630, and my email address is nathan@foxlsat.com. I get far fewer questions than you might think. (This is my third book, and I still haven't been forced to change my contact info.) So try me—I'm here to help.

—San Francisco, June 4, 2012

# How To Use This Book

The fastest way to learn to ride a bike is to crash. A lot. The technique seems mysterious at first. How the hell do the other kids make it look so easy? You skin your knees, you shed a few tears, you get back up, and you try it one more time. And then one day—maybe when you're on the verge of giving up—you don't crash. Suddenly, before you even realize it, you're halfway down the block. You've done it!

And, of course, as soon as you realize this, you panic and you crash once more.

You never stop crashing, really. But the crashes become less and less frequent, until they're almost nonexistent. You're never a perfect rider, but you never stop getting better. The more you practice, the better you become.

The LSAT is exactly the same. There is no amount of abstract theory that can help you learn. (*The Theory of Bicycle Physics* would be worthless to a kid.) Instead, you need to try, and fail, and learn from your mistakes. That is the purpose of this book—with emphasis on the last part, of course.

The instructions are simple:
1. **Do one section of PrepTest 63.** Time yourself, 35 minutes per section. When time is up, check your answers.
2. **Read the strategy introduction.** At the beginning of each section, you'll find a brief primer on my general strategies for that set of questions.
3. **Read the explanations.** And *not* just for the ones you got wrong! The LSAT is notorious for allowing students to choose the right answer for the wrong reasons. (You might get it right this time, but you'll miss it next time.) The explanations in this book will help you avoid that pattern and answer future questions with more certainty.
4. **Repeat.**

Don't focus too intently on any one question. Perfection is not a useful, or even reasonable, goal on the LSAT. Time yourself, but remember that most people don't finish each section. Most people randomly guess on a few questions at the end of each section—there's no penalty for guessing. Focus on repeatedly nailing the easier questions instead of occasionally getting the harder ones correct, because some of the harder ones are so convoluted that little can be gained from studying them, something I'll point out in the explanations. (Easier questions tend to appear near the beginning of each section.)

The goal here is to try to eliminate your repeated, systematic mistakes. Eventually, just like riding a bike, you'll start to get a feel for it.

Until then, put 35 minutes on the clock—and have fun crashing.

# THE JUNE 2011 LSAT

SECTION I

Time—35 minutes

25 Questions

Directions: The questions in this section are based on the reasoning contained in brief statements or passages. For some questions, more than one of the choices could conceivably answer the question. However, you are to choose the best answer; that is, the response that most accurately and completely answers the question. You should not make assumptions that are by commonsense standards implausible, superfluous, or incompatible with the passage. After you have chosen the best answer, blacken the corresponding space on your answer sheet.

1. Backyard gardeners who want to increase the yields of their potato plants should try growing stinging nettles alongside the plants, since stinging nettles attract insects that kill a wide array of insect pests that damage potato plants. It is true that stinging nettles also attract aphids, and that many species of aphids are harmful to potato plants, but that fact in no way contradicts this recommendation, because _____.

Which one of the following most logically completes the argument?

(A) stinging nettles require little care and thus are easy to cultivate
(B) some types of aphids are attracted to stinging nettle plants but do not damage them
(C) the types of aphids that stinging nettles attract do not damage potato plants
(D) insect pests typically cause less damage to potato plants than other harmful organisms do
(E) most aphid species that are harmful to potato plants cause greater harm to other edible food plants

2. Jocko, a chimpanzee, was once given a large bunch of bananas by a zookeeper after the more dominant members of the chimpanzee's troop had wandered off. In his excitement, Jocko uttered some loud "food barks." The other chimpanzees returned and took the bananas away. The next day, Jocko was again found alone and was given a single banana. This time, however, he kept silent. The zookeeper concluded that Jocko's silence was a stratagem to keep the other chimpanzees from his food.

Which one of the following, if true, most seriously calls into question the zookeeper's conclusion?

(A) Chimpanzees utter food barks only when their favorite foods are available.
(B) Chimpanzees utter food barks only when they encounter a sizable quantity of food.
(C) Chimpanzees frequently take food from other chimpanzees merely to assert dominance.
(D) Even when they are alone, chimpanzees often make noises that appear to be signals to other chimpanzees.
(E) Bananas are a food for which all of the chimpanzees at the zoo show a decided preference.

3. A recent survey quizzed journalism students about the sorts of stories they themselves wished to read. A significant majority said they wanted to see stories dealing with serious governmental and political issues and had little tolerance for the present popularity of stories covering lifestyle trends and celebrity gossip. This indicates that today's trends in publishing are based on false assumptions about the interests of the public.

Which one of the following most accurately describes a flaw in the argument's reasoning?

(A) It takes what is more likely to be the effect of a phenomenon to be its cause.
(B) It regards the production of an effect as incontrovertible evidence of an intention to produce that effect.
(C) It relies on the opinions of a group unlikely to be representative of the group at issue in the conclusion.
(D) It employs language that unfairly represents those who are likely to reject the argument's conclusion.
(E) It treats a hypothesis as fact even though it is admittedly unsupported.

GO ON TO THE NEXT PAGE.

4. Electric bug zappers, which work by attracting insects to light, are a very effective means of ridding an area of flying insects. Despite this, most pest control experts now advise against their use, recommending instead such remedies as insect-eating birds or insecticide sprays.

Which one of the following, if true, most helps to account for the pest control experts' recommendation?

(A) Insect-eating birds will take up residence in any insect-rich area if they are provided with nesting boxes, food, and water.

(B) Bug zappers are less effective against mosquitoes, which are among the more harmful insects, than they are against other harmful insects.

(C) Bug zappers use more electricity but provide less light than do most standard outdoor light sources.

(D) Bug zappers kill many more beneficial insects and fewer harmful insects than do insect-eating birds and insecticide sprays.

(E) Developers of certain new insecticide sprays claim that their products contain no chemicals that are harmful to humans, birds, or pets.

5. Gardener: The design of Japanese gardens should display harmony with nature. Hence, rocks chosen for placement in such gardens should vary widely in appearance, since rocks found in nature also vary widely in appearance.

The gardener's argument depends on assuming which one of the following?

(A) The selection of rocks for placement in a Japanese garden should reflect every key value embodied in the design of Japanese gardens.

(B) In the selection of rocks for Japanese gardens, imitation of nature helps to achieve harmony with nature.

(C) The only criterion for selecting rocks for placement in a Japanese garden is the expression of harmony with nature.

(D) Expressing harmony with nature and being natural are the same thing.

(E) Each component of a genuine Japanese garden is varied.

6. Small experimental vacuum tubes can operate in heat that makes semiconductor components fail. Any component whose resistance to heat is greater than that of semiconductors would be preferable for use in digital circuits, but only if that component were also comparable to semiconductors in all other significant respects, such as maximum current capacity. However, vacuum tubes' maximum current capacity is presently not comparable to that of semiconductors.

If the statements above are true, which one of the following must also be true?

(A) Vacuum tubes are not now preferable to semiconductors for use in digital circuits.

(B) Once vacuum tubes and semiconductors have comparable maximum current capacity, vacuum tubes will be used in some digital circuits.

(C) The only reason that vacuum tubes are not now used in digital circuits is that vacuum tubes' maximum current capacity is too low.

(D) Semiconductors will always be preferable to vacuum tubes for use in many applications other than digital circuits.

(E) Resistance to heat is the only advantage that vacuum tubes have over semiconductors.

7. The cause of the epidemic that devastated Athens in 430 B.C. can finally be identified. Accounts of the epidemic mention the hiccups experienced by many victims, a symptom of no known disease except that caused by the recently discovered Ebola virus. Moreover, other symptoms of the disease caused by the Ebola virus are mentioned in the accounts of the Athenian epidemic.

Each of the following, if true, weakens the argument EXCEPT:

(A) Victims of the Ebola virus experience many symptoms that do not appear in any of the accounts of the Athenian epidemic.

(B) Not all of those who are victims of the Ebola virus are afflicted with hiccups.

(C) The Ebola virus's host animals did not live in Athens at the time of the Athenian epidemic.

(D) The Ebola virus is much more contagious than the disease that caused the Athenian epidemic was reported to have been.

(E) The epidemics known to have been caused by the Ebola virus are usually shorter-lived than was the Athenian epidemic.

GO ON TO THE NEXT PAGE.

8.  Letter to the editor: Your article was unjustified in criticizing environmentalists for claiming that more wolves on Vancouver Island are killed by hunters than are born each year. You stated that this claim was disproven by recent studies that indicate that the total number of wolves on Vancouver Island has remained roughly constant for 20 years. But you failed to account for the fact that, fearing the extinction of this wolf population, environmentalists have been introducing new wolves into the Vancouver Island wolf population for 20 years.

Which one of the following most accurately expresses the conclusion of the argument in the letter to the editor?

(A)  Environmentalists have been successfully maintaining the wolf population on Vancouver Island for 20 years.

(B)  As many wolves on Vancouver Island are killed by hunters as are born each year.

(C)  The population of wolves on Vancouver Island should be maintained by either reducing the number killed by hunters each year or introducing new wolves into the population.

(D)  The recent studies indicating that the total number of wolves on Vancouver Island has remained roughly constant for 20 years were flawed.

(E)  The stability in the size of the Vancouver Island wolf population does not warrant the article's criticism of the environmentalists' claim.

9.  Computer scientist: For several decades, the number of transistors on new computer microchips, and hence the microchips' computing speed, has doubled about every 18 months. However, from the mid-1990s into the next decade, each such doubling in a microchip's computing speed was accompanied by a doubling in the cost of producing that microchip.

Which one of the following can be properly inferred from the computer scientist's statements?

(A)  The only effective way to double the computing speed of computer microchips is to increase the number of transistors per microchip.

(B)  From the mid-1990s into the next decade, there was little if any increase in the retail cost of computers as a result of the increased number of transistors on microchips.

(C)  For the last several decades, computer engineers have focused on increasing the computing speed of computer microchips without making any attempt to control the cost of producing them.

(D)  From the mid-1990s into the next decade, a doubling in the cost of fabricating new computer microchips accompanied each doubling in the number of transistors on those microchips.

(E)  It is unlikely that engineers will ever be able to increase the computing speed of microchips without also increasing the cost of producing them.

GO ON TO THE NEXT PAGE.

10. Ms. Sandstrom's newspaper column describing a strange natural phenomenon on the Mendels' farm led many people to trespass on and extensively damage their property. Thus, Ms. Sandstrom should pay for this damage if, as the Mendels claim, she could have reasonably expected that the column would lead people to damage the Mendels' farm.

The argument's conclusion can be properly inferred if which one of the following is assumed?

(A) One should pay for any damage that one's action leads other people to cause if one could have reasonably expected that the action would lead other people to cause damage.

(B) One should pay for damage that one's action leads other people to cause only if, prior to the action, one expected that the action would lead other people to cause that damage.

(C) It is unlikely that the people who trespassed on and caused the damage to the Mendels' property would themselves pay for the damage they caused.

(D) Ms. Sandstrom knew that her column could incite trespassing that could result in damage to the Mendels' farm.

(E) The Mendels believe that Ms. Sandstrom is able to form reasonable expectations about the consequences of her actions.

11. Meyer was found by his employer to have committed scientific fraud by falsifying data. The University of Williamstown, from which Meyer held a PhD, validated this finding and subsequently investigated whether he had falsified data in his doctoral thesis, finding no evidence that he had. But the university decided to revoke Meyer's PhD anyway.

Which one of the following university policies most justifies the decision to revoke Meyer's PhD?

(A) Anyone who holds a PhD from the University of Williamstown and is found to have committed academic fraud in the course of pursuing that PhD will have the PhD revoked.

(B) No PhD program at the University of Williamstown will admit any applicant who has been determined to have committed any sort of academic fraud.

(C) Any University of Williamstown student who is found to have submitted falsified data as academic work will be dismissed from the university.

(D) Anyone who holds a PhD from the University of Williamstown and is found to have committed scientific fraud will have the PhD revoked.

(E) The University of Williamstown will not hire anyone who is under investigation for scientific fraud.

12. Aerobics instructor: Compared to many forms of exercise, kickboxing aerobics is highly risky. Overextending when kicking often leads to hip, knee, or lower-back injuries. Such overextension is very likely to occur when beginners try to match the high kicks of more skilled practitioners.

Which one of the following is most strongly supported by the aerobics instructor's statements?

(A) Skilled practitioners of kickboxing aerobics are unlikely to experience injuries from overextending while kicking.

(B) To reduce the risk of injuries, beginners at kickboxing aerobics should avoid trying to match the high kicks of more skilled practitioners.

(C) Beginners at kickboxing aerobics will not experience injuries if they avoid trying to match the high kicks of more skilled practitioners.

(D) Kickboxing aerobics is more risky than forms of aerobic exercise that do not involve high kicks.

(E) Most beginners at kickboxing aerobics experience injuries from trying to match the high kicks of more skilled practitioners.

13. A large company has been convicted of engaging in monopolistic practices. The penalty imposed on the company will probably have little if any effect on its behavior. Still, the trial was worthwhile, since it provided useful information about the company's practices. After all, this information has emboldened the company's direct competitors, alerted potential rivals, and forced the company to restrain its unfair behavior toward customers and competitors.

Which one of the following most accurately expresses the overall conclusion drawn in the argument?

(A) Even if the company had not been convicted of engaging in monopolistic practices, the trial probably would have had some effect on the company's behavior.

(B) The light shed on the company's practices by the trial has emboldened its competitors, alerted potential rivals, and forced the company to restrain its unfair behavior.

(C) The penalty imposed on the company will likely have little or no effect on its behavior.

(D) The company's trial on charges of engaging in monopolistic practices was worthwhile.

(E) The penalty imposed on the company in the trial should have been larger.

GO ON TO THE NEXT PAGE.

14. Waller: If there were really such a thing as extrasensory perception, it would generally be accepted by the public since anyone with extrasensory powers would be able to convince the general public of its existence by clearly demonstrating those powers. Indeed, anyone who was recognized to have such powers would achieve wealth and renown.

Chin: It's impossible to demonstrate anything to the satisfaction of all skeptics. So long as the cultural elite remains closed-minded to the possibility of extrasensory perception, the popular media reports, and thus public opinion, will always be biased in favor of such skeptics.

Waller's and Chin's statements commit them to disagreeing on whether

(A)    extrasensory perception is a real phenomenon
(B)    extrasensory perception, if it were a real phenomenon, could be demonstrated to the satisfaction of all skeptics
(C)    skeptics about extrasensory perception have a weak case
(D)    the failure of the general public to believe in extrasensory perception is good evidence against its existence
(E)    the general public believes that extrasensory perception is a real phenomenon

15. Counselor: Hagerle sincerely apologized to the physician for lying to her. So Hagerle owes me a sincere apology as well, because Hagerle told the same lie to both of us.

Which one of the following principles, if valid, most helps to justify the counselor's reasoning?

(A)    It is good to apologize for having done something wrong to a person if one is capable of doing so sincerely.
(B)    If someone tells the same lie to two different people, then neither of those lied to is owed an apology unless both are.
(C)    Someone is owed a sincere apology for having been lied to by a person if someone else has already received a sincere apology for the same lie from that same person.
(D)    If one is capable of sincerely apologizing to someone for lying to them, then one owes that person such an apology.
(E)    A person should not apologize to someone for telling a lie unless he or she can sincerely apologize to all others to whom the lie was told.

16. A survey of address changes filed with post offices and driver's license bureaus over the last ten years has established that households moving out of the city of Weston outnumbered households moving into the city two to one. Therefore, we can expect that next year's census, which counts all residents regardless of age, will show that the population of Weston has declined since the last census ten years ago.

Which one of the following, if true, most helps to strengthen the argument?

(A)    Within the past decade many people both moved into the city and also moved out of it.
(B)    Over the past century any census of Weston showing a population loss was followed ten years later by a census showing a population gain.
(C)    Many people moving into Weston failed to notify either the post office or the driver's license bureau that they had moved to the city.
(D)    Most adults moving out of Weston were parents who had children living with them, whereas most adults remaining in or moving into the city were older people who lived alone.
(E)    Most people moving out of Weston were young adults who were hoping to begin a career elsewhere, whereas most adults remaining in or moving into the city had long-standing jobs in the city.

17. Psychologist: People tend to make certain cognitive errors when they predict how a given event would affect their future happiness. But people should not necessarily try to rid themselves of this tendency. After all, in a visual context, lines that are actually parallel often appear to people as if they converge. If a surgeon offered to restructure your eyes and visual cortex so that parallel lines would no longer ever appear to converge, it would not be reasonable to take the surgeon up on the offer.

The psychologist's argument does which one of the following?

(A)    attempts to refute a claim that a particular event is inevitable by establishing the possibility of an alternative event
(B)    attempts to undermine a theory by calling into question an assumption on which the theory is based
(C)    argues that an action might not be appropriate by suggesting that a corresponding action in an analogous situation is not appropriate
(D)    argues that two situations are similar by establishing that the same action would be reasonable in each situation
(E)    attempts to establish a generalization and then uses that generalization to argue against a particular action

18. Principle: Even if an art auction house identifies the descriptions in its catalog as opinions, it is guilty of misrepresentation if such a description is a deliberate attempt to mislead bidders.

Application: Although Healy's, an art auction house, states that all descriptions in its catalog are opinions, Healy's was guilty of misrepresentation when its catalog described a vase as dating from the mid-eighteenth century when it was actually a modern reproduction.

Which one of the following, if true, most justifies the above application of the principle?

(A)    An authentic work of art from the mid-eighteenth century will usually sell for at least ten times more than a modern reproduction of a similar work from that period.

(B)    Although pottery that is similar to the vase is currently extremely popular among art collectors, none of the collectors who are knowledgeable about such pottery were willing to bid on the vase.

(C)    The stated policy of Healy's is to describe works in its catalogs only in terms of their readily perceptible qualities and not to include any information about their age.

(D)    Some Healy's staff members believe that the auction house's catalog should not contain any descriptions that have not been certified to be true by independent experts.

(E)    Without consulting anyone with expertise in authenticating vases, Healy's described the vase as dating from the mid-eighteenth century merely in order to increase its auction price.

19. Anthropologist: It was formerly believed that prehistoric *Homo sapiens* ancestors of contemporary humans interbred with Neanderthals, but DNA testing of a Neanderthal's remains indicates that this is not the case. The DNA of contemporary humans is significantly different from that of the Neanderthal.

Which one of the following is an assumption required by the anthropologist's argument?

(A)    At least some Neanderthals lived at the same time and in the same places as prehistoric *Homo sapiens* ancestors of contemporary humans.

(B)    DNA testing of remains is significantly less reliable than DNA testing of samples from living species.

(C)    The DNA of prehistoric *Homo sapiens* ancestors of contemporary humans was not significantly more similar to that of Neanderthals than is the DNA of contemporary humans.

(D)    Neanderthals and prehistoric *Homo sapiens* ancestors of contemporary humans were completely isolated from each other geographically.

(E)    Any similarity in the DNA of two species must be the result of interbreeding.

20. Council member: The profits of downtown businesses will increase if more consumers live in the downtown area, and a decrease in the cost of living in the downtown area will guarantee that the number of consumers living there will increase. However, the profits of downtown businesses will not increase unless downtown traffic congestion decreases.

If all the council member's statements are true, which one of the following must be true?

(A)    If downtown traffic congestion decreases, the number of consumers living in the downtown area will increase.

(B)    If the cost of living in the downtown area decreases, the profits of downtown businesses will increase.

(C)    If downtown traffic congestion decreases, the cost of living in the downtown area will increase.

(D)    If downtown traffic congestion decreases, the cost of living in the downtown area will decrease.

(E)    If the profits of downtown businesses increase, the number of consumers living in the downtown area will increase.

GO ON TO THE NEXT PAGE.

21. On the Discount Phoneline, any domestic long-distance call starting between 9 A.M. and 5 P.M. costs 15 cents a minute, and any other domestic long-distance call costs 10 cents a minute. So any domestic long-distance call on the Discount Phoneline that does not cost 10 cents a minute costs 15 cents a minute.

The pattern of reasoning in which one of the following arguments is most similar to that in the argument above?

(A) If a university class involves extensive lab work, the class will be conducted in a laboratory; otherwise, it will be conducted in a normal classroom. Thus, if a university class does not involve extensive lab work, it will not be conducted in a laboratory.

(B) If a university class involves extensive lab work, the class will be conducted in a laboratory; otherwise, it will be conducted in a normal classroom. Thus, if a university class is not conducted in a normal classroom, it will involve extensive lab work.

(C) If a university class involves extensive lab work, the class will be conducted in a laboratory; otherwise, it will be conducted in a normal classroom. Thus, if a university class is conducted in a normal classroom, it will not be conducted in a laboratory.

(D) If a university class involves extensive lab work, the class will be conducted in a laboratory; otherwise, it will be conducted in a normal classroom. Thus, if a university class involves extensive lab work, it will not be conducted in a normal classroom.

(E) If a university class involves extensive lab work, the class will be conducted in a laboratory; otherwise, it will be conducted in a normal classroom. Thus, if a university class is not conducted in a normal classroom, it will be conducted in a laboratory.

22. One child pushed another child from behind, injuring the second child. The first child clearly understands the difference between right and wrong, so what was done was wrong if it was intended to injure the second child.

Which one of the following principles, if valid, most helps to justify the reasoning in the argument?

(A) An action that is intended to harm another person is wrong only if the person who performed the action understands the difference between right and wrong.

(B) It is wrong for a person who understands the difference between right and wrong to intentionally harm another person.

(C) Any act that is wrong is done with the intention of causing harm.

(D) An act that harms another person is wrong if the person who did it understands the difference between right and wrong and did not think about whether the act would injure the other person.

(E) A person who does not understand the difference between right and wrong does not bear any responsibility for harming another person.

23. Researcher: Each subject in this experiment owns one car, and was asked to estimate what proportion of all automobiles registered in the nation are the same make as the subject's car. The estimate of nearly every subject has been significantly higher than the actual national statistic for the make of that subject's car. I hypothesize that certain makes of car are more common in some regions of the nation than in other regions; obviously, that would lead many people to overestimate how common their make of car is nationally. That is precisely the result found in this experiment, so certain makes of car must indeed be more common in some areas of the nation than in others.

Which one of the following most accurately expresses a reasoning flaw in the researcher's argument?

(A) The argument fails to estimate the likelihood that most subjects in the experiment did not know the actual statistics about how common their make of car is nationwide.

(B) The argument treats a result that supports a hypothesis as a result that proves a hypothesis.

(C) The argument fails to take into account the possibility that the subject pool may come from a wide variety of geographical regions.

(D) The argument attempts to draw its main conclusion from a set of premises that are mutually contradictory.

(E) The argument applies a statistical generalization to a particular case to which it was not intended to apply.

GO ON TO THE NEXT PAGE.

24. In university towns, police issue far more parking citations during the school year than they do during the times when the students are out of town. Therefore, we know that most parking citations in university towns are issued to students.

Which one of the following is most similar in its flawed reasoning to the flawed reasoning in the argument above?

(A) We know that children buy most of the snacks at cinemas, because popcorn sales increase as the proportion of child moviegoers to adult moviegoers increases.

(B) We know that this houseplant gets more of the sunlight from the window, because it is greener than that houseplant.

(C) We know that most people who go to a university are studious because most of those people study while they attend the university.

(D) We know that consumers buy more fruit during the summer than they buy during the winter, because there are far more varieties of fruit available in the summer than in the winter.

(E) We know that most of the snacks parents buy go to other people's children, because when other people's children come to visit, parents give out more snacks than usual.

25. Counselor: Those who believe that criticism should be gentle rather than harsh should consider the following: change requires a motive, and criticism that is unpleasant provides a motive. Since harsh criticism is unpleasant, harsh criticism provides a motive. Therefore, only harsh criticism will cause the person criticized to change.

The reasoning in the counselor's argument is most vulnerable to criticism on the grounds that the argument

(A) infers that something that is sufficient to provide a motive is necessary to provide a motive

(B) fails to address the possibility that in some cases the primary goal of criticism is something other than bringing about change in the person being criticized

(C) takes for granted that everyone who is motivated to change will change

(D) confuses a motive for doing something with a motive for avoiding something

(E) takes the refutation of an argument to be sufficient to show that the argument's conclusion is false

# S  T  O  P

IF YOU FINISH BEFORE TIME IS CALLED, YOU MAY CHECK YOUR WORK ON THIS SECTION ONLY.
DO NOT WORK ON ANY OTHER SECTION IN THE TEST.

SECTION II

Time—35 minutes

23 Questions

<u>Directions:</u> Each group of questions in this section is based on a set of conditions. In answering some of the questions, it may be useful to draw a rough diagram. Choose the response that most accurately and completely answers each question and blacken the corresponding space on your answer sheet.

Questions 1–5

Each of seven candidates for the position of judge—Hamadi, Jefferson, Kurtz, Li, McDonnell, Ortiz, and Perkins—will be appointed to an open position on one of two courts—the appellate court or the trial court. There are three open positions on the appellate court and six open positions on the trial court, but not all of them will be filled at this time. The judicial appointments will conform to the following conditions:

Li must be appointed to the appellate court.

Kurtz must be appointed to the trial court.

Hamadi cannot be appointed to the same court as Perkins.

1. Which one of the following is an acceptable set of appointments of candidates to courts?

(A)    appellate: Hamadi, Ortiz
      trial: Jefferson, Kurtz, Li, McDonnell, Perkins
(B)    appellate: Hamadi, Li, Perkins
      trial: Jefferson, Kurtz, McDonnell, Ortiz
(C)    appellate: Kurtz, Li, Perkins
      trial: Hamadi, Jefferson, McDonnell, Ortiz
(D)    appellate: Li, McDonnell, Ortiz
      trial: Hamadi, Jefferson, Kurtz, Perkins
(E)    appellate: Li, Perkins
      trial: Hamadi, Jefferson, Kurtz, McDonnell, Ortiz

2. Which one of the following CANNOT be true?

(A)    Hamadi and McDonnell are both appointed to the appellate court.
(B)    McDonnell and Ortiz are both appointed to the appellate court.
(C)    Ortiz and Perkins are both appointed to the appellate court.
(D)    Hamadi and Jefferson are both appointed to the trial court.
(E)    Ortiz and Perkins are both appointed to the trial court.

3. Which one of the following CANNOT be true?

(A)    Jefferson and McDonnell are both appointed to the appellate court.
(B)    Jefferson and McDonnell are both appointed to the trial court.
(C)    McDonnell and Ortiz are both appointed to the trial court.
(D)    McDonnell and Perkins are both appointed to the appellate court.
(E)    McDonnell and Perkins are both appointed to the trial court.

4. If Ortiz is appointed to the appellate court, which one of the following must be true?

(A)    Hamadi is appointed to the appellate court.
(B)    Jefferson is appointed to the appellate court.
(C)    Jefferson is appointed to the trial court.
(D)    Perkins is appointed to the appellate court.
(E)    Perkins is appointed to the trial court.

5. Which one of the following, if substituted for the condition that Hamadi cannot be appointed to the same court as Perkins, would have the same effect on the appointments of the seven candidates?

(A)    Hamadi and Perkins cannot both be appointed to the appellate court.
(B)    If Hamadi is not appointed to the trial court, then Perkins must be.
(C)    If Perkins is appointed to the same court as Jefferson, then Hamadi cannot be.
(D)    If Hamadi is appointed to the same court as Li, then Perkins must be appointed to the same court as Kurtz.
(E)    No three of Hamadi, Kurtz, Li, and Perkins can be appointed to the same court as each other.

GO ON TO THE NEXT PAGE.

## Questions 6–10

Exactly six members of a skydiving team—Larue, Ohba, Pei, Treviño, Weiss, and Zacny—each dive exactly once, one at a time, from a plane, consistent with the following conditions:

Treviño dives from the plane at some time before Weiss does.

Larue dives from the plane either first or last.

Neither Weiss nor Zacny dives from the plane last.

Pei dives from the plane at some time after either Ohba or Larue but not both.

6. Which one of the following could be an accurate list of the members in the order in which they dive from the plane, from first to last?

   (A)   Larue, Treviño, Ohba, Zacny, Pei, Weiss
   (B)   Larue, Treviño, Pei, Zacny, Weiss, Ohba
   (C)   Weiss, Ohba, Treviño, Zacny, Pei, Larue
   (D)   Treviño, Weiss, Pei, Ohba, Zacny, Larue
   (E)   Treviño, Weiss, Zacny, Larue, Pei, Ohba

7. Which one of the following must be true?

   (A)   At least two of the members dive from the plane after Larue.
   (B)   At least two of the members dive from the plane after Ohba.
   (C)   At least two of the members dive from the plane after Pei.
   (D)   At least two of the members dive from the plane after Treviño.
   (E)   At least two of the members dive from the plane after Weiss.

8. If Larue dives from the plane last, then each of the following could be true EXCEPT:

   (A)   Treviño dives from the plane fourth.
   (B)   Weiss dives from the plane fourth.
   (C)   Ohba dives from the plane fifth.
   (D)   Pei dives from the plane fifth.
   (E)   Zacny dives from the plane fifth.

9. If Zacny dives from the plane immediately after Weiss, then which one of the following must be false?

   (A)   Larue dives from the plane first.
   (B)   Treviño dives from the plane third.
   (C)   Zacny dives from the plane third.
   (D)   Pei dives from the plane fourth.
   (E)   Zacny dives from the plane fourth.

10. If Treviño dives from the plane immediately after Larue, then each of the following could be true EXCEPT:

    (A)   Ohba dives from the plane third.
    (B)   Weiss dives from the plane third.
    (C)   Zacny dives from the plane third.
    (D)   Pei dives from the plane fourth.
    (E)   Weiss dives from the plane fourth.

GO ON TO THE NEXT PAGE.

Questions 11–17

A company's six vehicles—a hatchback, a limousine, a pickup, a roadster, a sedan, and a van—are serviced during a certain week—Monday through Saturday—one vehicle per day. The following conditions must apply:

At least one of the vehicles is serviced later in the week than the hatchback.

The roadster is serviced later in the week than the van and earlier in the week than the hatchback.

Either the pickup and the van are serviced on consecutive days, or the pickup and the sedan are serviced on consecutive days, but not both.

The sedan is serviced earlier in the week than the pickup or earlier in the week than the limousine, but not both.

11. Which one of the following could be the order in which the vehicles are serviced, from Monday through Saturday?

(A)   the hatchback, the pickup, the sedan, the limousine, the van, the roadster
(B)   the pickup, the sedan, the van, the roadster, the hatchback, the limousine
(C)   the pickup, the van, the sedan, the roadster, the limousine, the hatchback
(D)   the van, the roadster, the pickup, the hatchback, the sedan, the limousine
(E)   the van, the sedan, the pickup, the roadster, the hatchback, the limousine

12. Which one of the following CANNOT be the vehicle serviced on Thursday?

(A)   the hatchback
(B)   the limousine
(C)   the pickup
(D)   the sedan
(E)   the van

13. If neither the pickup nor the limousine is serviced on Monday, then which one of the following must be true?

(A)   The hatchback and the limousine are serviced on consecutive days.
(B)   The hatchback and the sedan are serviced on consecutive days.
(C)   The van is serviced on Monday.
(D)   The limousine is serviced on Saturday.
(E)   The pickup is serviced on Saturday.

14. If the limousine is not serviced on Saturday, then each of the following could be true EXCEPT:

(A)   The limousine is serviced on Monday.
(B)   The roadster is serviced on Tuesday.
(C)   The hatchback is serviced on Wednesday.
(D)   The roadster is serviced on Wednesday.
(E)   The sedan is serviced on Wednesday.

15. If the sedan is serviced earlier in the week than the pickup, then which one of the following could be true?

(A)   The limousine is serviced on Wednesday.
(B)   The sedan is serviced on Wednesday.
(C)   The van is serviced on Wednesday.
(D)   The hatchback is serviced on Friday.
(E)   The limousine is serviced on Saturday.

16. If the limousine is serviced on Saturday, then which one of the following must be true?

(A)   The pickup is serviced earlier in the week than the roadster.
(B)   The pickup is serviced earlier in the week than the sedan.
(C)   The sedan is serviced earlier in the week than the roadster.
(D)   The hatchback and the limousine are serviced on consecutive days.
(E)   The roadster and the hatchback are serviced on consecutive days.

17. Which one of the following could be the list of the vehicles serviced on Tuesday, Wednesday, and Friday, listed in that order?

(A)   the pickup, the hatchback, the limousine
(B)   the pickup, the roadster, the hatchback
(C)   the sedan, the limousine, the hatchback
(D)   the van, the limousine, the hatchback
(E)   the van, the roadster, the limousine

GO ON TO THE NEXT PAGE.

Questions 18–23

A street entertainer has six boxes stacked one on top of the other and numbered consecutively 1 through 6, from the lowest box up to the highest. Each box contains a single ball, and each ball is one of three colors—green, red, or white. Onlookers are to guess the color of each ball in each box, given that the following conditions hold:

There are more red balls than white balls.

There is a box containing a green ball that is lower in the stack than any box that contains a red ball.

There is a white ball in a box that is immediately below a box that contains a green ball.

18. If there are exactly two white balls, then which one of the following boxes could contain a green ball?

(A)    box 1
(B)    box 3
(C)    box 4
(D)    box 5
(E)    box 6

19. If there are green balls in boxes 5 and 6, then which one of the following could be true?

(A)    There are red balls in boxes 1 and 4.
(B)    There are red balls in boxes 2 and 4.
(C)    There is a white ball in box 1.
(D)    There is a white ball in box 2.
(E)    There is a white ball in box 3.

20. The ball in which one of the following boxes must be the same color as at least one of the other balls?

(A)    box 2
(B)    box 3
(C)    box 4
(D)    box 5
(E)    box 6

21. Which one of the following must be true?

(A)    There is a green ball in a box that is lower than box 4.
(B)    There is a green ball in a box that is higher than box 4.
(C)    There is a red ball in a box that is lower than box 4.
(D)    There is a red ball in a box that is higher than box 4.
(E)    There is a white ball in a box that is lower than box 4.

22. If there are red balls in boxes 2 and 3, then which one of the following could be true?

(A)    There is a red ball in box 1.
(B)    There is a white ball in box 1.
(C)    There is a green ball in box 4.
(D)    There is a red ball in box 5.
(E)    There is a white ball in box 6.

23. If boxes 2, 3, and 4 all contain balls that are the same color as each other, then which one of the following must be true?

(A)    Exactly two of the boxes contain a green ball.
(B)    Exactly three of the boxes contain a green ball.
(C)    Exactly three of the boxes contain a red ball.
(D)    Exactly one of the boxes contains a white ball.
(E)    Exactly two of the boxes contain a white ball.

# S T O P

IF YOU FINISH BEFORE TIME IS CALLED, YOU MAY CHECK YOUR WORK ON THIS SECTION ONLY.
DO NOT WORK ON ANY OTHER SECTION IN THE TEST.

SECTION III
Time—35 minutes
27 Questions

Directions: Each set of questions in this section is based on a single passage or a pair of passages. The questions are to be answered on the basis of what is <u>stated</u> or <u>implied</u> in the passage or pair of passages. For some of the questions, more than one of the choices could conceivably answer the question. However, you are to choose the <u>best</u> answer; that is, the response that most accurately and completely answers the question, and blacken the corresponding space on your answer sheet.

In Alaska, tradition is a powerful legal concept, appearing in a wide variety of legal contexts relating to natural-resource and public-lands activities. Both state and federal laws in the United States assign
(5) privileges and exemptions to individuals engaged in "traditional" activities using otherwise off-limits land and resources. But in spite of its prevalence in statutory law, the term "tradition" is rarely defined. Instead, there seems to be a presumption that its
(10) meaning is obvious. Failure to define "tradition" clearly in written law has given rise to problematic and inconsistent legal results.

One of the most prevalent ideas associated with the term "tradition" in the law is that tradition is based
(15) on long-standing practice, where "long-standing" refers not only to the passage of time but also to the continuity and regularity of a practice. But two recent court cases involving indigenous use of sea otter pelts illustrate the problems that can arise in the application
(20) of this sense of "traditional."

The hunting of sea otters was initially prohibited by the Fur Seal Treaty of 1910. The Marine Mammal Protection Act (MMPA) of 1972 continued the prohibition, but it also included an Alaska Native
(25) exemption, which allowed takings of protected animals for use in creating authentic native articles by means of "traditional native handicrafts." The U.S. Fish and Wildlife Service (FWS) subsequently issued regulations defining authentic native articles as those
(30) "commonly produced" before 1972, when the MMPA took effect. Not covered by the exemption, according to the FWS, were items produced from sea otter pelts, because Alaska Natives had not produced such handicrafts "within living memory."
(35) In 1986, FWS agents seized articles of clothing made from sea otter pelts from Marina Katelnikoff, an Aleut. She sued, but the district court upheld the FWS regulations. Then in 1991 Katelnikoff joined a similar suit brought by Boyd Dickinson, a Tlingit from whom
(40) articles of clothing made from sea otter pelts had also been seized. After hearing testimony establishing that Alaska Natives had made many uses of sea otters before the occupation of the territory by Russia in the late 1700s, the court reconsidered what constituted a
(45) traditional item under the statute. The court now held that the FWS's regulations were based on a "strained interpretation" of the word "traditional," and that the reference to "living memory" imposed an excessively restrictive time frame. The court stated, "The fact that
(50) Alaskan natives were prevented, by circumstances beyond their control, from exercising a tradition for a

given period of time does not mean that it has been lost forever or that it has become any less a 'tradition.' It defies common sense to define 'traditional' in such
(55) a way that only those traditions that were exercised during a comparatively short period in history could qualify as 'traditional.'"

1. Which one of the following most accurately expresses the main point of the passage?

(A) Two cases involving the use of sea otter pelts by Alaska Natives illustrate the difficulties surrounding the application of the legal concept of tradition in Alaska.

(B) Two court decisions have challenged the notion that for an activity to be considered "traditional," it must be shown to be a long-standing activity that has been regularly and continually practiced.

(C) Two court cases involving the use of sea otter pelts by Alaska Natives exemplify the wave of lawsuits that are now occurring in response to changes in natural-resource and public-lands regulations.

(D) Definitions of certain legal terms long taken for granted are being reviewed in light of new evidence that has come from historical sources relating to Alaska Native culture.

(E) Alaskan state laws and U.S. federal laws are being challenged by Alaska Natives because the laws are not sufficiently sensitive to indigenous peoples' concerns.

GO ON TO THE NEXT PAGE.

2. The court in the 1991 case referred to the FWS's interpretation of the term "traditional" as "strained" (line 46) because, in the court's view, the interpretation

   (A) ignored the ways in which Alaska Natives have historically understood the term "traditional"
   (B) was not consonant with any dictionary definition of "traditional"
   (C) was inconsistent with what the term "traditional" is normally understood to mean
   (D) led the FWS to use the word "traditional" to describe a practice that should not have been described as such
   (E) failed to specify which handicrafts qualified to be designated as "traditional"

3. According to the passage, the court's decision in the 1991 case was based on which one of the following?

   (A) a narrow interpretation of the term "long-standing"
   (B) a common-sense interpretation of the phrase "within living memory"
   (C) strict adherence to the intent of FWS regulations
   (D) a new interpretation of the Fur Seal Treaty of 1910
   (E) testimony establishing certain historical facts

4. The passage most strongly suggests that the court in the 1986 case believed that "traditional" should be defined in a way that

   (A) reflects a compromise between the competing concerns surrounding the issue at hand
   (B) emphasizes the continuity and regularity of practices to which the term is applied
   (C) reflects the term's usage in everyday discourse
   (D) encourages the term's application to recently developed, as well as age-old, activities
   (E) reflects the concerns of the people engaging in what they consider to be traditional activities

5. Which one of the following is most strongly suggested by the passage?

   (A) Between 1910 and 1972, Alaska Natives were prohibited from hunting sea otters.
   (B) Traditional items made from sea otter pelts were specifically mentioned in the Alaska Native exemption of the MMPA.
   (C) In the late 1700s, Russian hunters pressured the Russian government to bar Alaska Natives from hunting sea otters.
   (D) By 1972, the sea otter population in Alaska had returned to the levels at which it had been prior to the late 1700s.
   (E) Prior to the late 1700s, sea otters were the marine animal most often hunted by Alaska Natives.

6. The author's reference to the Fur Seal Treaty (line 22) primarily serves to

   (A) establish the earliest point in time at which fur seals were considered to be on the brink of extinction
   (B) indicate that several animals in addition to sea otters were covered by various regulatory exemptions issued over the years
   (C) demonstrate that there is a well-known legal precedent for prohibiting the hunting of protected animals
   (D) suggest that the sea otter population was imperiled by Russian seal hunters and not by Alaska Natives
   (E) help explain the evolution of Alaska Natives' legal rights with respect to handicrafts defined as "traditional"

7. The ruling in the 1991 case would be most relevant as a precedent for deciding in a future case that which one of the following is a "traditional" Alaska Native handicraft?

   (A) A handicraft no longer practiced but shown by archaeological evidence to have been common among indigenous peoples several millennia ago
   (B) A handicraft that commonly involves taking the pelts of more than one species that has been designated as endangered
   (C) A handicraft that was once common but was discontinued when herd animals necessary for its practice abandoned their local habitat due to industrial development
   (D) A handicraft about which only a very few indigenous craftspeople were historically in possession of any knowledge
   (E) A handicraft about which young Alaska Natives know little because, while it was once common, few elder Alaska Natives still practice it

GO ON TO THE NEXT PAGE.

The literary development of Kate Chopin, author of *The Awakening* (1899), took her through several phases of nineteenth-century women's fiction. Born in 1850, Chopin grew up with the sentimental novels that

(5) formed the bulk of the fiction of the mid–nineteenth century. In these works, authors employed elevated, romantic language to portray female characters whose sole concern was to establish their social positions through courtship and marriage. Later, when she

(10) started writing her own fiction, Chopin took as her models the works of a group of women writers known as the local colorists.

After 1865, what had traditionally been regarded as "women's culture" began to dissolve as women

(15) entered higher education, the professions, and the political world in greater numbers. The local colorists, who published stories about regional life in the 1870s and 1880s, were attracted to the new worlds opening up to women, and felt free to move within these worlds

(20) as artists. Like anthropologists, the local colorists observed culture and character with almost scientific detachment. However, as "women's culture" continued to disappear, the local colorists began to mourn its demise by investing its images with mythic significance.

(25) In their stories, the garden became a paradisal sanctuary; the house became an emblem of female nurturing; and the artifacts of domesticity became virtual totemic objects.

Unlike the local colorists, Chopin devoted herself

(30) to telling stories of loneliness, isolation, and frustration. But she used the conventions of the local colorists to solve a specific narrative problem: how to deal with extreme psychological states without resorting to the excesses of the sentimental novels she read as a youth.

(35) By reporting narrative events as if they were part of a region's "local color," Chopin could tell rather shocking or even melodramatic tales in an uninflected manner.

Chopin did not share the local colorists' growing nostalgia for the past, however, and by the 1890s she

(40) was looking beyond them to the more ambitious models offered by a movement known as the New Women. In the form as well as the content of their work, the New Women writers pursued freedom and innovation. They modified the form of the sentimental

(45) novel to make room for interludes of fantasy and parable, especially episodes in which women dream of an entirely different world than the one they inhabit. Instead of the crisply plotted short stories that had been the primary genre of the local colorists, the New

(50) Women writers experimented with impressionistic methods in an effort to explore hitherto unrecorded aspects of female consciousness. In *The Awakening*, Chopin embraced this impressionistic approach more fully to produce 39 numbered sections of uneven

(55) length unified less by their style or content than by their sustained focus on faithfully rendering the workings of the protagonist's mind.

8. Which one of the following statements most accurately summarizes the content of the passage?

(A) Although Chopin drew a great deal of the material for *The Awakening* from the concerns of the New Women, she adapted them, using the techniques of the local colorists, to recapture the atmosphere of the novels she had read in her youth.

(B) Avoiding the sentimental excesses of novels she read in her youth, and influenced first by the conventions of the local colorists and then by the innovative methods of the New Women, Chopin developed the literary style she used in *The Awakening*.

(C) With its stylistic shifts, variety of content, and attention to the internal psychology of its characters, Chopin's *The Awakening* was unlike any work of fiction written during the nineteenth century.

(D) In *The Awakening*, Chopin rebelled against the stylistic restraint of the local colorists, choosing instead to tell her story in elevated, romantic language that would more accurately convey her protagonist's loneliness and frustration.

(E) Because she felt a kinship with the subject matter but not the stylistic conventions of the local colorists, Chopin turned to the New Women as models for the style she was struggling to develop in *The Awakening*.

9. With which one of the following statements about the local colorists would Chopin have been most likely to agree?

(A) Their idealization of settings and objects formerly associated with "women's culture" was misguided.

(B) Their tendency to observe character dispassionately caused their fiction to have little emotional impact.

(C) Their chief contribution to literature lay in their status as inspiration for the New Women.

(D) Their focus on regional life prevented them from addressing the new realms opening up to women.

(E) Their conventions prevented them from portraying extreme psychological states with scientific detachment.

GO ON TO THE NEXT PAGE.

10. According to the passage, which one of the following conventions did Chopin adopt from other nineteenth-century women writers?

    (A) elevated, romantic language
    (B) mythic images of "women's culture"
    (C) detached narrative stance
    (D) strong plot lines
    (E) lonely, isolated protagonists

11. As it is used by the author in line 14 of the passage, "women's culture" most probably refers to a culture that was expressed primarily through women's

    (A) domestic experiences
    (B) regional customs
    (C) artistic productions
    (D) educational achievements
    (E) political activities

12. The author of the passage describes the sentimental novels of the mid–nineteenth century in lines 3–9 primarily in order to

    (A) argue that Chopin's style represents an attempt to mimic these novels
    (B) explain why Chopin later rejected the work of the local colorists
    (C) establish the background against which Chopin's fiction developed
    (D) illustrate the excesses to which Chopin believed nostalgic tendencies would lead
    (E) prove that women's literature was already flourishing by the time Chopin began to write

13. The passage suggests that one of the differences between *The Awakening* and the work of the New Women was that *The Awakening*

    (A) attempted to explore aspects of female consciousness
    (B) described the dream world of female characters
    (C) employed impressionism more consistently throughout
    (D) relied more on fantasy to suggest psychological states
    (E) displayed greater unity of style and content

14. The primary purpose of the passage is to

    (A) educate readers of *The Awakening* about aspects of Chopin's life that are reflected in the novel
    (B) discuss the relationship between Chopin's artistic development and changes in nineteenth-century women's fiction
    (C) trace the evolution of nineteenth-century women's fiction using Chopin as a typical example
    (D) counter a claim that Chopin's fiction was influenced by external social circumstances
    (E) weigh the value of Chopin's novels and stories against those of other writers of her time

15. The work of the New Women, as it is characterized in the passage, gives the most support for which one of the following generalizations?

    (A) Works of fiction written in a passionate, engaged style are more apt to effect changes in social customs than are works written in a scientific, detached style.
    (B) Even writers who advocate social change can end up regretting the change once it has occurred.
    (C) Changes in social customs inevitably lead to changes in literary techniques as writers attempt to make sense of the new social realities.
    (D) Innovations in fictional technique grow out of writers' attempts to describe aspects of reality that have been neglected in previous works.
    (E) Writers can most accurately depict extreme psychological states by using an uninflected manner.

GO ON TO THE NEXT PAGE.

Until the 1950s, most scientists believed that the geology of the ocean floor had remained essentially unchanged for many millions of years. But this idea became insupportable as new discoveries were made.
(5) First, scientists noticed that the ocean floor exhibited odd magnetic variations. Though unexpected, this was not entirely surprising, because it was known that basalt—the volcanic rock making up much of the ocean floor—contains magnetite, a strongly magnetic
(10) mineral that was already known to locally distort compass readings on land. This distortion is due to the fact that although some basalt has so-called "normal" polarity—that is, the magnetite in it has the same polarity as the earth's present magnetic field—other
(15) basalt has reversed polarity, an alignment opposite that of the present field. This occurs because in magma (molten rock), grains of magnetite—behaving like little compass needles—align themselves with the earth's magnetic field, which has reversed at various
(20) times throughout history. When magma cools to form solid basalt, the alignment of the magnetite grains is "locked in," recording the earth's polarity at the time of cooling.

As more of the ocean floor was mapped, the
(25) magnetic variations revealed recognizable patterns, particularly in the area around the other great oceanic discovery of the 1950s: the global mid-ocean ridge, an immense submarine mountain range that winds its way around the earth much like the seams of a baseball.
(30) Alternating stripes of rock with differing polarities are laid out in rows on either side of the mid-ocean ridge: one stripe with normal polarity and the next with reversed polarity. Scientists theorized that mid-ocean ridges mark structurally weak zones where the ocean
(35) floor is being pulled apart along the ridge crest. New magma from deep within the earth rises easily through these weak zones and eventually erupts along the crest of the ridges to create new oceanic crust. Over millions of years, this process, called ocean floor spreading,
(40) built the mid-ocean ridge.

This theory was supported by several lines of evidence. First, at or near the ridge crest, the rocks are very young, and they become progressively older away from the crest. Further, the youngest rocks all
(45) have normal polarity. Finally, because geophysicists had already determined the ages of continental volcanic rocks and, by measuring the magnetic orientation of these same rocks, had assigned ages to the earth's recent magnetic reversals, they were able to compare
(50) these known ages of magnetic reversals with the ocean floor's magnetic striping pattern, enabling scientists to show that, if we assume that the ocean floor moved away from the spreading center at a rate of several centimeters per year, there is a remarkable correlation
(55) between the ages of the earth's magnetic reversals and the striping pattern.

16. Which one of the following most accurately expresses the main idea of the passage?

(A) In the 1950s, scientists refined their theories concerning the process by which the ocean floor was formed many millions of years ago.
(B) The discovery of basalt's magnetic properties in the 1950s led scientists to formulate a new theory to account for the magnetic striping on the ocean floor.
(C) In the 1950s, two significant discoveries led to the transformation of scientific views about the geology of the oceans.
(D) Local distortions to compass readings are caused, scientists have discovered, by magma that rises through weak zones in the ocean floor to create new oceanic crust.
(E) The discovery of the ocean floor's magnetic variations convinced scientists of the need to map the entire ocean floor, which in turn led to the discovery of the global mid-ocean ridge.

17. The author characterizes the correlation mentioned in the last sentence of the passage as "remarkable" in order to suggest that the correlation

(A) indicates that ocean floor spreading occurs at an extremely slow rate
(B) explains the existence of the global mid-ocean ridge
(C) demonstrates that the earth's magnetic field is considerably stronger than previously believed
(D) provides strong confirmation of the ocean floor spreading theory
(E) reveals that the earth's magnetic reversals have occurred at very regular intervals

18. According to the passage, which one of the following is true of magnetite grains?

(A) In the youngest basalt, they are aligned with the earth's current polarity.
(B) In magma, most but not all of them align themselves with the earth's magnetic field.
(C) They are not found in other types of rock besides basalt.
(D) They are about the size of typical grains of sand.
(E) They are too small to be visible to the naked eye.

GO ON TO THE NEXT PAGE.

19. If the time intervals between the earth's magnetic field reversals fluctuate greatly, then, based on the passage, which one of the following is most likely to be true?

    (A) Compass readings are most likely to be distorted near the peaks of the mid-ocean ridge.
    (B) It is this fluctuation that causes the ridge to wind around the earth like the seams on a baseball.
    (C) Some of the magnetic stripes of basalt on the ocean floor are much wider than others.
    (D) Continental rock is a more reliable indicator of the earth's magnetic field reversals than is oceanic rock.
    (E) Within any given magnetic stripe on the ocean floor, the age of the basalt does not vary.

20. Which one of the following would, if true, most help to support the ocean floor spreading theory?

    (A) There are types of rock other than basalt that are known to distort compass readings.
    (B) The ages of the earth's magnetic reversals have been verified by means other than examining magnetite grains in rock.
    (C) Pieces of basalt similar to the type found on the mid-ocean ridge have been found on the continents.
    (D) Along its length, the peak of the mid-ocean ridge varies greatly in height above the ocean floor.
    (E) Basalt is the only type of volcanic rock found in portions of the ocean floor nearest to the continents.

21. Which one of the following is most strongly supported by the passage?

    (A) Submarine basalt found near the continents is likely to be some of the oldest rock on the ocean floor.
    (B) The older a sample of basalt is, the more times it has reversed its polarity.
    (C) Compass readings are more likely to become distorted at sea than on land.
    (D) The magnetic fields surrounding magnetite grains gradually weaken over millions of years on the ocean floor.
    (E) Any rock that exhibits present-day magnetic polarity was formed after the latest reversal of the earth's magnetic field.

GO ON TO THE NEXT PAGE.

**Passage A**

Central to the historian's profession and scholarship has been the ideal of objectivity. The assumptions upon which this ideal rests include a commitment to the reality of the past, a sharp separation
(5) between fact and value, and above all, a distinction between history and fiction.

According to this ideal, historical facts are prior to and independent of interpretation: the value of an interpretation should be judged by how well it accounts
(10) for the facts; if an interpretation is contradicted by facts, it should be abandoned. The fact that successive generations of historians have ascribed different meanings to past events does not mean, as relativist historians claim, that the events themselves lack fixed
(15) or absolute meanings.

Objective historians see their role as that of a neutral judge, one who must never become an advocate or, worse, propagandist. Their conclusions should display the judicial qualities of balance and
(20) evenhandedness. As with the judiciary, these qualities require insulation from political considerations, and avoidance of partisanship or bias. Thus objective historians must purge themselves of external loyalties; their primary allegiance is to objective historical truth
(25) and to colleagues who share a commitment to its discovery.

**Passage B**

The very possibility of historical scholarship as an enterprise distinct from propaganda requires of its practitioners that self-discipline that enables them to
(30) do such things as abandon wishful thinking, assimilate bad news, and discard pleasing interpretations that fail elementary tests of evidence and logic.

Yet objectivity, for the historian, should not be confused with neutrality. Objectivity is perfectly
(35) compatible with strong political commitment. The objective thinker does not value detachment as an end in itself but only as an indispensable means of achieving deeper understanding. In historical scholarship, the ideal of objectivity is most compellingly embodied in
(40) the *powerful argument*—one that reveals by its every twist and turn its respectful appreciation of the alternative arguments it rejects. Such a text attains power precisely because its author has managed to suspend momentarily his or her own perceptions so as
(45) to anticipate and take into account objections and alternative constructions—not those of straw men, but those that truly issue from the rival's position, understood as sensitively and stated as eloquently as the rival could desire. To mount a telling attack on a
(50) position, one must first inhabit it. Those so habituated to their customary intellectual abode that they cannot even explore others can never be persuasive to anyone but fellow habitués.

Such arguments are often more faithful to the
(55) complexity of historical interpretation—more faithful even to the irreducible plurality of human perspectives— than texts that abjure position-taking altogether. The powerful argument is the highest fruit of the kind of thinking I would call objective, and in it neutrality

(60) plays no part. Authentic objectivity bears no resemblance to the television newscaster's mechanical gesture of allocating the same number of seconds to both sides of a question, editorially splitting the difference between them, irrespective of their perceived merits.

22. Both passages are concerned with answering which one of the following questions?

(A) What are the most serious flaws found in recent historical scholarship?
(B) What must historians do in order to avoid bias in their scholarship?
(C) How did the ideal of objectivity first develop?
(D) Is the scholarship produced by relativist historians sound?
(E) Why do the prevailing interpretations of past events change from one era to the next?

23. Both passages identify which one of the following as a requirement for historical research?

(A) the historian's willingness to borrow methods of analysis from other disciplines when evaluating evidence
(B) the historian's willingness to employ methodologies favored by proponents of competing views when evaluating evidence
(C) the historian's willingness to relinquish favored interpretations in light of the discovery of facts inconsistent with them
(D) the historian's willingness to answer in detail all possible objections that might be made against his or her interpretation
(E) the historian's willingness to accord respectful consideration to rival interpretations

GO ON TO THE NEXT PAGE.

24. The author of passage B and the kind of objective historian described in passage A would be most likely to disagree over whether

    (A) detachment aids the historian in achieving an objective view of past events

    (B) an objective historical account can include a strong political commitment

    (C) historians today are less objective than they were previously

    (D) propaganda is an essential tool of historical scholarship

    (E) historians of different eras have arrived at differing interpretations of the same historical events

25. Which one of the following most accurately describes an attitude toward objectivity present in each passage?

    (A) Objectivity is a goal that few historians can claim to achieve.

    (B) Objectivity is essential to the practice of historical scholarship.

    (C) Objectivity cannot be achieved unless historians set aside political allegiances.

    (D) Historians are not good judges of their own objectivity.

    (E) Historians who value objectivity are becoming less common.

26. Both passages mention propaganda primarily in order to

    (A) refute a claim made by proponents of a rival approach to historical scholarship

    (B) suggest that scholars in fields other than history tend to be more biased than historians

    (C) point to a type of scholarship that has recently been discredited

    (D) identify one extreme to which historians may tend

    (E) draw contrasts with other kinds of persuasive writing

27. The argument described in passage A and the argument made by the author of passage B are both advanced by

    (A) citing historical scholarship that fails to achieve objectivity

    (B) showing how certain recent developments in historical scholarship have undermined the credibility of the profession

    (C) summarizing opposing arguments in order to point out their flaws

    (D) suggesting that historians should adopt standards used by professionals in certain other fields

    (E) identifying what are seen as obstacles to achieving objectivity

# S T O P

SECTION IV

Time—35 minutes

26 Questions

<u>Directions:</u> The questions in this section are based on the reasoning contained in brief statements or passages. For some questions, more than one of the choices could conceivably answer the question. However, you are to choose the <u>best</u> answer; that is, the response that most accurately and completely answers the question. You should not make assumptions that are by commonsense standards implausible, superfluous, or incompatible with the passage. After you have chosen the best answer, blacken the corresponding space on your answer sheet.

1. Commentator: In last week's wreck involving one of Acme Engines' older locomotives, the engineer lost control of the train when his knee accidentally struck a fuel shut-down switch. Acme claims it is not liable because it never realized that the knee-level switches were a safety hazard. When asked why it relocated knee-level switches in its newer locomotives, Acme said engineers had complained that they were simply inconvenient. However, it is unlikely that Acme would have spent the $500,000 it took to relocate switches in the newer locomotives merely because of inconvenience. Thus, Acme Engines should be held liable for last week's wreck.

The point that Acme Engines spent $500,000 relocating knee-level switches in its newer locomotives is offered in the commentator's argument as

(A) proof that the engineer is not at all responsible for the train wreck
(B) a reason for believing that the wreck would have occurred even if Acme Engines had remodeled their older locomotives
(C) an explanation of why the train wreck occurred
(D) evidence that knee-level switches are not in fact hazardous
(E) an indication that Acme Engines had been aware of the potential dangers of knee-level switches before the wreck occurred

2. Artist: Almost everyone in this country really wants to be an artist even though they may have to work other jobs to pay the rent. After all, just about everyone I know hopes to someday be able to make a living as a painter, musician, or poet even if they currently work as dishwashers or discount store clerks.

The reasoning in the artist's argument is flawed in that the argument

(A) contains a premise that presupposes the truth of the conclusion
(B) presumes that what is true of each person in a country is also true of the country's population as a whole
(C) defends a view solely on the grounds that the view is widely held
(D) bases its conclusion on a sample that is unlikely to accurately represent people in the country as a whole
(E) fails to make a needed distinction between wanting to be an artist and making a living as an artist

3. The qwerty keyboard became the standard keyboard with the invention of the typewriter and remains the standard for typing devices today. If an alternative known as the Dvorak keyboard were today's standard, typists would type significantly faster. Nevertheless, it is not practical to switch to the Dvorak keyboard because the cost to society of switching, in terms of time, money, and frustration, would be greater than the benefits that would be ultimately gained from faster typing.

The example above best illustrates which one of the following propositions?

(A) Often it is not worthwhile to move to a process that improves speed if it comes at the expense of accuracy.
(B) People usually settle on a standard because that standard is more efficient than any alternatives.
(C) People often remain with an entrenched standard rather than move to a more efficient alternative simply because they dislike change.
(D) The emotional cost associated with change is a factor that sometimes outweighs financial considerations.
(E) The fact that a standard is already in wide use can be a crucial factor in making it a more practical choice than an alternative.

GO ON TO THE NEXT PAGE.

4. Sam: Mountain lions, a protected species, are preying on bighorn sheep, another protected species. We must let nature take its course and hope the bighorns survive.

 Meli: Nonsense. We must do what we can to ensure the survival of the bighorn, even if that means limiting the mountain lion population.

Which one of the following is a point of disagreement between Meli and Sam?

(A)  Humans should not intervene to protect bighorn sheep from mountain lions.

(B)  The preservation of a species as a whole is more important than the loss of a few individuals.

(C)  The preservation of a predatory species is easier to ensure than the preservation of the species preyed upon.

(D)  Any measures to limit the mountain lion population would likely push the species to extinction.

(E)  If the population of mountain lions is not limited, the bighorn sheep species will not survive.

5. Parent: Pushing very young children into rigorous study in an effort to make our nation more competitive does more harm than good. Curricula for these young students must address their special developmental needs, and while rigorous work in secondary school makes sense, the same approach in the early years of primary school produces only short-term gains and may cause young children to burn out on schoolwork. Using very young students as pawns in the race to make the nation economically competitive is unfair and may ultimately work against us.

Which one of the following can be inferred from the parent's statements?

(A)  For our nation to be competitive, our secondary school curriculum must include more rigorous study than it now does.

(B)  The developmental needs of secondary school students are not now being addressed in our high schools.

(C)  Our country can be competitive only if the developmental needs of all our students can be met.

(D)  A curriculum of rigorous study does not adequately address the developmental needs of primary school students.

(E)  Unless our nation encourages more rigorous study in the early years of primary school, we cannot be economically competitive.

6. A transit company's bus drivers are evaluated by supervisors riding with each driver. Drivers complain that this affects their performance, but because the supervisor's presence affects every driver's performance, those drivers performing best with a supervisor aboard will likely also be the best drivers under normal conditions.

Which one of the following is an assumption on which the argument depends?

(A)  There is no effective way of evaluating the bus drivers' performance without having supervisors ride with them.

(B)  The supervisors are excellent judges of a bus driver's performance.

(C)  For most bus drivers, the presence of a supervisor makes their performance slightly worse than it otherwise would be.

(D)  The bus drivers are each affected in roughly the same way and to the same extent by the presence of the supervisor.

(E)  The bus drivers themselves are able to deliver accurate assessments of their driving performance.

7. Economic growth accelerates business demand for the development of new technologies. Businesses supplying these new technologies are relatively few, while those wishing to buy them are many. Yet an acceleration of technological change can cause suppliers as well as buyers of new technologies to fail.

Which one of the following is most strongly supported by the information above?

(A)  Businesses supplying new technologies are more likely to prosper in times of accelerated technological change than other businesses.

(B)  Businesses that supply new technologies may not always benefit from economic growth.

(C)  The development of new technologies may accelerate economic growth in general.

(D)  Businesses that adopt new technologies are most likely to prosper in a period of general economic growth.

(E)  Economic growth increases business failures.

GO ON TO THE NEXT PAGE.

8. Energy analyst: During this record-breaking heat wave, air conditioner use has overloaded the region's electrical power grid, resulting in frequent power blackouts throughout the region. For this reason, residents have been asked to cut back voluntarily on air conditioner use in their homes. But even if this request is heeded, blackouts will probably occur unless the heat wave abates.

Which one of the following, if true, most helps to resolve the apparent discrepancy in the information above?

(A) Air-conditioning is not the only significant drain on the electrical system in the area.

(B) Most air-conditioning in the region is used to cool businesses and factories.

(C) Most air-conditioning systems could be made more energy efficient by implementing simple design modifications.

(D) Residents of the region are not likely to reduce their air conditioner use voluntarily during particularly hot weather.

(E) The heat wave is expected to abate in the near future.

9. Long-term and short-term relaxation training are two common forms of treatment for individuals experiencing problematic levels of anxiety. Yet studies show that on average, regardless of which form of treatment one receives, symptoms of anxiety decrease to a normal level within the short-term-training time period. Thus, for most people the generally more expensive long-term training is unwarranted.

Which one of the following, if true, most weakens the argument?

(A) A decrease in symptoms of anxiety often occurs even with no treatment or intervention by a mental health professional.

(B) Short-term relaxation training conducted by a more experienced practitioner can be more expensive than long-term training conducted by a less experienced practitioner.

(C) Recipients of long-term training are much less likely than recipients of short-term training to have recurrences of problematic levels of anxiety.

(D) The fact that an individual thinks that a treatment will reduce his or her anxiety tends, in and of itself, to reduce the individual's anxiety.

(E) Short-term relaxation training involves the teaching of a wider variety of anxiety-combating relaxation techniques than does long-term training.

10. Editorial: Many critics of consumerism insist that advertising persuades people that they need certain consumer goods when they merely desire them. However, this accusation rests on a fuzzy distinction, that between wants and needs. In life, it is often impossible to determine whether something is merely desirable or whether it is essential to one's happiness.

Which one of the following most accurately expresses the conclusion drawn in the editorial's argument?

(A) The claim that advertising persuades people that they need things that they merely want rests on a fuzzy distinction.

(B) Many critics of consumerism insist that advertising attempts to blur people's ability to distinguish between wants and needs.

(C) There is nothing wrong with advertising that tries to persuade people that they need certain consumer goods.

(D) Many critics of consumerism fail to realize that certain things are essential to human happiness.

(E) Critics of consumerism often use fuzzy distinctions to support their claims.

11. People who browse the web for medical information often cannot discriminate between scientifically valid information and quackery. Much of the quackery is particularly appealing to readers with no medical background because it is usually written more clearly than scientific papers. Thus, people who rely on the web when attempting to diagnose their medical conditions are likely to do themselves more harm than good.

Which one of the following is an assumption the argument requires?

(A) People who browse the web for medical information typically do so in an attempt to diagnose their medical conditions.

(B) People who attempt to diagnose their medical conditions are likely to do themselves more harm than good unless they rely exclusively on scientifically valid information.

(C) People who have sufficient medical knowledge to discriminate between scientifically valid information and quackery will do themselves no harm if they rely on the web when attempting to diagnose their medical conditions.

(D) Many people who browse the web assume that information is not scientifically valid unless it is clearly written.

(E) People attempting to diagnose their medical conditions will do themselves more harm than good only if they rely on quackery instead of scientifically valid information.

GO ON TO THE NEXT PAGE.

12. When adults toss balls to very young children they generally try to toss them as slowly as possible to compensate for the children's developing coordination. But recent studies show that despite their developing coordination, children actually have an easier time catching balls that are thrown at a faster speed.

Which one of the following, if true, most helps to explain why very young children find it easier to catch balls that are thrown at a faster speed?

(A) Balls thrown at a faster speed, unlike balls thrown at a slower speed, trigger regions in the brain that control the tracking of objects for self-defense.

(B) Balls that are tossed more slowly tend to have a higher arc that makes it less likely that the ball will be obscured by the body of the adult tossing it.

(C) Adults generally find it easier to catch balls that are thrown slowly than balls that are thrown at a faster speed.

(D) Children are able to toss balls back to the adults with more accuracy when they throw fast than when they throw the ball back more slowly.

(E) There is a limit to how fast the balls can be tossed to the children before the children start to have more difficulty in catching them.

13. Like a genetic profile, a functional magnetic-resonance image (fMRI) of the brain can contain information that a patient wishes to keep private. An fMRI of a brain also contains enough information about a patient's skull to create a recognizable image of that patient's face. A genetic profile can be linked to a patient only by referring to labels or records.

The statements above, if true, most strongly support which one of the following?

(A) It is not important that medical providers apply labels to fMRIs of patients' brains.

(B) An fMRI has the potential to compromise patient privacy in circumstances in which a genetic profile would not.

(C) In most cases patients cannot be reasonably sure that the information in a genetic profile will be kept private.

(D) Most of the information contained in an fMRI of a person's brain is also contained in that person's genetic profile.

(E) Patients are more concerned about threats to privacy posed by fMRIs than they are about those posed by genetic profiles.

14. Council member: I recommend that the abandoned shoe factory be used as a municipal emergency shelter. Some council members assert that the courthouse would be a better shelter site, but they have provided no evidence of this. Thus, the shoe factory would be a better shelter site.

A questionable technique used in the council member's argument is that of

(A) asserting that a lack of evidence against a view is proof that the view is correct

(B) accepting a claim simply because advocates of an opposing claim have not adequately defended their view

(C) attacking the proponents of the courthouse rather than addressing their argument

(D) attempting to persuade its audience by appealing to their fear

(E) attacking an argument that is not held by any actual council member

15. It was misleading for James to tell the Core Curriculum Committee that the chair of the Anthropology Department had endorsed his proposal. The chair of the Anthropology Department had told James that his proposal had her endorsement, but only if the draft proposal she saw included all the recommendations James would ultimately make to the Core Curriculum Committee.

The argument relies on which one of the following assumptions?

(A) If the chair of the Anthropology Department did not endorse James's proposed recommendations, the Core Curriculum Committee would be unlikely to implement them.

(B) The chair of the Anthropology Department would have been opposed to any recommendations James proposed to the Core Curriculum Committee other than those she had seen.

(C) James thought that the Core Curriculum Committee would implement the proposed recommendations only if they believed that the recommendations had been endorsed by the chair of the Anthropology Department.

(D) James thought that the chair of the Anthropology Department would have endorsed all of the recommendations that he proposed to the Core Curriculum Committee.

(E) The draft proposal that the chair of the Anthropology Department had seen did not include all of the recommendations in James's proposal to the Core Curriculum Committee.

GO ON TO THE NEXT PAGE.

16. Travaillier Corporation has recently hired employees with experience in the bus tour industry, and its executives have also been negotiating with charter bus companies that subcontract with bus tour companies. But Travaillier has traditionally focused on serving consumers who travel primarily by air, and marketing surveys show that Travaillier's traditional consumers have not changed their vacation preferences. Therefore, Travaillier must be attempting to enlarge its consumer base by attracting new customers.

Which one of the following, if true, would most weaken the argument?

(A) In the past, Travaillier has found it very difficult to change its customers' vacation preferences.

(B) Several travel companies other than Travaillier have recently tried and failed to expand into the bus tour business.

(C) At least one of Travaillier's new employees not only has experience in the bus tour industry but has also designed air travel vacation packages.

(D) Some of Travaillier's competitors have increased profits by concentrating their attention on their customers who spend the most on vacations.

(E) The industry consultants employed by Travaillier typically recommend that companies expand by introducing their current customers to new products and services.

17. Educator: Traditional classroom education is ineffective because education in such an environment is not truly a social process and only social processes can develop students' insights. In the traditional classroom, the teacher acts from outside the group and interaction between teachers and students is rigid and artificial.

The educator's conclusion follows logically if which one of the following is assumed?

(A) Development of insight takes place only if genuine education also occurs.

(B) Classroom education is effective if the interaction between teachers and students is neither rigid nor artificial.

(C) All social processes involve interaction that is neither rigid nor artificial.

(D) Education is not effective unless it leads to the development of insight.

(E) The teacher does not act from outside the group in a nontraditional classroom.

18. The probability of avoiding heart disease is increased if one avoids fat in one's diet. Furthermore, one is less likely to eat fat if one avoids eating dairy foods. Thus the probability of maintaining good health is increased by avoiding dairy foods.

The reasoning in the argument is most vulnerable to criticism on which one of the following grounds?

(A) The argument ignores the possibility that, even though a practice may have potentially negative consequences, its elimination may also have negative consequences.

(B) The argument fails to consider the possibility that there are more ways than one of decreasing the risk of a certain type of occurrence.

(C) The argument presumes, without providing justification, that factors that carry increased risks of negative consequences ought to be eliminated.

(D) The argument fails to show that the evidence appealed to is relevant to the conclusion asserted.

(E) The argument fails to consider that what is probable will not necessarily occur.

19. Professor: One cannot frame an accurate conception of one's physical environment on the basis of a single momentary perception, since each such glimpse occurs from only one particular perspective. Similarly, any history book gives only a distorted view of the past, since it reflects the biases and prejudices of its author.

The professor's argument proceeds by

(A) attempting to show that one piece of reasoning is incorrect by comparing it with another, presumably flawed, piece of reasoning

(B) developing a case for one particular conclusion by arguing that if that conclusion were false, absurd consequences would follow

(C) making a case for the conclusion of one argument by showing that argument's resemblance to another, presumably cogent, argument

(D) arguing that because something has a certain group of characteristics, it must also have another, closely related, characteristic

(E) arguing that a type of human cognition is unreliable in one instance because it has been shown to be unreliable under similar circumstances

GO ON TO THE NEXT PAGE.

20. To date, most of the proposals that have been endorsed by the Citizens League have been passed by the city council. Thus, any future proposal that is endorsed by the Citizens League will probably be passed as well.

The pattern of reasoning in which one of the following arguments is most similar to that in the argument above?

(A) Most of the Vasani grants that have been awarded in previous years have gone to academic biologists. Thus, if most of the Vasani grants awarded next year are awarded to academics, most of these will probably be biologists.

(B) Most of the individual trees growing on the coastal islands in this area are deciduous. Therefore, most of the tree species on these islands are probably deciduous varieties.

(C) Most of the editors who have worked for the local newspaper have not been sympathetic to local farmers. Thus, if the newspaper hires someone who is sympathetic to local farmers, they will probably not be hired as an editor.

(D) Most of the entries that were received after the deadline for last year's photography contest were rejected by the judges' committee. Thus, the people whose entries were received after the deadline last year will probably send them in well before the deadline this year.

(E) Most of the stone artifacts that have been found at the archaeological site have been domestic tools. Thus, if the next artifact found at the site is made of stone, it will probably be a domestic tool.

21. Chemist: The molecules of a certain weed-killer are always present in two forms, one the mirror image of the other. One form of the molecule kills weeds, while the other has no effect on them. As a result, the effectiveness of the weed-killer in a given situation is heavily influenced by which of the two forms is more concentrated in the soil, which in turn varies widely because local soil conditions will usually favor the breakdown of one form or the other. Thus, much of the data on the effects of this weed-killer are probably misleading.

Which one of the following, if true, most strengthens the chemist's argument?

(A) In general, if the molecules of a weed-killer are always present in two forms, then it is likely that weeds are killed by one of those two forms but unaffected by the other.

(B) Almost all of the data on the effects of the weed-killer are drawn from laboratory studies in which both forms of the weed-killer's molecules are equally concentrated in the soil and equally likely to break down in that soil.

(C) Of the two forms of the weed-killer's molecules, the one that kills weeds is found in most local soil conditions to be the more concentrated form.

(D) The data on the effects of the weed-killer are drawn from studies of the weed-killer under a variety of soil conditions similar to those in which the weed-killer is normally applied.

(E) Data on the weed-killer's effects that rely solely on the examination of the effects of only one of the two forms of the weed-killer's molecules will almost certainly be misleading.

GO ON TO THE NEXT PAGE.

22. Principle: A police officer is eligible for a Mayor's Commendation if the officer has an exemplary record, but not otherwise; an officer eligible for the award who did something this year that exceeded what could be reasonably expected of a police officer should receive the award if the act saved someone's life.

Conclusion: Officer Franklin should receive a Mayor's Commendation but Officer Penn should not.

From which one of the following sets of facts can the conclusion be properly drawn using the principle?

(A)  In saving a child from drowning this year, Franklin and Penn both risked their lives beyond what could be reasonably expected of a police officer. Franklin has an exemplary record but Penn does not.

(B)  Both Franklin and Penn have exemplary records, and each officer saved a child from drowning earlier this year. However, in doing so, Franklin went beyond what could be reasonably expected of a police officer; Penn did not.

(C)  Neither Franklin nor Penn has an exemplary record. But, in saving the life of an accident victim, Franklin went beyond what could be reasonably expected of a police officer. In the only case in which Penn saved someone's life this year, Penn was merely doing what could be reasonably expected of an officer under the circumstances.

(D)  At least once this year, Franklin has saved a person's life in such a way as to exceed what could be reasonably expected of a police officer. Penn has not saved anyone's life this year.

(E)  Both Franklin and Penn have exemplary records. On several occasions this year Franklin has saved people's lives, and on many occasions this year Franklin has exceeded what could be reasonably expected of a police officer. On no occasions this year has Penn saved a person's life or exceeded what could be reasonably expected of an officer.

23. Essayist: It is much less difficult to live an enjoyable life if one is able to make lifestyle choices that accord with one's personal beliefs and then see those choices accepted by others. It is possible for people to find this kind of acceptance by choosing friends and associates who share many of their personal beliefs. Thus, no one should be denied the freedom to choose the people with whom he or she will associate.

Which one of the following principles, if valid, most helps to justify the essayist's argument?

(A)  No one should be denied the freedom to make lifestyle choices that accord with his or her personal beliefs.

(B)  One should associate with at least some people who share many of one's personal beliefs.

(C)  If having a given freedom could make it less difficult for someone to live an enjoyable life, then no one should be denied that freedom.

(D)  No one whose enjoyment of life depends, at least in part, on friends and associates who share many of the same personal beliefs should be deliberately prevented from having such friends and associates.

(E)  One may choose for oneself the people with whom one will associate, if doing so could make it easier to live an enjoyable life.

24. Physician: The rise in blood pressure that commonly accompanies aging often results from a calcium deficiency. This deficiency is frequently caused by a deficiency in the active form of vitamin D needed in order for the body to absorb calcium. Since the calcium in one glass of milk per day can easily make up for any underlying calcium deficiency, some older people can lower their blood pressure by drinking milk.

The physician's conclusion is properly drawn if which one of the following is assumed?

(A)  There is in milk, in a form that older people can generally utilize, enough of the active form of vitamin D and any other substances needed in order for the body to absorb the calcium in that milk.

(B)  Milk does not contain any substance that is likely to cause increased blood pressure in older people.

(C)  Older people's drinking one glass of milk per day does not contribute to a deficiency in the active form of vitamin D needed in order for the body to absorb the calcium in that milk.

(D)  People who consume high quantities of calcium together with the active form of vitamin D and any other substances needed in order for the body to absorb calcium have normal blood pressure.

(E)  Anyone who has a deficiency in the active form of vitamin D also has a calcium deficiency.

GO ON TO THE NEXT PAGE.

25. Political philosopher: A just system of taxation would require each person's contribution to correspond directly to the amount the society as a whole contributes to serve that person's interests. For purposes of taxation, wealth is the most objective way to determine how well the society has served the interest of any individual. Therefore, each person should be taxed solely in proportion to her or his income.

The flawed reasoning in the political philosopher's argument is most similar to that in which one of the following?

(A) Cars should be taxed in proportion to the danger that they pose. The most reliable measure of this danger is the speed at which a car can travel. Therefore, cars should be taxed only in proportion to their ability to accelerate quickly.

(B) People should be granted autonomy in proportion to their maturity. A certain psychological test was designed to provide an objective measure of maturity. Therefore, those scoring above high school level on the test should be granted complete autonomy.

(C) Everyone should pay taxes solely in proportion to the benefits they receive from government. Many government programs provide subsidies for large corporations. Therefore, a just tax would require corporations to pay a greater share of their income in taxes than individual citizens pay.

(D) Individuals who confer large material benefits upon society should receive high incomes. Those with high incomes should pay correspondingly high taxes. Therefore, we as a society should place high taxes on activities that confer large benefits upon society.

(E) Justice requires that health care be given in proportion to each individual's need. Therefore, we need to ensure that the most seriously ill hospital patients are given the highest priority for receiving care.

26. A recent poll showed that almost half of the city's residents believe that Mayor Walker is guilty of ethics violations. Surprisingly, however, 52 percent of those surveyed judged Walker's performance as mayor to be good or excellent, which is no lower than it was before anyone accused him of ethics violations.

Which one of the following, if true, most helps to explain the surprising fact stated above?

(A) Almost all of the people who believe that Walker is guilty of ethics violations had thought, even before he was accused of those violations, that his performance as mayor was poor.

(B) In the time since Walker was accused of ethics violations, there has been an increase in the percentage of city residents who judge the performance of Walker's political opponents to be good or excellent.

(C) About a fifth of those polled did not know that Walker had been accused of ethics violations.

(D) Walker is currently up for reelection, and anticorruption groups in the city have expressed support for Walker's opponent.

(E) Walker has defended himself against the accusations by arguing that the alleged ethics violations were the result of honest mistakes by his staff members.

# S T O P

IF YOU FINISH BEFORE TIME IS CALLED, YOU MAY CHECK YOUR WORK ON THIS SECTION ONLY.
DO NOT WORK ON ANY OTHER SECTION IN THE TEST.

# COMPUTING YOUR SCORE

## Directions:

1. Use the Answer Key on the next page to check your answers.

2. Use the Scoring Worksheet below to compute your raw score.

3. Use the Score Conversion Chart to convert your raw score into the 120–180 scale.

### Scoring Worksheet

1. Enter the number of questions you answered correctly in each section.

|  | Number Correct |
|---|---|
| SECTION I................. | _____ |
| SECTION II................ | _____ |
| SECTION III.............. | _____ |
| SECTION IV ............. | _____ |

2. Enter the sum here: _____

**This is your Raw Score.**

### Conversion Chart
### For Converting Raw Score to the 120–180 LSAT Scaled Score
### LSAT Form 2LSN93

| Reported Score | Raw Score Lowest | Raw Score Highest |
|---|---|---|
| 180 | 100 | 101 |
| 179 | 99 | 99 |
| 178 | 98 | 98 |
| 177 | 97 | 97 |
| 176 | —* | —* |
| 175 | 96 | 96 |
| 174 | 95 | 95 |
| 173 | 94 | 94 |
| 172 | 93 | 93 |
| 171 | 92 | 92 |
| 170 | 90 | 91 |
| 169 | 89 | 89 |
| 168 | 88 | 88 |
| 167 | 86 | 87 |
| 166 | 85 | 85 |
| 165 | 83 | 84 |
| 164 | 82 | 82 |
| 163 | 80 | 81 |
| 162 | 78 | 79 |
| 161 | 77 | 77 |
| 160 | 75 | 76 |
| 159 | 73 | 74 |
| 158 | 71 | 72 |
| 157 | 69 | 70 |
| 156 | 67 | 68 |
| 155 | 66 | 66 |
| 154 | 64 | 65 |
| 153 | 62 | 63 |
| 152 | 60 | 61 |
| 151 | 58 | 59 |
| 150 | 56 | 57 |
| 149 | 54 | 55 |
| 148 | 53 | 53 |
| 147 | 51 | 52 |
| 146 | 49 | 50 |
| 145 | 47 | 48 |
| 144 | 46 | 46 |
| 143 | 44 | 45 |
| 142 | 42 | 43 |
| 141 | 41 | 41 |
| 140 | 39 | 40 |
| 139 | 38 | 38 |
| 138 | 36 | 37 |
| 137 | 35 | 35 |
| 136 | 33 | 34 |
| 135 | 32 | 32 |
| 134 | 30 | 31 |
| 133 | 29 | 29 |
| 132 | 28 | 28 |
| 131 | 27 | 27 |
| 130 | 25 | 26 |
| 129 | 24 | 24 |
| 128 | 23 | 23 |
| 127 | 22 | 22 |
| 126 | 21 | 21 |
| 125 | 20 | 20 |
| 124 | 19 | 19 |
| 123 | 18 | 18 |
| 122 | —* | —* |
| 121 | 17 | 17 |
| 120 | 0 | 16 |

*There is no raw score that will produce this scaled score for this form.

# ANSWER KEY

## SECTION I

| | | | | | | | |
|---|---|---|---|---|---|---|---|
| 1. | C | 8. | E | 15. | C | 22. | B |
| 2. | B | 9. | D | 16. | D | 23. | B |
| 3. | C | 10. | A | 17. | C | 24. | E |
| 4. | D | 11. | D | 18. | E | 25. | A |
| 5. | B | 12. | B | 19. | C | | |
| 6. | A | 13. | D | 20. | B | | |
| 7. | B | 14. | D | 21. | E | | |

## SECTION II

| | | | | | | | |
|---|---|---|---|---|---|---|---|
| 1. | E | 8. | C | 15. | A | 22. | C |
| 2. | B | 9. | D | 16. | B | 23. | D |
| 3. | A | 10. | A | 17. | B | | |
| 4. | C | 11. | B | 18. | B | | |
| 5. | E | 12. | E | 19. | C | | |
| 6. | B | 13. | C | 20. | E | | |
| 7. | D | 14. | E | 21. | A | | |

## SECTION III

| | | | | | | | |
|---|---|---|---|---|---|---|---|
| 1. | A | 8. | B | 15. | D | 22. | B |
| 2. | C | 9. | A | 16. | C | 23. | C |
| 3. | E | 10. | C | 17. | D | 24. | B |
| 4. | B | 11. | A | 18. | A | 25. | B |
| 5. | A | 12. | C | 19. | C | 26. | D |
| 6. | E | 13. | C | 20. | B | 27. | E |
| 7. | C | 14. | B | 21. | A | | |

## SECTION IV

| | | | | | | | |
|---|---|---|---|---|---|---|---|
| 1. | E | 8. | B | 15. | E | 22. | A |
| 2. | D | 9. | C | 16. | E | 23. | C |
| 3. | E | 10. | A | 17. | D | 24. | A |
| 4. | A | 11. | B | 18. | A | 25. | A |
| 5. | D | 12. | A | 19. | C | 26. | A |
| 6. | D | 13. | B | 20. | E | | |
| 7. | B | 14. | B | 21. | B | | |

# SECTION
# ONE

# Logical Reasoning

## (Or: Exposing the Bullshit)

The LSAT is simpler than you think it is. When you read an argument, and it doesn't seem to make sense to you, it's *not* because you're missing something. The arguments don't make sense *because they don't fucking make sense.* The arguments are often incomplete at best, and sometimes downright flawed. It's a *good* thing if most of them sound confusing to you. If they don't, then you're simply not being critical enough.

Your most important job on the Logical Reasoning section is to complete this sentence: "This argument is bullshit because _____." If you can fill in that blank, then you are well on your way to answering whatever question is asked. It doesn't matter if the question eventually asks you to strengthen the argument, or weaken it, or identify an assumption, or find a similar pattern of reasoning. We'll discuss each of these various types of questions (and more!) below, and I'll offer a few simple tricks for certain types. But most of the time, it all boils down to the same thing. You must *argue* with the speaker as you carefully read the argument. Listen closely, then tell him he's full of shit. The reason *why* he's full of shit is almost always directly related to the correct answer. Here we go.

# QUESTION 1:

Backyard gardeners who want to increase the yields of their potato plants should try growing stinging nettles alongside the plants, since stinging nettles attract insects that kill a wide array of insect pests that damage potato plants. It is true that stinging nettles also attract aphids, and that many species of aphids are harmful to potato plants, but that fact in no way contradicts this recommendation, because _____.

**Which one of the following most logically completes the argument?**

A) stinging nettles require little care and thus are easy to cultivate
B) some types of aphids are attracted to stinging nettle plants but do not damage them
C) the types of aphids that stinging nettles attract do not damage potato plants
D) insect pests typically cause less damage to potato plants than other harmful organisms do
E) most aphid species that are harmful to potato plants cause greater harm to other edible food plants

The June 2011 test starts off with a mystery. The LSAC calls this an "Explanation" question. The mystery we are supposed to explain is this: Stinging nettles are good for potato plants, because they attract insects that kill pests that damage potato plants. But stinging nettles also attract aphids, some species of which are themselves pests that damage potato plants. The argument ultimately concludes that farmers who want to increase their potato yields should still go ahead and plant stinging nettles—aphids be damned—because... wait, *why*? Well, let's fill in the blank: The argument is bullshit because *it says stinging nettles will attract aphids, but proceeds to recommend that farmers plant the nettles anyway*. If aphids are harmful, why the hell should potato farmers do something that will attract aphids?

We're asked to "logically complete" the argument, which means we need to make it make sense. My guess is that the aphids attracted by the stinging nettles are eaten up by the *other* insects attracted by the stinging nettles. If that's true, then the recommendation seems to be a logical one. Let's see.

A) This does nothing to explain why the aphids aren't a problem. No way.
B) Whether aphids harm stinging nettles or not is a distraction. The issue is: Are the aphids going to hurt the potatoes? This answer does nothing to tell us one way or the other.
C) Ohhhh, this could be it. The facts we were given said that *some species* of aphids damage potato plants. But if stinging nettles only attract species of aphids that do *not* damage potato plants, then potato farmers shouldn't worry about plant-ing stinging nettles. This is a good explanation of the mystery, so it's probably our answer.
D) Just because insect pests "typically cause less damage" than other organisms doesn't mean you'd *want* them around. This answer doesn't explain why farmers shouldn't worry about attracting aphids. Answer C was better.
E) Just because aphids cause *worse* damage to other plants (tomatoes, let's say) doesn't mean potato farmers wouldn't worry about the damage aphids cause to potatoes.

The best explanation for why potato farmers shouldn't worry about aphids attracted by stinging nettles was C. So C is our answer.

## QUESTION 2:

Jocko, a chimpanzee, was once given a large bunch of bananas by a zookeeper after the more dominant members of the chimpanzee's troop had wandered off. In his excitement, Jocko uttered some loud "food barks." The other chimpanzees returned and took the bananas away. The next day, Jocko was again found alone and was given a single banana. This time, however, he kept silent. The zookeeper concluded that Jocko's silence was a stratagem to keep the other chimpanzees from his food.

Which one of the following, if true, most seriously calls into question the zookeeper's conclusion?

A) Chimpanzees utter food barks only when their favorite foods are available.
B) Chimpanzees utter food barks only when they encounter a sizable quantity of food.
C) Chimpanzees frequently take food from other chimpanzees merely to assert dominance.
D) Even when they are alone, chimpanzees often make noises that appear to be signals to other chimpanzees.
E) Bananas are a food for which all of the chimpanzees at the zoo show a decided preference.

The zookeeper is a dumbass. It's possible that Jocko might have learned to shut up in order to keep the other chimps from stealing his food, but it's also possible that Jocko simply isn't as excited by a single banana as he was by a large bunch. The argument is bullshit because *Jocko might just be spoiled*. We're asked to find an answer that "seriously calls into question" the zookeeper's conclusion. The LSAC calls this a Weaken question. We're asked to find a piece of additional information that, if true, would cause the conclusion of the zookeeper's argument to fail. So I'm putting myself in the shoes of an attorney who is trying to disprove the zookeeper's conclusion that Jocko is learning. My dream answer would be "chimps only ever bark for large bunches of bananas." The answer might not be exactly that, but we'll see.

A) This is close, but no cigar. Jocko got the same food both times, so even if Answer A is true, then Jocko should have barked both times he got bananas (if they are his favorite) or neither time (if they are not). I want an answer that says Jocko is more excited about a higher *quantity* of food.
B) Oh, well lookie here. This is pretty much exactly what we were hoping for, so we've gotta love this answer. Let's scan Answers C–E, and hope they suck so that we can pick B.
C) So what? How is this relevant to whether Jocko is learning or not?
D) Again: So what? The issue isn't whether Jocko sometimes appears to signal other chimps, the issue is whether Jocko learned to shut up in order to keep his food.
E) And yet again: so what? This answer wouldn't weaken the idea that Jocko has learned to shut up.

B was the only answer that attacked the argument, and it did so very nicely. So B is our answer.

3

# QUESTION 3:

A recent survey quizzed journalism students about the sorts of stories they themselves wished to read. A significant majority said they wanted to see stories dealing with serious governmental and political issues and had little tolerance for the present popularity of stories covering lifestyle trends and celebrity gossip. This indicates that today's trends in publishing are based on false assumptions about the interests of the public.

Which one of the following most accurately describes a flaw in the argument's reasoning?

A)  It takes what is more likely to be the effect of a phenomenon to be its cause.
B)  It regards the production of an effect as incontrovertible evidence of an intention to produce that effect.
C)  It relies on the opinions of a group unlikely to be representative of the group at issue in the conclusion.
D)  It employs language that unfairly represents those who are likely to reject the argument's conclusion.
E)  It treats a hypothesis as fact even though it is admittedly unsupported.

The flaw here is a biased or unrepresentative sample. The argument is bullshit because *the survey was given to journalism students, but the conclusion was about the interests of the public.* I've been to journalism school, and I've never seen a bigger bunch of government/politics nerds. (Not even in law school.) The question asks us to identify a flaw in the reasoning, and that flaw is clearly something wrong with the sample—this flaw is tested all the time, so by the time you're ready to take the LSAT, this one should jump out at you. The correct answer will say something like "The argument uses a study about one narrow population to make a conclusion about a much broader population."

A)  Nah. This would be the answer if the argument had said, "Law students are poor, therefore being poor causes you to go to law school." This is a very common flaw on the LSAT, but it's not the flaw on this question.
B)  This would be the answer if the argument had said, "Law school makes you poor, therefore going to law school proves you want to be poor." This is a less common flaw on the LSAT, and it's not the flaw on this question.
C)  Unrepresentative sample? That's exactly what we were looking for. It's probably the correct answer.
D)  I don't think I've ever seen an LSAT question where this would be the correct answer. I suppose if the argument would have been something like "People who disagree are douchebags," then this would be the answer. I've never seen that on the test though.
E)  This would be the answer if the argument had said, "The Bible can't be proven to be fact, but it says homosexuality is a sin, therefore homosexuality is a sin." That's flawed logic, but it isn't the flaw found in this argument.

Our answer is C.

4

# QUESTION 4:

Electric bug zappers, which work by attracting insects to light, are a very effective means of ridding an area of flying insects. Despite this, most pest control experts now advise against their use, recommending instead such remedies as insect-eating birds or insecticide sprays.

Which one of the following, if true, most helps to account for the pest control experts' recommendation?

A) Insect-eating birds will take up residence in any insect-rich area if they are provided with nesting boxes, food, and water.
B) Bug zappers are less effective against mosquitoes, which are among the more harmful insects, than they are against other harmful insects.
C) Bug zappers use more electricity but provide less light than do most standard outdoor light sources.
D) Bug zappers kill many more beneficial insects and fewer harmful insects than do insect-eating birds and insecticide sprays.
E) Developers of certain new insecticide sprays claim that their products contain no chemicals that are harmful to humans, birds, or pets.

This is another Explanation question (like Question 1). We are asked to explain the following mystery: Why would pest control experts advise pest-eating birds or insecticide sprays instead of bug zappers, if bug zappers are "a very effective means of ridding an area of flying insects"? Well, I have a few ideas.

First, aren't those things dangerous? I have a crazy little cousin named Noah. He's two years old, and he thinks he's indestructible. Suppose Noah climbed up on a ladder and peed on the bug zapper, just for fun? (He *would* do this.) If Noah's around, maybe you might want to go with alternative pest control methods. That's one explanation.

Another explanation might have something to do with the fact that bug zappers first "attract insects to light." Aren't we supposed to be getting rid of insects? Suppose bug zappers work by attracting every bug in the neighborhood to your house, then killing any that come within an 18-inch area around the zapper—leaving the rest of your house full of mosquitoes. Would that be good? I don't think so.

The final potential explanation I have in mind has to do with the difference between "insects" and "flying insects." The facts say that the bug zapper attracts "insects" and then is effective at killing "flying insects." Does this mean that my house is going to be clear of mosquitoes but completely infested with roaches? I don't think I like the sound of that.

Any of these explanations would be a great answer. Or it might be something different. I love our predictions here, because even if they aren't exactly right they'll help us more quickly dismiss answer choices that don't explain anything.

A) This doesn't explain why birds are better than the bug zapper. Actually, this makes it sound like birds are a pain in the ass. No way.
B) Hmm. I can make a case for this answer, but it also feels like a trap. My problem with this answer is that the facts say the zappers are "very effective means of ridding an area of flying insects." That means they have to be very effective against mosquitoes, even if they are, as B proposes, "less effective" than they are against other insects. I'll only choose B if the rest of the answers are horrible.
C) This may be true, and maybe I want to conserve, and maybe I want more light on my porch, but what I'm really interested in here is *killing bugs*. The mystery was "Why do pest control experts recommend other methods over bug zappers?" This doesn't seem to address the pest control issue at all, so I don't think this can be it.
D) Okay, I like this answer. If this is true, then your bug zapper might kill every ladybug in the neighborhood. If ladybugs are good at eating the aphids on your tomato plants, then maybe you'd prefer to use birds or sprays instead of the bug zapper. This wasn't what we predicted, but it addressed the mystery in the same way that our predictions did. This answer is best so far.
E) If this answer went a bit further and said "...and bug zappers *are* harmful to humans, birds, and pets," then it would be pretty good. But as is, it's an incomplete answer. D is our answer.

This was an interesting question, because I can definitely see how B, C, or E could have been the best answer if the rest of the answers really sucked. But we were asked to identify the answer that "most helped" to explain the mystery, and that answer was D.

# QUESTION 5:

Gardener: The design of Japanese gardens should display harmony with nature. Hence, rocks chosen for placement in such gardens should vary widely in appearance, since rocks found in nature also vary widely in appearance.

**The gardener's argument depends on assuming which one of the following?**

A) The selection of rocks for placement in a Japanese garden should reflect every key value embodied in the design of Japanese gardens.
B) In the selection of rocks for Japanese gardens, imitation of nature helps to achieve harmony with nature.
C) The only criterion for selecting rocks for placement in a Japanese garden is the expression of harmony with nature.
D) Expressing harmony with nature and being natural are the same thing.
E) Each component of a genuine Japanese garden is varied.

Um, don't most of the rocks in any given piece of nature look mostly the same? Like Yosemite is mostly granite, and Hawaii is mostly lava, and the Grand Canyon is mostly... that reddish shit? Would it really make sense to have granite and lava and... that reddish shit... all in one Japanese garden? Sounds like a mess to me.

The question asks us to identify an assumption that the argument "depends on." This is one way of describing what the LSAC calls a "Necessary Assumption." We're looking for something that has to be true in order for the conclusion of the argument to be true. In other words the correct answer, if untrue, will cause the argument to fail. If the correct answer is related to our objection, above, it will look something like, "To display harmony with nature, one must have all the elements of nature all at once." I think that's a *necessary assumption* of the argument because if it is *not* true, then why does a Japanese garden have to have different types of rock?

A) This isn't the answer, because "every key value" is not at issue here. Only one key value—"harmony with nature"—was discussed by the argument. Even if A is not true, it could still be true that the "harmony with nature" value should be followed. Therefore A is not *necessary* to the argument.
B) This is not what we predicted, but I like it anyway. If B is untrue, this answer becomes, "Imitation of nature does not help to achieve harmony of nature." And if *that's* true, then the fact that nature has many types of rocks would be no justification for putting many kinds of rocks into a Japanese garden. Therefore I think Answer B's "imitation helps achieve harmony" is a necessary assumption of the argument. I like it so far.
C) No way. There could be plenty of other considerations. Cost, for example. Weight. Size. Etcetera. The argument would still make sense even if harmony were not the *only* criterion. So C is not necessary.
D) This answer proves too much. The gardener did not claim that the Japanese garden had to actually *be* nature, only that it had to *display harmony* with nature. If D is untrue, this answer becomes, "Expressing harmony with nature and being natural are not the same thing." That wouldn't destroy the gardener's argument—the gardener would probably say, "Yeah, no shit." Therefore D is not necessary.
E) Again, this answer proves too much. Nobody said the sand, for example, had to be varied. If E is untrue, this answer becomes, "Not every component of a Japanese garden is varied." That wouldn't destroy the gardener's argument—again, the gardener would probably say "No shit." Therefore E is not necessary.

B did not exactly match our prediction, but if it is not true it really hurts the argument. Therefore we can say B is *necessary*, and it's our answer.

## QUESTION 6:

Small experimental vacuum tubes can operate in heat that makes semiconductor components fail. Any component whose resistance to heat is greater than that of semiconductors would be preferable for use in digital circuits, but only if that component were also comparable to semiconductors in all other significant respects, such as maximum current capacity. However, vacuum tubes' maximum current capacity is presently not comparable to that of semiconductors.

If the statements above are true, which one of the following must also be true?

A) Vacuum tubes are not now preferable to semiconductors for use in digital circuits.
B) Once vacuum tubes and semiconductors have comparable maximum current capacity, vacuum tubes will be used in some digital circuits.
C) The only reason that vacuum tubes are not now used in digital circuits is that vacuum tubes' maximum current capacity is too low.
D) Semiconductors will always be preferable to vacuum tubes for use in many applications other than digital circuits.
E) Resistance to heat is the only advantage that vacuum tubes have over semiconductors.

There's really no "argument" here, because I don't see a conclusion. However, I do think the premises would *justify* (*i.e.* prove) a conclusion. Let's put the pieces together: If it's true that digital circuits require components that are comparable to semiconductors in maximum current capacity (second sentence), and if it's also true that vacuum tubes' maximum current capacity is presently not comparable to that of semiconductors (third sentence), then it *must* also be true vacuum tubes are presently not preferable for use in digital circuits. Even though the passage didn't actually state this conclusion, it definitely implied it.

The question asks us to find a statement that must be true according to the facts we were given. The correct answer on this type of question does not *have* to be the conclusion of the argument, but I won't be surprised if it is. Let's see.

## Weird Science

It's worth noting that there is not a damn bit of scientific knowledge required to answer this question. It's actually one of the easiest questions in this section, as long as you don't let the scientific-sounding terms scare you off. There is no science on the LSAT—only stuff that looks like science. "Vacuum tubes" and "current capacity" don't have to mean anything to you to get this one right. They mean nothing to me.

A) This seems pretty good to me. It's a lot like what we predicted. We should be happy with A if the other answers are weak.
B) This is a prediction about the future that is simply not justified by the facts we were given. Answer A *must* be true according to the facts. Answer B is, at best, *probably* true—and we could even argue about that. A was better.
C) This doesn't have to be true, because there can be lots of things wrong with a component. Maybe they are too big, too expensive, too heavy, too hard to manufacture, too hard to install. We simply don't know. Answer A was proven by the given facts, but C is speculative. Answer A is still the best so far.
D) This may currently be the case, because vacuum tubes don't presently have enough maximum current capacity. But it's purely speculative to predict that this will *always* be the case. No way.
E) This answer is an analogue of C. Like C, it doesn't have to be true, because there can be lots of advantages to a component. Maybe they are small, and cheap, and light, and easy to manufacture, and easy to install. We simply don't know.

The only answer that is proven by the given facts is A, so that's our answer.

# QUESTION 7:

The cause of the epidemic that devastated Athens in 430 B.C. can finally be identified. Accounts of the epidemic mention the hiccups experienced by many victims, a symptom of no known disease except that caused by the recently discovered Ebola virus. Moreover, other symptoms of the disease caused by the Ebola virus are mentioned in the accounts of the Athenian epidemic.

Each of the following, if true, weakens the argument EXCEPT:

A) Victims of the Ebola virus experience many symptoms that do not appear in any of the accounts of the Athenian epidemic.
B) Not all of those who are victims of the Ebola virus are afflicted with hiccups.
C) The Ebola virus's host animals did not live in Athens at the time of the Athenian epidemic.
D) The Ebola virus is much more contagious than the disease that caused the Athenian epidemic was reported to have been.
E) The epidemics known to have been caused by the Ebola virus are usually shorter-lived than was the Athenian epidemic.

This argument simultaneously violates two of the most-commonly violated LSAT Ten Commandments. The first is The Arrow Only Goes One Way: The second and third sentences of the argument claim that Ebola has certain symptoms, including hiccups. So Ebola → hiccups (and other symptoms). The proper contrapositive here (reverse the terms and negate the terms) would have been ~~Hiccups (and other symptoms)~~ → ~~Ebola~~. But the argument instead concludes, on the basis that the Athenians were known to have hiccups (and other Ebola-like symptoms), that the Athenians had Ebola. In other words, they simply (and stupidly) turned the arrow around without negating: Hiccups (and other symptoms) → Ebola. Did they do that? Yes they did. The problem with this reasoning is that lots of stuff, like too much Athens Light Beer, can cause hiccups. As for the other unnamed symptoms, I think it's safe to assume that we could invent plenty of unnamed alternate causes for those as well. So this argument confuses a necessary condition for a sufficient condition. *Please see the next page for an explanation of the difference between necessary and sufficient.*

In doing so, the argument also violates another commandment: Thou Shalt Not Confuse Correlation With Causation. Even if victims of the epidemic did have Ebola-like symptoms (correlation), that doesn't mean Ebola *caused* their symptoms. It's possible that some other cause made it look like they had Ebola, or even if they did have Ebola (correlation) it's possible that Ebola didn't *cause* the epidemic. This should be a very easy argument to weaken.

The question uses EXCEPT, so it's telling us that the four incorrect answer choices will each weaken the argument. The one correct answer will either strengthen the argument or be irrelevant.

A) This is a pretty sad weakener, because you don't have to have all the symptoms of a disease to have that disease. Furthermore, maybe the victims *did* have all the Ebola symptoms but the symptoms just didn't get recorded on the stone tablets or whatever. I do see how this answer choice hurts the conclusion slightly, but it doesn't hurt it a lot. So this could be the answer on an EXCEPT question, unless we find something even sorrier.
B) I think this is even worse than A. This one is like trying to say "not all gunshot victims die, so if you die then you weren't a gunshot victim." (Obviously wrong, because you could have been eaten by a tiger at the zoo.) This answer choice is especially pathetic because the second sentence in the argument says "many" of the victims had hiccups, which seems to leave open the possibility that not all victims had hiccups. This could be it.
C) This is a decent weakener, because it undermines the possibility that Ebola could have been present in Athens at that time. So this is out.

D) This is a tricky answer to get past. At first blush, it looks like a strengthener (Ebola is nasty, so the epidemic must have been Ebola!), but it's really a fairly good weakener, because if the reported epidemic wasn't as contagious as Ebola, then that's a *difference* between the epidemic and Ebola, which suggests that the epidemic was *not* Ebola. A very tough incorrect answer.

E) This, like D, is a decent weakener, because it points out a discrepancy between the typical Ebola epidemic and the Athenian epidemic.

The worst weakener of the lot is B, so that's our answer.

---

Many students struggle with assumption questions because they don't understand that there are two very different types of assumptions: sufficient and necessary. The purpose of this sidebar is to teach you the difference, and to do so, I'm going to use a super-simple bit of math. Don't panic! If you passed third grade, you've seen this math before.

# Sufficient Assumption

• Premise: Anything times zero equals zero.
• Conclusion: Therefore A times B equals zero.
• Question: "Which one of the following, if true, would allow the conclusion to be properly inferred?" Or, stated another way, "Which one of the following, if assumed, would justify the argument's conclusion?" Both of these are asking for *sufficient* assumptions. (You might want to memorize the wording of those questions, so that you can differentiate a sufficient assumption question from a necessary assumption question.)

This question is asking you to *prove* the argument's conclusion. In order to prove a conclusion on the LSAT, the conclusion of the argument must be connected, with no gaps, to the evidence offered. So we need an answer that connects the evidence "anything times zero is zero" to the conclusion "A times B is zero."

It's pretty simple. The answer must contain one of the following:

"A equals zero." If it's true that A is zero, and if it's true that anything times zero equals zero, then no matter what B is, the conclusion "A times B equals zero" would be *proven* correct. And proof is what we're looking for on a sufficient assumption question.

"B equals 0" would be just as good, because no matter what A is, the conclusion "A times B equals zero" would be proven correct.

Here's the really interesting part (if you're a nerd like me, which I hope you are). While "A equals zero" and "B equals zero" are each *sufficient* to prove the conclusion correct, neither of these statements, independently, is *necessary* in order for the argument to possibly make sense. A could be 1,000,000, and the conclusion "A times B equals zero" could still be conceivable (if B equals zero). Likewise, B could be 1,000,000 and the conclusion could still be possible (as long as A equals zero.) So if the question had said "which one of the following is an assumption *required by* the argument," (that's asking for a *necessary* component of the argument) then "A equals zero" would not be a good answer. Nor would "B equals zero."

The definition of *sufficient assumption* is "something that would prove the argument's conclusion to be correct." Go ahead and memorize that. And don't worry, once I'm done explaining *necessary assumption*, I won't use any math for a while, I promise.

# Necessary Assumption

• Premise: Anything times zero equals zero.
• Conclusion: Therefore A times B is *not* zero.
• Question: "Which one of the following is an assumption on which the argument depends?" Or, stated another way, "Which one of the following is necessary support for the argument's conclusion?" Or, stated still another way, "Which one of the following is an assumption required by the argument?"

These three questions are all asking you to do the same thing. Your task is to identify an answer that *must be true*, in order for the argument to even conceivably be true. In other words, it's asking you to identify an answer that, *if untrue*, would cause the argument to fail. In other words, it's asking for a necessary condition.

There are two answers here. "A does not equal zero" is one of them, and "B does not equal zero" is the other. If either of these statements is untrue, then the conclusion of the argument would fail (because anything times zero equals zero). It is *necessary* that A not be zero, and it is *necessary* that B not be zero, because if either A or B is zero, the argument is complete nonsense. Since "A does not equal zero" and "B does not equal zero" were unstated, they are *assumptions*. So "A does not equal zero" and "B does not equal zero" are both *necessary assumptions* of the argument.

Note! Both of these statements are *necessary*, but neither is *sufficient*. If A does not equal zero, that doesn't *prove* that A times B is not zero (because B might equal zero). Likewise, if B does not equal zero, that doesn't *prove* that A times B is not zero (because A might equal zero). So neither of these would be a correct answer to the question "Which one of the following, if assumed, would allow the conclusion to be properly drawn," which is a *sufficient assumption* question.

But the questions listed above were all asking for necessary assumptions, and "A does not equal zero" and "B does not equal zero" *must be true* or else the argument will fail–thus we know they are "necessary."

The definition of a *necessary assumption* is "something that must be true, or else the argument will fail." (Alternatively: "something that, if untrue, will prove the argument invalid.") Go ahead and memorize that. Thanks for bearing with my math example. I'll put away my abacus for a while now.

## QUESTION 8:

**Letter to the editor: Your article was unjustified in criticizing environmentalists for claiming that more wolves on Vancouver Island are killed by hunters than are born each year. You stated that this claim was disproven by recent studies that indicate that the total number of wolves on Vancouver Island has remained roughly constant for 20 years. But you failed to account for the fact that, fearing the extinction of this wolf population, environmentalists have been introducing new wolves into the Vancouver Island wolf population for 20 years.**

**Which one of the following most accurately expresses the conclusion of the argument in the letter to the editor?**

**A)  Environmentalists have been successfully maintaining the wolf population on Vancouver Island for 20 years.**
**B)  As many wolves on Vancouver Island are killed by hunters as are born each year.**
**C)  The population of wolves on Vancouver Island should be maintained by either reducing the number killed by hunters each year or introducing new wolves into the population.**
**D)  The recent studies indicating that the total number of wolves on Vancouver Island has remained roughly constant for 20 years were flawed.**
**E)  The stability in the size of the Vancouver Island wolf population does not warrant the article's criticism of the environmentalists' claim.**

I usually like to argue with the speaker, but here I'm actually on the speaker's side. The facts seem to play out like this:

• Environmentalists claim that more wolves are killed by hunters than are born each year.
• Paper disputes this claim, on the grounds that the total number of wolves has remained constant.
• Letter writer says "Hey, dumbass editor, you forgot that new wolves have been added to the population for 20 years, so if the total number of wolves has remained constant, then that's evidence *for* the assertion that more wolves are dying than being born, not *against* it."

(I like when one party calls another party a dumbass. When this happens on the LSAT, the accusing party is generally correct.)

The question simply asks us to identify the conclusion of the argument. Any time somebody calls someone else a dumbass, that's usually her conclusion. An accusation needs to be backed up by evidence, so the argument will usually contain "you're a dumbass," and some evidence in support of that conclusion. Here, the accusation came in the very first sentence and the rest of the argument backed it up. So I think the answer will match the first sentence of the argument: "Your article was unjustified in criticizing environmentalists for claiming that more wolves on Vancouver Island are killed by hunters than are born each year." Let's see.

A)  Nope! The conclusion wasn't to do with whether or not the wolf population has been maintained. The conclusion was "you shouldn't have criticized the environmentalists."
B)  No, this was evidence in support of the conclusion that the paper shouldn't have criticized the environmentalists.
C)  No, it's definitely not about whether wolves *should* or *should not* be maintained on the island. Presumably the environmentalists think they should, but the letter writer didn't take a position on this issue. The letter writer is solely calling out the editor on one very narrow issue—printing an "unjustified" critique of the environmentalist's claim.
D)  No, the letter writer is criticizing the editor, not the studies.
E)  Yep. "Does not warrant" matches "unjustified." They both mean "you didn't have proper evidence to claim what you claimed." This answer choice really doesn't match our prediction, but A-D were all fatally flawed.

Answer E hits the nail on the head: The letter writer thinks the article should not have criticized the environmentalist's claim. So E is our answer.

## QUESTION 9:

Computer scientist: For several decades, the number of transistors on new computer microchips, and hence the microchips' computing speed, has doubled about every 18 months. However, from the mid-1990s into the next decade, each such doubling in a microchip's computing speed was accompanied by a doubling in the cost of producing that microchip.

Which one of the following can be properly inferred from the computer scientist's statements?

A) The only effective way to double the computing speed of computer microchips is to increase the number of transistors per microchip.
B) From the mid-1990s into the next decade, there was little if any increase in the retail cost of computers as a result of the increased number of transistors on microchips.
C) For the last several decades, computer engineers have focused on increasing the computing speed of computer microchips without making any attempt to control the cost of producing them.
D) From the mid-1990s into the next decade, a doubling in the cost of fabricating new computer microchips accompanied each doubling in the number of transistors on those microchips.
E) It is unlikely that engineers will ever be able to increase the computing speed of microchips without also increasing the cost of producing them.

OK, so the number of transistors per chip, and hence the processing speed of that chip, has doubled every 18 months for "several decades." And since the mid-90s each doubling of speed has been accompanied by a doubling in cost. Those are the facts.

We're asked to find a statement that can be "properly inferred" from these facts. *Do not* be Sherlock Holmes here (not in the classical Sherlock sense, of making amazing leaps of deductive reasoning, nor in the shitty Hollywood sense of speaking in a fake accent and inexplicably knowing how to do Kung Fu). The point here isn't to solve a crazy mystery, it's just to pick an answer choice that *must be true* based on the given facts. The correct answer here is hard to predict in advance, but easy to identify once we see it in the answer choices. We're going to pick the one that seems boring and obvious, given the stated facts. We're going to avoid anything that seems remotely speculative.

A) No. I stopped reading this one after the first four words. There's no way that the evidence can be used to prove that "the only effective way" to do anything is anything else. The evidence is simply not about methods of doing something versus methods of doing something else. The evidence is simply about what's happened in the past.
B) No. Retail cost? Who said anything about retail cost? Pure speculation.
C) Huh? The facts said nothing about engineers, or cost control, let alone whether or not engineers are ignoring cost control.
D) Well, um, that seems pretty boring and obvious, given the facts. The doubling in number of transistors has been happening "for decades," and the doubling in cost has been happening since the mid-90s. So yeah, the two have "accompanied" each other. Boring and obvious is exactly what we are looking for on a "must be true" question. This is probably it.
E) What? No. The statement made *no* prediction about the future whatsoever.

A, B, C, and E are all horrible answers. We're going with D.

# 10

## QUESTION 10:

Ms. Sandstrom's newspaper column describing a strange natural phenomenon on the Mendels' farm led many people to trespass on and extensively damage their property. Thus, Ms. Sandstrom should pay for this damage if, as the Mendels claim, she could have reasonably expected that the column would lead people to damage the Mendels' farm.

The argument's conclusion can be properly inferred if which one of the following is assumed?

A) One should pay for any damage that one's action leads other people to cause if one could have reasonably expected that the action would lead other people to cause damage.

B) One should pay for damage that one's action leads other people to cause only if, prior to the action, one expected that the action would lead other people to cause that damage.

C) It is unlikely that the people who trespassed on and caused the damage to the Mendels' property would themselves pay for the damage they caused.

D) Ms. Sandstrom knew that her column could incite trespassing that could result in damage to the Mendels' farm.

E) The Mendels believe that Ms. Sandstrom is able to form reasonable expectations about the consequences of her actions.

*Mens rea* (state of mind) is an important element of a crime. Some laws only assign liability if you *actually knew* you were doing harm (subjective standard). Other laws assign liability whether or not you *actually* knew you were doing harm—you're liable if you did something that you *should have known* would cause harm (objective standard). In these cases, we won't need to prove that the guilty party *actually* knew. We simply get ordinary people to say "yes, she *should have known* in those circumstances." We don't know if Sandstrom actually knew she was causing harm, but the Mendels claim she *should* have known. And whether or not she *actually* knew is irrelevant because the conclusion is "if she should have known, then she should pay." If the law holds people to an objective standard, ("should have known = should pay") then she's guilty.

The question asks, "The argument's conclusion can be properly inferred if which one of the following is assumed?" That's a Sufficient Assumption question. (See the box on pg. 51 and the appendix for more on Sufficient Assumption.) Basically, "find the missing piece that will prove the argument to be true." We can almost always predict this type of answer in advance: connect the evidence to the conclusion. Luckily, we already did that above. We said "if the law holds people to an objective standard, then she's going to have to pay." The argument doesn't actually claim that there's an objective standard, just assumes it. But in court, we can't assume *anything*. We must find a law to convict Sandstrom of her crime. The law we want is "One should pay for all damages that could have reasonably been expected to occur as a result of one's actions." Sandstrom is screwed if we find that law.

A) Yep, this is exactly what we predicted. If this is the law, Sandstrom is liable. We'd add this to the evidence and submit it to the judge. We'd win.

B) No, this answer choice would only apply if Sandstrom had *actually* expected that the damage would be caused. (Subjective standard.) And we don't know if Sandstrom actually knew. Sandstrom walks.

C) What? No. Just because the people who did the damage probably wouldn't pay for it doesn't mean Sandstrom should pay for it. (What about the owner of the property? What about the government? What about the publisher of the newspaper? Etc.) Sandstrom walks again.

D) No, we still lack a law that says "those who know should pay." The correct answer has to be a law. This additional fact is probably bad for Sandstrom, but maybe the law says "only property owners are ever liable for any damage on their property." If that's the law, then Sandstrom walks. We're looking for a bulletproof case against Sandstrom.

E) No, just because she "is able to form" reasonable expectations, generally, doesn't mean she would have reasonably been able to expect *this particular outcome*.

Our answer is A, because it's the only one that lets us string up Sandstrom.

## QUESTION 11:

**Meyer was found by his employer to have committed scientific fraud by falsifying data. The University of Williamstown, from which Meyer held a PhD, validated this finding and subsequently investigated whether he had falsified data in his doctoral thesis, finding no evidence that he had. But the university decided to revoke Meyer's PhD anyway.**

**Which one of the following university policies most justifies the decision to revoke Meyer's PhD?**

A) Anyone who holds a PhD from the University of Williamstown and is found to have committed academic fraud in the course of pursuing that PhD will have the PhD revoked.

B) No PhD program at the University of Williamstown will admit any applicant who has been determined to have committed any sort of academic fraud.

C) Any University of Williamstown student who is found to have submitted falsified data as academic work will be dismissed from the university.

D) Anyone who holds a PhD from the University of Williamstown and is found to have committed scientific fraud will have the PhD revoked.

E) The University of Williamstown will not hire anyone who is under investigation for scientific fraud.

Wow, really? That's fucked up. Since when did all previous achievements get revoked on the basis of one alleged mistake? What the University did to Meyer is like an attorney graduating from law school, going into practice, his employer firing him for allegedly cheating a client, and then having his law school say, "Yeah, we're going to go back and revoke his J.D. as well, even though there's no evidence he ever cheated on his exams." It ain't right. Meyer may be a dick—he is alleged to have committed fraud, after all—but we don't usually take everything away from someone who might have made a mistake. I'm on Meyer's side here.

Except I'm not, because the question asks us to find an answer that, if it were the policy of the University, would "most justify" the University's action. So we have to switch teams, and be the attorney for the University. This question is similar to #10, in that we're asked to look for a law that would, when combined with the evidence, make it okay to "convict" Meyer (i.e. revoke his Ph.D.). We should be able to predict the answer here. The evidence is that Meyer's employer alleges he committed scientific fraud by falsifying data. The desired outcome is the University revokes his Ph.D. So a perfect answer would be "the University shall revoke the degree of any alumnus who is ever accused of anything." If that's the rule, then the University must revoke Meyer's Ph.D.

A) Nah. Meyer was not found to have committed academic fraud during his Ph.D. The University couldn't even find a shred of evidence, let alone enough to convict him.

B) Not even close. Meyer isn't applying for admission.

C) This answer is wrong for two reasons. First, Meyer's wrongdoing occurred at his place of employment, which may not be an "academic" institution. And second, Meyer isn't at the University, so he wouldn't give a shit about being "dismissed." Terrible answer.

D) Yeah, this seems pretty good. Meyer's employer "found" him to have committed scientific fraud. So if this is the rule, then Williamstown gets to revoke his Ph.D.

E) No. The argument isn't about whether or not Williamstown should hire Meyer, although that would be nice, because the dude is probably unemployed.

D is our answer, because if D is the University policy, then they are "justified" (at least according to their own policies) in revoking his Ph.D.

## QUESTION 12:

Aerobics instructor: Compared to many forms of exercise, kickboxing aerobics is highly risky. Overextending when kicking often leads to hip, knee, or lower-back injuries. Such overextension is very likely to occur when beginners try to match the high kicks of more skilled practitioners.

Which one of the following is most strongly supported by the aerobics instructor's statements?

A) Skilled practitioners of kickboxing aerobics are unlikely to experience injuries from overextending while kicking.
B) To reduce the risk of injuries, beginners at kickboxing aerobics should avoid trying to match the high kicks of more skilled practitioners.
C) Beginners at kickboxing aerobics will not experience injuries if they avoid trying to match the high kicks of more skilled practitioners.
D) Kickboxing aerobics is more risky than forms of aerobic exercise that do not involve high kicks.
E) Most beginners at kickboxing aerobics experience injuries from trying to match the high kicks of more skilled practitioners.

## Master this Question

"Must be true" / "most strongly supported" is a very common type of question, which sucks when you don't get the concept. But it's also a very *learnable* type of question, and since there are so many of them you might be able to increase your LSAT score by 5 points just by mastering this one type. Question #12 is a terrific example, so make sure you understand it before moving on. Email me (seriously!) if you read the explanation a couple times and still don't get it: nathan@foxlsat.com

When I started out, I thought that an answer like B seemed "too obvious" to be the correct answer. Many of my new students—especially, for some reason, the highest achieving ones—share this same misconception. "It seems like the speaker already said this. Don't I have to go an extra step, and pick something that is *probably* true, like A or D?"

Hell no. When the LSAT asks you to pick an answer that is "strongly supported," they're testing your ability to distinguish between solid evidence and mere conjecture. If an answer seems boring or obvious, on this type of question, that's probably the correct one.

I think the first sentence, "compared to many forms of exercise, kickboxing aerobics is highly risky," is the conclusion of this argument. And it's supported by the second and third sentences, which describe one type of injury that can be caused by overextension during kickboxing. If I were to argue here, I'd say "Yeah, but don't other forms of exercise have their own risks, too?" I mean downhill skiing is "aerobic exercise" too, and I'm pretty sure that's not safer than pretend fighting while wearing a leotard. Right?

Anyway, this is all immaterial because the question asks us to find a statement "most strongly supported by" the given statements. This is like question #9, above: all we have to do is find the answer choice that seems most obvious according to the given information. No fancy deduction necessary. Ignore any outside information you might have about kickboxing, especially if you picked it up watching *Bloodsport* (which was a bitchin' movie when I was about 13... and now). Avoid answers that seem speculative. We're going to pick the one that, ideally, has been *proven true by the given facts.* If we can't find one that's been proven, then we'll find the one that is closest to proven.

A) No, this feels like a trap to me. The fact that beginners often get hurt when attempting high kicks does *not* imply that skilled or professional practitioners don't also get hurt doing these kicks.
B) Well, yeah, this is at least strongly *suggested* by the given facts. The facts are that overextension leads to injury, and overextension often happens when beginners try to match the high kicks of experts. So, if you're a beginner trying to avoid injury—*duh*—then don't try to do those kicks. I like this answer.
C) No way. There are probably a million other ways to get hurt in kickboxing besides attempting high kicks. Jean-Claude Van Damme would be happy to show you a few.
D) Mmmm... no. There are no high kicks involved in downhill skiing, remember? The aerobics instructor gave no actual evidence about other forms of aerobic exercise—just a conclusion. So this can't be "strongly supported" by the given statements.
E) No, the statement never said that "most beginners" even attempt the high kicks.

Our answer is B.

# QUESTION 13:

A large company has been convicted of engaging in monopolistic practices. The penalty imposed on the company will probably have little if any effect on its behavior. Still, the trial was worthwhile, since it provided useful information about the company's practices. After all, this information has emboldened the company's direct competitors, alerted potential rivals, and forced the company to restrain its unfair behavior toward customers and competitors.

Which one of the following most accurately expresses the overall conclusion drawn in the argument?

A) Even if the company had not been convicted of engaging in monopolistic practices, the trial probably would have had some effect on the company's behavior.
B) The light shed on the company's practices by the trial has emboldened its competitors, alerted potential rivals, and forced the company to restrain its unfair behavior.
C) The penalty imposed on the company will likely have little or no effect on its behavior.
D) The company's trial on charges of engaging in monopolistic practices was worthwhile.
E) The penalty imposed on the company in the trial should have been larger.

OK, so a large company got convicted of monopolistic practices, but the penalty they'll have to pay will have "little if any effect on its behavior." That's a bummer, right? Not so, says the argument. Oh really? Why? Well, goes the argument, the *trial itself* provided useful information about the company's practices, which emboldened competitors, alerted rivals, and forced the company to restrain its unfair behavior. THEREFORE, the trial was worthwhile regardless of the penalty imposed.

What I've just done is rearrange the argument, using a "oh really... *why*?" to introduce the evidence and a big, all-caps THEREFORE to introduce the conclusion. On the actual test, I wouldn't write this down—it would take too long, plus there's no scratch paper available. But this is *exactly* the process I'll go through in my head when I need to clarify exactly what part of an argument is evidence and what part is conclusion. I bet you can do this too. (Just don't do it out loud, or the proctor will give you the stink-eye.)

Here, since we're simply asked to identify the overall conclusion, I'm pretty sure we've already predicted the correct answer. It's whatever comes after the THERE-FORE in my rearranged argument above. My prediction is "the trial was worthwhile." An answer choice *must* include this in order for me to consider it.

A) Hmmm... I don't think so. This is speculative, because we simply don't know what would have happened if the company had been found not liable. It's an alternate universe, and we have no information about that universe. Sure it's *possible* that the company might have changed its ways, but isn't it just as likely that it would have continued, or even expanded, its monopolistic practices? An answer that is supposedly describing the conclusion of an argument can't go *further* than the argument actually went, and I think this answer does just that. Check out my explanation for #12, above, for more on why you shouldn't speculate.
B) No, this is part of the *evidence*, not the conclusion.
C) This was also part of the evidence, not the conclusion.
D) Yep. This is exactly what we predicted. It's non-speculative, it's the exact conclusion that the argument actually made—no more, no less—and it's gonna be our answer.
E) I'm sure the plaintiff would argue that a penalty is worthless unless it means something to whoever is being penalized. So let's triple it. But, counters the defense, since the trial itself already changed the company's behavior, then why not make the penalty smaller? Matter of fact, let's just make it zero!

Our answer is D, because it best describes the *actual* conclusion of the argument.

# QUESTION 14:

**Waller:** If there were really such a thing as extrasensory perception, it would generally be accepted by the public since anyone with extrasensory powers would be able to convince the general public of its existence by clearly demonstrating those powers. Indeed, anyone who was recognized to have such powers would achieve wealth and renown.

**Chin:** It's impossible to demonstrate anything to the satisfaction of all skeptics. So long as the cultural elite remains closed-minded to the possibility of extrasensory perception, the popular media reports, and thus public opinion, will always be biased in favor of such skeptics.

**Waller's and Chin's statements commit them to disagreeing on whether**

A) extrasensory perception is a real phenomenon
B) extrasensory perception, if it were a real phenomenon, could be demonstrated to the satisfaction of all skeptics
C) skeptics about extrasensory perception have a weak case
D) the failure of the general public to believe in extrasensory perception is good evidence against its existence
E) the general public believes that extrasensory perception is a real phenomenon

I'm on Waller's side here. Waller says, basically, "If anybody really has ESP, they could easily prove it, get famous, and make millions." And I don't buy Chin's counterargument at all. Chin says "yeah but there will still be some *skeptics*, and they are the *cultural elite*, and they *run the media*, so the guy with ESP wouldn't be able to convince the public!" Sounds like a crock of shit to me. If some dude was able to use ESP to solve cold murder cases, or win at gambling, or find water on a previously barren property, that dude would be *useful,* immediately *rich*, and fucking *famous*. I don't know who the supposed "cultural elite" are, but if they exist, they are not going to be able to keep this guy off of television. No way.

It's great to be able to pick a side, because it usually means we understand the argument. But we have to ensure that personal feelings don't cloud our judgment. The question asks us to find the point at issue between Waller and Chin. Regardless of who is right and who is wrong, the two speakers have disagreed about whether a person with ESP would be able to convince the public that ESP exists. Our job is simply to find that in the answer choices.

A) Nope. Waller definitely says no to this, but Chin didn't go so far as to say "yes, ESP *does* exist." Instead, Chin just made a (weak) attack on Waller's logic. We need to pick the answer choice to which one speaker has clearly said "yes" and the other has said "no." This can't be our answer, because Chin hasn't really taken a position.

B) A bit tricky, but nah. Chin has definitely said no to this, since he said there will *always* be skeptics. But Waller never even mentioned the skeptics, nor did he make any broad claim like "eventually *everyone* will believe." We don't know whether Waller thinks all skeptics will be convinced... Waller just thinks that "the general public" will be convinced. There's room for a few holdouts in that position.

C) What the? Neither speaker took a position on this statement. Not even close.

D) Yeah, I think so. Waller says yes to this statement (if ESP existed then the general public would believe in it) and Chin says no (the cultural elite would prevent the public from believing even if it existed). This is not exactly like our prediction, but at its heart it kinda means the same thing. I bet this is our answer.

E) No. Both Waller and Chin are speaking in hypotheticals. Neither of them takes a position on what the general public *actually* believes. (Which is a good thing, because there are a shocking number of hippies out there who actually *do* believe in things like ESP, UFOs, astrology, the moon landing was faked, and the twin towers were an inside job. Jenny McCarthy gets TV time to claim that vaccinations cause autism... God*damn* it, I'm getting upset...) Anyway, this can't be the answer because neither speaker has addressed actual public beliefs.

So our answer is D.

# QUESTION 15:

Counselor: Hagerle sincerely apologized to the physician for lying to her. So Hagerle owes me a sincere apology as well, because Hagerle told the same lie to both of us.

Which one of the following principles, if valid, most helps to justify the counselor's reasoning?

A) It is good to apologize for having done something wrong to a person if one is capable of doing so sincerely.
B) If someone tells the same lie to two different people, then neither of those lied to is owed an apology unless both are.
C) Someone is owed a sincere apology for having been lied to by a person if someone else has already received a sincere apology for the same lie from that same person.
D) If one is capable of sincerely apologizing to someone for lying to them, then one owes that person such an apology.
E) A person should not apologize to someone for telling a lie unless he or she can sincerely apologize to all others to whom the lie was told.

Who is this counselor, George Costanza? Only someone very *Seinfeld*-esque would do this sort of whining about not getting an equal apology. And even aside from the whining, the counselor's argument is weak.

Just because Hagerle apologized to the physician doesn't mean that Hagerle also owes the counselor an apology. No, not even if Hagerle wronged the counselor and the physician in the same way. I can think of lots of reasons why not. To start with, who is to say that Hagerle "owed" the physician an apology in the first place? Is there a rule that says, "if you lie to someone then you owe that person an apology?" I don't see that rule given as a fact, which means that rule doesn't exist. Second, maybe the physician is a nice guy and Counselor Costanza is a colossal dick! (It sure sounds like it.) Even if there *were* a rule about owing an apology to people you lie to, I would certainly argue for the inclusion of an "except if they are a dick" clause. And furthermore, what if Hagerle's lie had really bad effects when applied to the physician (it caused the physician to ac-cidentally kill a patient, for example) but it had no effect whatsoever on the counselor? Would Costanza still deserve his equal apology in those circumstances? I think not.

The question asks us to try to "justify" the counselor's reasoning—it's a Sufficient Assumption question. Just like question #11, earlier in the section, that means we now have to switch sides and try to complete the argument we hate so much. In other words, we're now on George Costanza's legal team. (If he pays your fee, then he's your client.) We need a rule that, if true, would get Costanza his apology. I think the answer will probably be something like "if anyone ever lies to you, then you are owed an apology." Alternatively, "if anyone wrongs two people in the same way, then the same apology is owed to both parties" would work. Let's see. Remember: On Sufficient Assumption questions, pick the answer that will make your client *win*. Let's get Costanza his coveted apology.

A) Just because it is "good" to apologize does not mean that anyone ever *must* apologize. Costanza needs a rule that will *force* (not merely recommend) some groveling. This ain't it.
B) I'll be pissed if this turns out to be the correct answer, because I don't think it's clear that the physician was "owed" an apology in the first place. Let's keep look-ing, and only choose B begrudgingly if none of the other answers is any good.
C) Yep. That's much better. Since someone else (the physician) already received a sincere apology from Hagerle for the same lie, this rule would *force* Hagerle to kneel in apology before the almighty Costanza. That's what we were looking for, so this is almost certainly our answer.
D) No, it's very possible (likely, even) that nobody would be able to sincerely apolo-gize to Costanza. If this were the rule, Hagerle would be able to say, "I don't have to apologize because I couldn't be sincere."
E) Again, the weak phrase "should not" isn't going to force anybody to apologize. And anyway, this rule only says, "*can* sincerely apologize" which indicates a loophole. Hagerle could say "yes I *can*... but I'm not gonna."

Our answer is C, because it's the only one that forces the apology our client is looking for.

# QUESTION 16:

A survey of address changes filed with post offices and driver's license bureaus over the last ten years has established that households moving out of the city of Weston outnumbered households moving into the city two to one. Therefore, we can expect that next year's census, which counts all residents regardless of age, will show that the population of Weston has declined since the last census ten years ago.

Which one of the following, if true, most helps strengthen the argument?

A) Within the past decade many people both moved into the city and also moved out of it.
B) Over the past century any census of Weston showing a population loss was followed ten years later by a census showing a population gain.
C) Many people moving into Weston failed to notify either the post office or the driver's license bureau that they had moved to the city.
D) Most adults moving out of Weston were parents who had children living with them, whereas most adults remaining in or moving into the city were older people who lived alone.
E) Most people moving out of Weston were young adults who were hoping to begin a career elsewhere, whereas most adults remaining in or moving into the city had long-standing jobs in the city.

Huh? This argument is bullshit because it ignores the possibility that different households can have different numbers of people in them. Fewer households *suggests* fewer people, but it certainly doesn't prove it. As a matter of fact, I think I can tell a story where fewer households might actually correspond to *more* people:

What if Weston just got its first university, and the university bought up a lot of the housing to use for classrooms and student housing? The conversion of some houses to classrooms would cause a decrease in *households*. The old couples who lived in those gigantic old houses take the cash and retire to Tahiti, so there's a small, temporary decrease in residents. But then the new university stuffs 20,000 incoming freshmen into the other houses—10 roommates in each house, and nobody ever does the dishes—so on balance the number of *residents* (and, most likely, cockroaches) has actually increased.

Storytime over. I used my story to *weaken* the argument, but now the question asks us to *strengthen* it. Because I think my attack was right on the money here, I think the correct answer probably needs to defend against this attack. So my first guess is going to be something like "the number of residents per household did not increase." (Or, even better, "the number of residents per household decreased.") If either of those is true, then my whole story about the new university wouldn't apply, and the argument would therefore be stronger. Let's see.

A) Who cares. This neither strengthens nor weakens the argument.
B) This is totally irrelevant, because we have no idea what kind of change the census ten years ago actually showed.
C) If this is true then it *weakens* the argument. We need a strengthener.
D) Boom. If this answer is true, then it seems likely that the number of residents per household decreased. If both the number of households *and* the number of residents per household have decreased, then it seems awful likely that the total number of residents has decreased. This fits our prediction very nicely.
E) Huh? This is a complete non sequitur. The reasons why some people stayed versus why other people moved have absolutely nothing to do with the logic of the argument. This neither strengthens nor weakens.

Our answer is D.

## QUESTION 17:

**Psychologist: People tend to make certain cognitive errors when they predict how a given event would affect their future happiness. But people should not necessarily try to rid themselves of this tendency. After all, in a visual context, lines that are actually parallel often appear to people as if they converge. If a surgeon offered to restructure your eyes and visual cortex so that parallel lines would no longer ever appear to converge, it would not be reasonable to take the surgeon up on the offer.**

**The psychologist's argument does which one of the following?**

A) attempts to refute a claim that a particular event is inevitable by establishing the possibility of an alternative event
B) attempts to undermine a theory by calling into question an assumption on which the theory is based
C) argues that an action might not be appropriate by suggesting that a corresponding action in an analogous situation is not appropriate
D) argues that two situations are similar by establishing that the same action would be reasonable in each situation
E) attempts to establish a generalization and then uses that generalization to argue against a particular action

What the fuck is *this*? The psychologist tries to justify a claim (people should not try to rid themselves of the tendency to predict how an event would affect their future happiness) on the basis of an analogy about how it probably wouldn't be a good idea to have a surgeon start hacking away at your visual cortex. *Huh?!* What does the first thing have to do with the other? This is completely bogus.

The question asks us to identify a type of reasoning in the argument. So all we have to do is pick the method actually used by the psychologist. The proper approach is somewhat similar to a must be true / most strongly supported question like #9 or #12 above: Use only what's on the page, and pick the answer that you have the most support for in the passage.

I think "the argument used a horseshit analogy" would be the perfect answer, because that's exactly what the argument did. Let's see what we've got.

A) No, the argument doesn't do this. This would be the answer if the argument had said, "The Red Sox won't win the World Series because it's possible the Giants will win it." That's an entirely different method of reasoning.
B) No, the argument doesn't do this either. This would be the answer if the argument had said, "Your theory that the Yankees will win the World Series is flawed because you've assumed that Derek Jeter is still a good player, which is untrue." That's not the type of reasoning employed by the psychologist's argument.
C) Analogy. Boom.
D) No, this is wrong for two reasons. First, the argument concludes that the same course of action would be unreasonable, not reasonable. And second, the terrible argument never "established" (*i.e.* proved), anything. It claimed, and it argued, but it did not prove. This answer sucks.
E) I don't see any "generalization" in this argument. Use of a generalization would sound like "history shows that the team with the highest payroll always wins. The Athletics do not have the highest payroll, therefore you should not bet on them to win."

## The Incredible Power of Incredulity

We dominated this question because we *argued* with the logic being presented. The second we said, "Dude, your stupid analogy does not apply," we had already answered the question. You should foster the same kind of skepticism if you want to conquer the LSAT. Most of the arguments suck! The questions are shockingly easy if you can articulate why.

Our answer is C.

## QUESTION 18:

**Principle:** Even if an art auction house identifies the descriptions in its catalog as opinions, it is guilty of misrepresentation if such a description is a deliberate attempt to mislead bidders.

**Application:** Although Healy's, an art auction house, states that all descriptions in its catalog are opinions, Healy's was guilty of misrepresentation when its catalog described a vase as dating from the mid-eighteenth century when it was actually a modern reproduction.

**Which one of the following, if true, most justifies the above application of the principle?**

A) An authentic work of art from the mid-eighteenth century will usually sell for at least ten times more than a modern reproduction of a similar work from that period.

B) Although pottery that is similar to the vase is currently extremely popular among art collectors, none of the collectors who are knowledgeable about such pottery were willing to bid on the vase.

C) The stated policy of Healy's is to describe works in its catalogs only in terms of their readily perceptible qualities and not to include any information about their age.

D) Some Healy's staff members believe that the auction house's catalog should not contain any descriptions that have not been certified to be true by independent experts.

E) Without consulting anyone with expertise in authenticating vases, Healy's described the vase as dating from the mid-eighteenth century merely in order to increase its auction price.

This is exactly the type of thing you'll be asked to do on a first-year Law School exam. Ready? Here are the exam instructions:

*You are a clerk for a state judge presiding over a case involving alleged misrepresentation. In your state, the pertinent statute reads "an art house is guilty of misrepresentation if it deliberately attempts to mislead bidders in a catalog description, even if the art auction house identifies its description as opinion." Plaintiff has sued defendant Healy's, an art auction house, for misrepresentation when its catalog described a vase as dating from the mid-eighteenth century when, in fact, it was actually a modern reproduction. Healy's catalog did state that the description was opinion. Please advise the judge on how she should rule.*

The correct answer to any law school question is always "it depends." The point isn't to find the correct ruling—there isn't one! (Not yet, anyway.) The point is to figure out what information is missing that would help *find* the correct answer. To do that, you have to look at the elements of the alleged misrepresentation and compare those elements to the facts. Your answer would need to hit the following points:

• First, the statute applies regardless of whether an art house makes the "opinion" caveat or not, so even though Healy's did make a disclaimer, their disclaimer is irrelevant.

• Second, the statute only applies to art houses. Is Healy's an art house? Yes it is, so the statute would apply to Healy's.

• Third, the statute only applies to catalog descriptions. Was the description in question printed in a catalog? Yes it was, so the statute would apply to this particular description.

• Fourth, the statute only applies to items that were misdescribed. Was the vase misdescribed? Yes it was, so the statute would still apply to this particular description.

• Fifth, the statute only applies to "deliberate attempts to mislead." Did Healy's deliberately attempt to mislead? Ohhhhh wait a minute! *There's* the missing information. We have no idea whether Healy's deliberately misdescribed the item. Was it a typo? Clerical error? Other honest mistake? Or did they know it was a fake and they were trying to fleece the customer? This is the issue your judge needs to focus on at trial. And that's going to be the answer to this question, I'm almost certain of it.

We're asked to "justify" the application of the principle. Since the application claims "Healy's was guilty," the only way to get there is to prove that Healy's did *deliberately* misdescribe the item. All the other facts seem to be in the record already. The missing link—the thing the plaintiff must prove at trial—is the deliberate intent to mislead. If they can prove that, then they'll win.

A) If this is true then it provides a reason why Healy's might have wanted to misdescribe the vase. But that's not the same thing as *proving* that they actually did have such intent, let alone act on that intent. This doesn't go far enough.

B) This has nothing whatsoever to do with intent. Let's move on.

C) Well, apparently they didn't follow their stated policy in this case. But that's not relevant. The point is: Was this an accident, or was it intentional? This answer doesn't address our key question.

D) No, the opinion of staff members is not relevant here. We know what we're looking for, and this ain't it.

E) Yep. If Healy's described the vase as mid-eighteenth century "merely in order to increase its auction price," without any attempt to discern whether the vase was actually from that time period, then that sure looks like a deliberate attempt to mislead. If E is true, then Healy's is going to lose. That's the outcome the application claimed was correct, so that's our answer.

THE FOX GUIDE TO A REAL LSAT, VOL. 3  **63**

## QUESTION 19:

Anthropologist: It was formerly believed that prehistoric *Homo sapiens* ancestors of contemporary humans interbred with Neanderthals, but DNA testing of a Neanderthal's remains indicates that this is not the case. The DNA of contemporary humans is significantly different from that of the Neanderthal.

**Which one of the following is an assumption required by the anthropologist's argument?**

A) At least some Neanderthals lived at the same time and in the same places as prehistoric *Homo sapiens* ancestors of contemporary humans.

B) DNA testing of remains is significantly less reliable than DNA testing of samples from living species.

C) The DNA of prehistoric *Homo sapiens* ancestors of contemporary humans was not significantly more similar to that of Neanderthals than is the DNA of contemporary humans.

D) Neanderthals and prehistoric *Homo sapiens* ancestors of contemporary humans were completely isolated from each other geographically.

E) Any similarity in the DNA of two species must be the result of interbreeding.

The evidence is "contemporary humans have significantly different DNA from those of the Neanderthal." The conclusion, based on this evidence, is "therefore *Homo sapiens*, the ancestor of contemporary humans, never interbred with the Neanderthal."

This is an incomplete argument. Do we know, for sure, that it's impossible for two creatures with vastly different DNA to nevertheless have ancestors who once interbred? If that's a fact, then the argument makes sense. But if it's *not* a fact, then the argument is ruined.

We're asked to identify "an assumption required by the anthropologist's argument." That means, "find the one that must be true, or else the argument is ruined." (It's a Necessary Assumption question.) I'm pretty sure we've already identified one necessary condition: The anthropologist's argument only makes sense if we assume that different DNA means ancestors who didn't interbreed. The anthropologist didn't explicitly state this, she just *assumed* it. So that's what we're looking for.

# The going gets tough

This question isn't a little bit harder than the previous questions—it's a lot harder. Not twice as hard, more like ten times as hard. This is a recurring pattern on the LSAT. Somewhere in the late teens or early 20s of each section, the questions, on average, get significantly harder. Please don't rush through the early questions, making silly mistakes, to get to these harder questions! Take your time harvesting the lower-hanging fruit. If you end up guessing on a few at the end of the section, at least you'll be guessing on the harder ones—and you'll have gotten the easier ones right.

A) Uh, no. If this is true, it could only weaken the anthropologist's claim that Neanderthals and Homo sapiens *didn't* interbreed. So there's no way this was a missing piece of the argument.

B) Nah. This is simply irrelevant.

C) Hmmm. This is a tough answer to parse. I actually scanned D and E before I tackled this one, hoping to find an answer that closely matched our prediction. When I didn't find what I was looking for, I took some more time with C. Remember, we're looking for an answer that must be true or else the anthropologist's argument fails. We can test this by looking at what happens if an answer is *not* true. If C is not true, we get "the DNA of prehistoric *Homo sapiens* ancestors of contemporary humans was significantly more similar to that of Neanderthals than is the DNA of contemporary humans." At first blush, this doesn't devastate the anthropologist's argument. But I can make a case that it certainly weakens the argument. Imagine if Homo sapiens and Neanderthal had basically identical DNA. If that were true, then how would it be possible to use DNA evidence today to claim that Homo sapiens and Neanderthal never interbred? I don't love this answer, but I hate A, B, D, and E. So we're going to have to choose C and move on.

D) No, the anthropologist never claimed (or implied) that *Homo sapiens* and Neanderthals were completely separated geographically. It's possible for two people to be in the same physical place without interbreeding, right? (Remember, beer hadn't been invented yet.) This answer isn't *necessary* in order for the anthropologist's argument to make sense.

E) This answer could be used to prove that two species *did* interbreed, but I don't see how it has to be true in order to support the anthropologist's claim that two species *didn't* interbreed.

Tough question, and our answer is C.

## QUESTION 20:

Council member: The profits of downtown businesses will increase if more consumers live in the downtown area, and a decrease in the cost of living in the downtown area will guarantee that the number of consumers living there will increase. However, the profits of downtown businesses will not increase unless downtown traffic congestion decreases.

If all the council member's statements are true, which one of the following must be true?

A) If downtown traffic congestion decreases, the number of consumers living in the downtown area will increase.
B) If the cost of living in the downtown area decreases, the profits of downtown businesses will increase.
C) If downtown traffic congestion decreases, the cost of living in the downtown area will increase.
D) If downtown traffic congestion decreases, the cost of living in the downtown area will decrease.
E) If the profits of downtown businesses increase, the number of consumers living in the downtown area will increase.

There's no *argument* here. (In other words, there's no conclusion, supported by facts.) Instead, we have only facts. The question asks us to identify a statement that must be true, if the given facts are true. I wouldn't try to predict this one in advance, because the given facts might be used to prove a lot of different propositions. Instead, let's just pick the answer that seems most proven, obvious, boring—and least speculative—based on the information we were given.

A) Nah. If downtown traffic congestion does *not* decrease, then we know that the profits of downtown businesses can't increase. But if downtown traffic congestion *does* decrease, then we really don't know anything at all. Downtown residents and downtown profits may or may not increase... who knows.

B) If the cost of living downtown decreases, then we know for sure that the number of downtown residents will increase. And if the number of downtown residents increases, then the profits of downtown businesses will increase. So this answer is proven to be true based solely on the first sentence of the council member's statement. Because it is *proven* true, it is our answer. It doesn't matter what the rest of the council member's statement says—if this answer must be true, then it's going to be our answer. Let's make sure we can get rid of C-E before moving on.

C) No, we weren't given any connection between downtown traffic congestion and downtown cost of living.

D) No, same explanation as C.

E) No, this answer gets the relationship between profits and number of residents exactly backward.

Our answer is B.

21

## QUESTION 21:

On the Discount Phoneline, any domestic long-distance call starting between 9 A.M. and 5 P.M. costs 15 cents a minute, and any other domestic long-distance call costs 10 cents a minute. So any domestic long-distance call on the Discount Phoneline that does not cost 10 cents a minute costs 15 cents a minute.

The pattern of reasoning in which one of the following arguments is most similar to that in the argument above?

A) If a university class involves extensive lab work, the class will be conducted in a laboratory; otherwise, it will be conducted in a normal classroom. Thus, if a university class does not involve extensive lab work, it will not be conducted in a laboratory.

B) If a university class involves extensive lab work, the class will be conducted in a laboratory; otherwise, it will be conducted in a normal classroom. Thus, if a university class is not conducted in a normal classroom, it will involve extensive lab work.

C) If a university class involves extensive lab work, the class will be conducted in a laboratory; otherwise, it will be conducted in a normal classroom. Thus, if a university class is conducted in a normal classroom, it will not be conducted in a laboratory.

D) If a university class involves extensive lab work, the class will be conducted in a laboratory; otherwise, it will be conducted in a normal classroom. Thus, if a university class involves extensive lab work, it will not be conducted in a normal classroom.

E) If a university class involves extensive lab work, the class will be conducted in a laboratory; otherwise, it will be conducted in a normal classroom. Thus, if a university class is not conducted in a normal classroom, it will be conducted in a laboratory.

Most students should skip this based on sheer length. If you consistently finish the Logical Reasoning sections with high accuracy (>80%) and time to spare, go ahead and do this question wherever it falls. But that probably applies to one out of ten students. Everyone else should skip it and come back if they have time. Remember, it's *your* test. I don't advocate a lot of skipping around, but if you're going to guess, guess on a question that takes up its own column.

The given argument is valid logic. The first sentence says that calls in a certain timeframe cost X, and all other domestic long-distance calls cost Y. The second sentence concludes, on the basis of the first statement, that any call that does not cost Y costs X. It's a valid conclusion, because it's essentially a restatement of the first sentence.

We're asked to find a similar pattern of reasoning, so the correct answer must also have valid logic.

Don't look at the answers just yet. First, predict the *pattern* we're looking for. The given argument took the pattern "If call category A, then cost equals B. If not call category A, then cost equals C. Therefore if cost doesn't equal C, then cost equals B."

Now we know what pattern we're looking for. We should find another argument with the same pattern of reasoning.

A) Premise: If lab work then lab, if no lab work then classroom. So far, this matches. "If class category A (lab work), then room B (laboratory). If not class category A (no lab work), then room C (normal classroom)." But the conclusion goes off the rails, because it says, "If not category A (lab work), then not room B (laboratory)." In order to match the given statement, the conclusion here needed to say "If not one category of classroom, then the other."

B) Premise: If lab work then lab, if no lab work then classroom. So far, this matches. Whoa. Wait a minute. That's exactly the same start as the previous answer choice. Quick scan... this is the same first sentence in all the answer choices. We've already predicted what the correct answer should be. ("If not one category of classroom, then the other.") B isn't a perfect match. Let's scan the rest of the list and see if it's there.

C) Close but no cigar. We wanted "If *not* one category of classroom, then the other." (With the sufficient condition in the negative.) This answer, on the other hand, says "If one category of classroom, then *not* the other." (With the necessary condition in the negative.) Those two statements look identical, but they're not. (See sidebar.) We're still looking.

D) No, this doesn't say "If not one category of classroom, then the other."

E) Yep. This is exactly what we predicted in our analysis of A. Wow, that was a nasty question though—10 out of 10 difficulty. Almost everyone would be better off answering the rest of the questions in the section before tackling a beast like this.

## A subtle difference that makes all the difference

My predicted answer here takes the pattern "if not one, then the other." This is like mom and dad taking care of a newborn baby: If one of them is gone, then the other one must be there. Answer E correctly matches this pattern.

Answer C is wrong because it flips the relationship and says "if one, then not the other." This is more like Superman and Clark Kent. If one of them is in the room, then the other one is certainly not there. This is a subtle but very important distinction... this concept appears at least once on almost every LSAT.

# 22

## QUESTION 22:

One child pushed another child from behind, injuring the second child. The first child clearly understands the difference between right and wrong, so what was done was wrong if it was intended to injure the second child.

Which one of the following principles, if valid, most helps to justify the reasoning in the argument?

A) An action that is intended to harm another person is wrong only if the person who performed the action understands the difference between right and wrong.

B) It is wrong for a person who understands the difference between right and wrong to intentionally harm another person.

C) Any act that is wrong is done with the intention of causing harm.

D) An act that harms another person is wrong if the person who did it understands the difference between right and wrong and did not think about whether the act would injure the other person.

E) A person who does not understand the difference between right and wrong does not bear any responsibility for harming another person.

Let's rearrange this argument. Premise: Child A understands the difference between right and wrong. Premise: Child A pushed Child B from behind, injuring Child B. Conclusion: *If* Child A's action was intended to injure child B, then that action was wrong. Because the conclusion begins with the word "if," we're looking for a *qualified* conclusion. The speaker isn't saying, "the action was wrong, period." Rather, "depending on the intent, the action may have been wrong." This question, like question #10 earlier, focuses on *mens rea* (state of mind) when assigning liability. We must "justify" the reasoning in the argument. "Justify" means "prove" or "complete." This is a Sufficient Assumption question. By filling in the blanks, the correct answer will *prove* that the conclusion of the argument is correct.

To get from the evidence (the kid knows the difference between right and wrong; the kid pushed another kid and injured him) to the conclusion (if the kid intended harm, then the action was wrong), we must find something like, "if you take an action intending harm, and you do cause harm, then you are in the wrong." The correct answer might not say *exactly* that, but it needs to do the exact same thing. Let's see.

A) Nope. The phrase "only if" introduces a necessary condition, rather than a sufficient one. We want a sufficient condition—we want an answer that says, "If X, then you are wrong." This answer says, "If you are wrong, then X."

B) Yes. This answer defines wrongness by saying, "If you do something (intentionally harm another person) then you are wrong." This matches our prediction. (The bit about understanding right and wrong is unnecessary, but it doesn't disqualify the answer, because the kid *knows* the difference between right and wrong, so the rule *would* apply to the kid.)

C) Nope. Just like A, this answer defines intent as a necessary condition of wrongness, when the author implies that intent is sufficient (*i.e.* enough) to prove wrongness.

D) No, the speaker said, "If you intended harm then you are wrong." This rule says an action is wrong if the actor "did not think about whether" it would cause harm. The speaker required actual intent, but D only requires negligence. Two different rules.

E) This wouldn't apply to the kid at all, because the kid *does* understand the difference between right and wrong.

## Necessary knowledge

It's *necessary* that you learn the difference between sufficient and necessary conditions. Learning this difference, by itself, is not *sufficient* to ensure your success on the LSAT, but without this knowledge you will surely fail. (That's how we know it's *necessary*.)

This can be difficult at first, but trust me: it's totally learnable, even obvious once you get it. Check out these resources:

• Definitions and examples for Sufficient Assumption and Necessary Assumption questions can be found in the appendices of this book and in the box on pg. 51.
• My LSAT blog (foxlsat.com/lsat-blog) has tons on this topic.
• Want a new perspective? Wikipedia has a good entry on "Necessity and Sufficiency"

Don't give up on this topic. It's very important.

The rule that applies to the kid, and leads to the same outcome the speaker wanted, is B. So that's our answer.

## QUESTION 23:

Researcher: Each subject in this experiment owns one car, and was asked to estimate what proportion of all automobiles registered in the nation are the same make as the subject's car. The estimate of nearly every subject has been significantly higher than the actual national statistic for the make of that subject's car. I hypothesize that certain makes of car are more common in some regions of the nation than in other regions; obviously, that would lead many people to overestimate how common their make of car is nationally. That is precisely the result found in this experiment, so certain makes of car must indeed be more common in some areas of the nation than in others.

**Which one of the following most accurately expresses a reasoning flaw in the researcher's argument?**

A) The argument fails to estimate the likelihood that most subjects in the experiment did not know the actual statistics about how common their make of car is nationwide.
B) The argument treats a result that supports a hypothesis as a result that proves a hypothesis.
C) The argument fails to take into account the possibility that the subject pool may come from a wide variety of geographical regions.
D) The argument attempts to draw its main conclusion from a set of premises that are mutually contradictory.
E) The argument applies a statistical generalization to a particular case to which it was not intended to apply.

What? No. Revoke that guy's nerd card for accepting his own hypothesis so quickly. He basically says, "I hypothesize that a certain cause could have a certain effect. The effect has been proven to exist, so my proposed cause must exist also." Hand over the nerd card, pal—we gotta cut that shit in half.

Let's propose similarly flawed arguments to show the ridiculousness. How about:

I hypothesize that astrological signs dictate personality and fortune in life. Because different personalities and fortunes are proven to exist, this proves that astrological signs have an effect.

I hypothesize that space aliens help me win football games if I ask them very very nicely. Because I won my last football game after asking them very very nicely, this proves that my space alien prayers helped me win.

You get the picture. We must find an answer that "most accurately expresses a reasoning flaw." The answer will be something like "The argument accepts a causal hypothesis when only the effect has been proven to exist."

A) Definitely not what we're looking for. Let's not bother trying to figure out what this means unless all the other answers are garbage.
B) This feels like a trap. The "result" mentioned in the argument (the study) doesn't even *support* the hypothesis. Did the fact that I won a football game "support" my hypothesis that space aliens are answering my prayers? Still, the argument does make a certain conclusion on the basis of very weak evidence. If all the other answers are totally off the mark, we'll come back.
C) This doesn't weaken the argument, and might actually strengthen it. If subjects from a wide variety of geographical regions are overestimating the prevalence of their particular car, then the researcher could say "yep, the cause and effect is nationwide... subjects all over the country overestimate the prevalence of their car, because pockets of popular cars exist all over the country." We were looking for a flaw, not a strengthener. This is out.
D) No, there aren't any premises in the argument that contradict. This would only be the answer if the argument had said "2+2 = 4, and 2+2 = 5, and therefore XYZ."
E) No inappropriate generalization here. This would only be the answer if the argument said, "because San Francisco summers are statistically proven to be moderate in temperature, this summer in Sacramento will also be very moderate."

I hate to say it, but our answer is B. All the other answers are terrible, and B describes *one* flaw in the argument, even if the argument had much bigger flaws. Very tough question.

24

## QUESTION 24:

In university towns, police issue far more parking citations during the school year than they do during the times when the students are out of town. Therefore, we know that most parking citations in university towns are issued to students.

Which one of the following is most similar in its flawed reasoning to the flawed reasoning in the argument above?

A) We know that children buy most of the snacks at cinemas, because popcorn sales increase as the proportion of child moviegoers to adult moviegoers increases.
B) We know that this houseplant gets more of the sunlight from the window, because it is greener than that houseplant.
C) We know that most people who go to a university are studious because most of those people study while they attend the university.
D) We know that consumers buy more fruit during the summer than they buy during the winter, because there are far more varieties of fruit available in the summer than in the winter.
E) We know that most of the snacks parents buy go to other people's children, because when other people's children come to visit, parents give out more snacks than usual.

Don't professors get tickets? Don't university administrators get tickets? School secretaries? Campus bus drivers? Fraternity beer keg deliverymen? The argument seems to assume that students are the only people that are in town during the school year. What about all those other seasonal folks?

Furthermore, what about the townies that are there all year-round, racking up tickets? What about the high school punks? They get tickets all year round, right? So of course, when the population doubles during the school year, the total number of tickets goes way up. But this is because the college folks are getting a few, *in addition to* the tickets that the high school punks keep getting.

We're asked to find a similarly flawed argument. So the correct answer has to be 1) flawed, and 2) flawed in the same way.

A) I don't think so. The big problem here is that adults probably buy snacks for the kids... kids don't buy snacks for themselves. I don't think this really matches.
B) This isn't even close. Nothing similar at all here.
C) The only thing similar here is the word "university." This is a trap for those who are being superlazy. (Is this argument even flawed? I think if you study then it is probably valid to call you "studious.")
D) No, I don't think the given argument had anything to do with number of types of items vs. total number of items. This is definitely flawed, but it's not the *same* flaw.
E) There we go. Of course it's true that Cartman and his friends gobble up lots of snacks during his birthday slumber party. But believe me, that fatass *also gobbles up snacks every other Goddamned day*, so even though total snack consumption spikes when Stan and Kyle and Kenny are over, Cartman still consumes 99 percent of all the snacks his mom buys. This matches the pattern we were looking for (townies keep getting tickets all year round).

Our answer is E.

## QUESTION 25:

**Counselor:** Those who believe that criticism should be gentle rather than harsh should consider the following: change requires a motive, and criticism that is unpleasant provides a motive. Since harsh criticism is unpleasant, harsh criticism provides a motive. Therefore, only harsh criticism will cause the person criticized to change.

The reasoning in the counselor's argument is most vulnerable to criticism on the grounds that the argument

A) infers that something that is sufficient to provide a motive is necessary to provide a motive
B) fails to address the possibility that in some cases the primary goal of criticism is something other than bringing about change in the person being criticized
C) takes for granted that everyone who is motivated to change will change
D) confuses a motive for doing something with a motive for avoiding something
E) takes the refutation of an argument to be sufficient to show that the argument's conclusion is false

Like Bernie Madoff, this one seems tight at the beginning but blows up in the end. I can rearrange the facts like this:

- If you are harshly criticized, then it is unpleasant.
- If you are unpleasantly criticized, then you have motive to change.
- In order to change, you must have motive.

A valid conclusion would have been, "So if you want to change, one way to get the motive you need is to be harshly criticized."

But that's not what the counselor claimed. Instead, the counselor claimed that harsh criticism is the *only* way to get the motive you need for change. The facts simply don't justify this conclusion—the facts *do* prove that harsh criticism will provide motive, but they *don't* eliminate all other possible ways of getting motivated.

The flaw here is the most egregious, or at least most commonly-tested, flaw in the history of the LSAT—the counselor has confused a sufficient condition for a necessary condition. (The facts indicate that harsh criticism is sufficient, *i.e.*, enough, to provide motive, but the conclusion suggests that harsh criticism is necessary, *i.e.* the only way, to get the motive you need). Let's look for an answer that says, "confuses a sufficient condition for a necessary condition."

A) Yep, that's what we were looking for. Number 25 is basically a freebie, after a very nasty stretch of questions from 19 through 24.
B) No, the goals of those doing the criticizing are simply irrelevant. And we've already found our answer in A. Basically, the only way to get us off of A would be another answer that also deals with sufficient vs. necessary.
C) No, the argument simply doesn't do this.
D) Avoiding? The argument is not about avoiding anything.
E) Well, this has the word "sufficient" in it, and the argument *is* designed to refute a certain position. But the argument doesn't go so far as to claim that a certain position is false, nor does it actually refute, *i.e.* prove wrong, any other argument. I guess this answer could be considered second-best, but it's a distant second.

Our answer is A because it very clearly describes the LSAT's most important flaw, which was present in the Counselor's argument.

# SECTION
# **TWO**

# Analytical Reasoning (Logic Games)

## (Or: Exposing the Patterns)

With Logic Games, just like the rest of the LSAT, you have to slow down in order to speed up. First, the good news: hardly anybody completes all four games. So our goal here is to slow down and focus on accuracy.

Unlike the rest of the LSAT, where we often have to pick the best of a bad bunch of answers, every question on the logic games has a single, objectively correct answer. There is no picking the "best" answer on the logic games. Rather, there are four terrible answers that we hate and one perfect answer that we love. *Focus on answering the questions with 100% certainty.* If you're just starting out, see if you can just get every answer right on a single game. If you can do this in 35 minutes, you're on the right track. Next, see if you can do two games perfectly in 35 minutes. Believe it or not, that would put you well ahead of the average test taker. If you can do three games perfectly, you'll be in the top ninety percent. But you have to walk before you can run. As long as you take your time in the beginning, eventually the patterns will start to reveal themselves.

My general process for Logic Games is as follows:

1. **Read through the entire scenario and all of the rules before doing anything else.** That lets you get the lay of the land before you start messing up the page. Fortunately, almost every game follows a "putting things in order" pattern, or "putting things in groups" pattern, or some combination of the two. Try to figure out which of these operations is most prominent in the game before you do anything else. Remember that there is no scratch paper allowed, so have a sharp pencil in hand, write small, and *think* before you write.

2. **Take plenty of time to understand exactly what each rule means.** Sometimes a single rule will have three pieces of information in it. For example, a rule might say, "B must go before A and after C, but can't go fourth." There are really *three* rules here. (1. B before A; 2. B after C; 3. B can't go fourth.) If you miss any one of these rules, you'll struggle with the game. Conversely, sometimes a rule will

mean *less* than you think it means at first blush. For example, the rule might say "A, B, C, D, and E are available for interviews." This does NOT mean that each of these people must interview! Look for another rule that says, "Each candidate must interview exactly once," or "there will be five interviews and no candidate can interview twice." If these rules are not present, then it's possible that one or more of the candidates might not interview at all, and/or one or more candidates might interview more than once. The slightest mistake can ruin the entire game, so read carefully, and absolutely do not rush.

3. **Make a diagram that incorporates as much information about the game as possible.** Sometimes, this will be a diagram that is exactly like something you've seen on a previous game. Frequently, you'll be able to use a diagram similar to a game you've seen before, but you'll have to make some minor tweaks. The LSAT has repeated a few basic patterns over and over and over: the more practice you've done, the more familiar the games will start to look. Still, on occasion, you'll have to invent something entirely new. Never fear: You'll be equipped to do this once you've practiced these methods.

4. **As you diagram, take the time to consider each rule in the context of all the rules, not just by itself.** The big prep companies will call this "making inferences," like it's some kind of magical process. But all we're really doing is writing down shit we know for sure. Usually, the first "inferences" come from simply combining two rules together. For example, if A comes before B and there are only seven spots, then A can't go last, because there would be no room left for B. This isn't rocket science. (Hey, B can't go first either, because where would A go?! I'm a genius.) Any time you learn something for sure, no matter how small, write it down. Like a Porta-Potty at a rock concert, little things will add up fast.

5. **Remember that more powerful inferences come from combining three rules together, or from combining a rule with an inference, or from combining two inferences together.** Every time you make a new inference, you get to consider that inference in light of everything else you know about the game, and frequently you'll be able to make another inference, which might lead to another, and another... Don't short-circuit this process by going to the questions too soon. Always remember that the questions are designed to confuse you! It's much better to invest the time up front in a solid solution rather than frantically trying to answer the questions without having a good foundation. Some of what you're writing down at this stage will directly answer some of the questions you'll see later.

6. **Move on to the questions when—and only when—you're ready.** "OK, but how do I know when it's time to go to the questions?" Every class asks me this question, and my answer is always the same: only *you* can really tell, through lots and lots of practice. I realize this isn't a very satisfactory answer, but it's the truth. Every game is different, and some games allow more inferences than others. Sometimes, I'll invest five or six minutes before going to the questions. On other games, I'll feel like I've learned all I can after a minute or two and go ahead to the questions. Personally, if I get stuck for 45-60 seconds without making any new inferences then I'm probably ready to proceed to the questions.

The logic games are partially art and partially science. You'll need to practice, practice, *practice* on the games until you get a feel for it. The payoff can be huge. I've never met a single student who couldn't eventually make a five or six question leap forward on the Logic Games. It's the most learnable section of the test. And it's also fun. These are *games*, dammit!

## Be a Pencil Pusher

Don't be afraid to take action. Each mark you make won't be an earth-shattering revelation, especially not at the beginning. The point is to simply write down the things you know for sure. Start by writing down your list of variables. Does this solve the game immediately? Of course not. But it gets you moving in the right direction, which is much better than freezing up and doing nothing at all.

## Solitaire Logic

Making inferences is like playing solitaire. You're only stuck in solitaire when you go through the entire deck without doing anything new. Every time you place even a single card, you get to go back through the whole deck to see what new possibilities have opened up. Tiny moves can have huge significance! Don't give up or panic too soon.

# Game One

Each of seven candidates for the position of judge—Hamadi, Jefferson, Kurtz, Li, McDonnell, Ortiz, and Perkins—will be appointed to an open position on one of two courts—the appellate court or the trial court. There are three open positions on the appellate court and six open positions on the trial court, but not all of them will be filled at this time. The judicial appointments will conform to the following conditions:

• Li must be appointed to the appellate court.
• Kurtz must be appointed to the trial court.
• Hamadi cannot be appointed to the same court as Perkins.

### Game One Setup (Questions 1-5)

The pattern here is clearly "putting things in groups." We have seven judges and two groups. Everyone has to go in one group or the other. Nobody goes in both groups, and nobody can be left out. Note that there is no *ordering* here at all. (There's no "chairman" of either group, and there's no "first" or "last" person assigned to either group.) All we have to do is figure out how to split the judges into two groups and we're done.

We'll start by listing my variables and making a picture of the two groups. Remember, there are three spots on the appellate court and six spots on the trial court:

H J K L M O P

A   T

Immediately we should notice that there are going to be two unfilled spots, since there are nine spots but only seven judges. The first rule couldn't possibly be any easier, since it simply tells us where one of the judges goes:

H J K M O P

L
A   T

Uh, the second rule is just as easy, since it also tells us where one of the judges goes:

H J M O P

L   K
A   T

The third rule is different. It doesn't tell me exactly where to put anybody—instead, it tells us that H and P, wherever they go, can't go in the same group. By itself, we'd denote that rule like this:

This last rule, combined with the fact that there are only two groups, creates an extremely common scenario. We don't know *where* H goes, but wherever it goes P has to go in the other group. And we don't know *where* P goes, but wherever it goes H has to go in the other group. So one spot in each group must be filled by either H or P. That's important! Let's add that to the diagram:

So in the end, we really only have three floaters (J, M, and O) for five spots (one on the appellate court and four on the trial court). We'll want to keep an eye on that appellate spot, because if it gets filled then everyone else has to go on the trial court.

We've only made one inference here (filling up a spot on both courts for the H/P split), but if past experience is any guide then that inference will turn out to be a huge one. I don't see anything else for us to do, so that means it's time to go on to the questions.

## QUESTION 1:

**Which one of the following is an acceptable set of appointments of candidates to courts?**

A) **appellate:** Hamadi, Ortiz
   **trial:** Jefferson, Kurtz, Li, McDonnell, Perkins
B) **appellate:** Hamadi, Li, Perkins
   **trial:** Jefferson, Kurtz, McDonnell, Ortiz
C) **appellate:** Kurtz, Li, Perkins
   **trial:** Hamadi, Jefferson, McDonnell, Ortiz
D) **appellate:** Li, McDonnell, Ortiz
   **trial:** Hamadi, Jefferson, Kurtz, Perkins
E) **appellate:** Li, Perkins
   **trial:** Hamadi, Jefferson, Kurtz, McDonnell, Ortiz

This is the most common type of question on the logic games. Every answer choice gives a full list of all the variables in their respective groups, and all we're asked to do is find the *one* answer choice that is acceptable. If there's only one that works, then there must be four answer choices that don't work. So a process of elimination should be pretty easy here.

There's a slower way and a faster way to do questions of this type. The slower way is to evaluate the answer choices, starting with A, and see what's wrong with each one. It'll work, but the problem with this approach is that you can get stuck on the correct answer. How long should you look at an answer choice without finding anything wrong with it before moving on to the other answers? It's a guessing game.

The more certain, and therefore faster, way to do this question is to take each *rule,* one at a time, and eliminate as many answer choices you can with that one rule. Like this:

- *Rule 1:* **L has to be on the appellate court.** That gets rid of A immediately. All other answer choices survive this rule. And now we're done with this rule, for the purposes of question 1.
- *Rule 2:* **K has to be on the trial court.** We don't have to look at A, because it's already eliminated. B, D, and E each pass this rule, but C does not. So C is eliminated.
- *Rule 3:* **H and P can't be on the same court.** This eliminates both B and D. The only remaining answer is E. Since we've tested all the rules, and E is the only answer to pass all the tests, we can be one hundred percent certain that our answer is E.

## Replacing Madness with Method

Pay close attention to the way I answer this first question. It might be only slightly faster than another method, but since this type of question appears first in almost every game, shaving off 30 seconds every time we see this type of question can shave 2 minutes off our total games time. It's also a great confidence builder to know we can quickly and accurately answer this question at the beginning of just about every game.

2

## QUESTION 2:

**Which one of the following CANNOT be true?**

A) Hamadi and McDonnell are both appointed to the appellate court.
B) McDonnell and Ortiz are both appointed to the appellate court.
C) Ortiz and Perkins are both appointed to the appellate court.
D) Hamadi and Jefferson are both appointed to the trial court.
E) Ortiz and Perkins are both appointed to the trial court.

This question asks us to find an answer choice that CANNOT be true. Unlike question 1, which was most easily answered using a process of elimination, we should look to positively ID the correct answer. All we have to do is pick the one that for sure won't work.

## Could be vs. must be

A quick rule of thumb is that a "could be true" (or "could be false") is easiest to answer via process of elimination. A "must be true" (or "must be false") is most easily answered by positively identifying the answer choice. This is because it's easier to see something that's certain than it is to see something that's merely possible. So on a "could be" question, it's quicker to eliminate the four "cannot be" answers.

A) I don't immediately see why this won't work, so I'll go on to B.
B) Bingo. The appellate court only has three positions, and two of them are already filled by L and *either* H or P. So there's room on the appellate court for either M or O, but not both at the same time. This answer cannot be true, so it's our answer. Let's just quickly scan C-E to make sure nothing else jumps out at us.
C) No, this seems fine. Note that A and C, like B, are about the appellate court, which doesn't have many spaces available—but both A and C list either H or P as one of the two judges on the appellate court. That'll work, unlike B.
D) Plenty of room on the trial court. No problem.
E) Again, plenty of room on the trial court.

Our answer is B.

## QUESTION 3:

**Which one of the following CANNOT be true?**

A) Jefferson and McDonnell are both appointed to the appellate court.
B) Jefferson and McDonnell are both appointed to the trial court.
C) McDonnell and Ortiz are both appointed to the trial court.
D) McDonnell and Perkins are both appointed to the appellate court.
E) McDonnell and Perkins are both appointed to the trial court.

Same strategy here as #2. Pick the one that looks like it'll be a problem.

A) Uh, wow. That was easy. Just like the previous question, there isn't enough room on the appellate court for these two candidates. The appellate court has to have L, along with either H or P, so there's only one other spot available. J and M can't be on the appellate court simultaneously. Again, let's scan the other answer choices just to be sure, but we can be ninety-nine percent certain this is our answer.
B) Plenty of room on the trial court.
C) Plenty of room on the trial court.
D) P with M on the appellate court? Sure, that'll work, unlike J with M, in answer A.
E) Plenty of room on the trial court.

Our answer is A. Our big inference made #2 and #3 basically freebies.

4

## QUESTION 4:

If Ortiz is appointed to the appellate court, which one of the following must be true?

A) Hamadi is appointed to the appellate court.
B) Jefferson is appointed to the appellate court.
C) Jefferson is appointed to the trial court.
D) Perkins is appointed to the appellate court.
E) Perkins is appointed to the trial court.

This question gives us a new rule that applies *only* to this question. So the first thing we have to do is adjust our diagram to incorporate the new information. Let's go ahead and put Ortiz on the appellate court:

$$
\begin{array}{cc}
J\ M & \underline{\phantom{X}} \\
 & \underline{\phantom{X}} \\
 & \underline{\phantom{X}} \\
\underline{O} & \underline{\phantom{X}} \\
\underline{H/P} & \underline{P/H} \\
\underline{L} & \underline{K} \\
\underline{A} & \underline{T}
\end{array}
$$

Notice anything? Yeah, the appellate court is now completely filled by L, O, and either H or P. That means everyone who isn't already assigned has to go on the trial court. Like this:

$$
\begin{array}{cc}
 & \underline{\phantom{X}} \\
 & \underline{M} \\
\underline{O} & \underline{J} \\
\underline{H/P} & \underline{P/H} \\
\underline{L} & \underline{K} \\
\underline{A} & \underline{T}
\end{array}
$$

So the only thing we don't know is where H and P go. (One's on one court, one's on the other.) The question asks us for something that must be true. This shouldn't be too tough, since we almost know everything about the game.

A) No, H and P can swap spots on the appellate and trial courts. It *could* be true that H is on the appellate court, but it doesn't *have* to be true.
B) No, J must be on the trial court.
C) Yep, he sure is.
D) Nah, same thing as A. Since H and P can swap spots on the appellate and trial courts, it *could* be true that P is on the appellate court, but it doesn't *have* to be true.
E) Same explanation as D.

Our answer is C.

## QUESTION 5:

Which one of the following, if substituted for the condition that Hamadi cannot be appointed to the same court as Perkins, would have the same effect on the appointments of the seven candidates?

A) Hamadi and Perkins cannot both be appointed to the appellate court.
B) If Hamadi is not appointed to the trial court, then Perkins must be.
C) If Perkins is appointed to the same court as Jefferson, then Hamadi cannot be.
D) If Hamadi is appointed to the same court as Li, then Perkins must be appointed to the same court as Kurtz.
E) No three of Hamadi, Kurtz, Li, and Perkins can be appointed to the same court as each other.

This is, by far, the hardest type of question that appears regularly on the Logic Games. It's not a little bit harder than the typical question, it's a *lot* harder. I strongly recommend that when you encounter a question of this type, you simply skip it and come back to it after you've done the remainder of the section, time permitting.

This question sucks because it changes the rules, which means we probably have to throw out all our existing work. And since this is always the last question in the game, there's nothing we can learn here that will help us on any subsequent question... our understanding of this question can get us, *at most*, one additional point. Your time is better spent on the subsequent games. I promise you that I would guess on this question, and then come back to it, time permitting, after finishing the section. That usually means you should skip it too.

The question is answerable, but extremely time-consuming. We have to find a new rule that does 1) no more than, and 2) no less than, one of the old rules. It's impossible to predict this type of question in advance, so we're going to have to eliminate four answer choices that have a different effect than the old rule. The rule we're replacing is "H cannot be appointed to the same court as P." Here we go:

A) It's true that H and P couldn't both be appointed to the appellate court under the old rule. So this rule wouldn't do *more* than the old rule. However, if this is the rule then it's permissible for H and P to both be on the trial court. So this rule does *less* than the old rule, and is therefore eliminated.

B) It's true that either H or P had to be on the trial court according to the old rule. So this rule wouldn't do more than the old rule. However, if this is the rule then it's permissible for H and P to *both* go on the trial court. (See sidebar if you're not sure why.) So this rule does *less* than the old rule, and is therefore eliminated.

C) Nope. This rule only applies if P is on the same court as J. So if P and J were *not* together, then P and H could be together. That wasn't permissible under the old rule. Since this answer does *less* than the old rule, it is eliminated.

D) Same thing as C, because this rule only applies if H is with L. If H is not with L, then P and H could be together. That wasn't permissible under the old rule. Since this answer does *less* than the old rule, it is eliminated.

E) This would do it. Under Rule 1 and Rule 2, L and K are *already* on separate groups. And if this were to replace Rule 3, it would have the exact same effect—there would be no way to put H and P together. This rule does no more, and no less, than the old rule—so it's our answer.

Trust me: You need to skip this question. It's about ten times more time-consuming and difficult than the other questions in this section. It's a lot smarter to pluck the lower-hanging fruit first, before busting out the extension ladder.

## Superman's baby, redux

I gave this example earlier, for Section 1 #21, but it definitely bears repeating:

"If Superman is in the room, then Clark Kent is not" is absolutely *not* the same rule as "If mom is not taking care of the baby, then dad must be."

It's okay for Superman and Clark Kent to both be *absent*, but they can't both be present.

It's okay for mom and dad to both be *present*, but they can't both be absent.

Answer B for this question makes a rule that if one of H and P is not on the trial court, then the other one must be there. But that wouldn't prevent them from *both* being there, which was impermissible under the old rule.

# Game Two

Exactly six members of a skydiving team—Larue, Ohba, Pei, Treviño, Weiss, and Zacny—each dive exactly once, one at a time, from a plane, consistent with the following conditions:

• Treviño dives from the plane at some time before Weiss does.
• Larue dives from the plane either first or last.
• Neither Weiss nor Zacny dives from the plane last.
• Pei dives from the plane at some time after either Ohba or Larue but not both.

### Game Two Setup (Questions 6-10)

Game One looked very familiar to anyone who has done more than a few tests, because all we had to do there was put things into two groups. That's a very common pattern. This game is even more familiar; almost every modern LSAT has at least one game (sometimes two!) that simply requires that its variables be put *in order* from first to last. This is the type of game that all my students eventually crush. After a few weeks in my classroom, I expect most students to score perfectly on a game like this, in no more than ten minutes or so, and frequently much, much quicker.

We're told that everybody has to jump out of the plane once. Nobody is allowed to puss out, and it would be pretty hard to jump out of the same plane twice on the same flight. Furthermore, nobody dives tandem. So it's six dudes for six spots, like this:

L O P T W Z
_ _ _ _ _ _

The first rule puts T before W. Not necessarily *immediately* before W, although that would be possible. T goes sometime before W. That rule looks like this:

T ... W

The second rule says L must go first or last. Because I prefer to write down things I know for sure, I'll write that rule like this:

_ _ _ _ _ _
  L̶ L̶ L̶ L̶

What I've done there is write the spots where L *definitely can't go*, rather than trying to denote the spots where L *could go*. (It's a subtle thing, but I think you'll be better served by preferring to see the rules in light of things that must be true or must be false rather than could be true or could be false.)

The third rule says W and Z can't go last.

_ _ _ _ _ _
  L̶ L̶ L̶ L̶ W
          Z

The last rule is the toughest one, but it's really not that bad. P has to go after O *or* L, but can't go after both. This means P has to go *in between* O and L. We can write that rule like this:

O/L ... P ... L/O

Now, before we rush blindly into the questions, let's try to predict some of the answers in advance. We'll do this by simply *combining the rules together*. First, because there are six spots, and because T has to be before W, we know that T can't go last (because we have to save room for W). Likewise, W can't go first (because we have to save room for T):

W̶ L̶ L̶ L̶ L̶ W
     Z̶
     T̶

Next, because W can't go last (Rule 3) and T has to go before W (Rule 1), we can infer that T can't go *fifth* either, because if T went fifth then W would be forced into the sixth spot, which isn't allowed:

W̶ L̶ L̶ L̶ L̶ W
    T̶ Z̶
     T̶

Finally, because there are exactly six spots and because P has to go in-between O and L, we know that P can't go first or last:

W̶ L̶ L̶ L̶ L̶ W
P̶   T̶ Z̶
     T̶
     P̶

The most restricted spot in the game seems to be the last one. Only L and O can go in that spot, since everybody else is restricted from that spot. And with that, I think we're ready to go on to the questions. See the sidebar on the next page for an extra credit approach to this game, but let's keep it simple.

## QUESTION 6:

**Which one of the following could be an accurate list of the members in the order in which they dive from the plane, from first to last?**

A) Larue, Treviño, Ohba, Zacny, Pei, Weiss
B) Larue, Treviño, Pei, Zacny, Weiss, Ohba
C) Weiss, Ohba, Treviño, Zacny, Pei, Larue
D) Treviño, Weiss, Pei, Ohba, Zacny, Larue
E) Treviño, Weiss, Zacny, Larue, Pei, Ohba

## Bonus World(s)

I came close to penciling out two separate scenarios or "worlds" here, triggered by the rule that L must go first or last. If L goes first, then P has to be before O in order to keep P between L and O. Similarly, if L goes last, then P has to be after O in order to keep P between L and O. (In class, I might do this game both ways on the board.) Space doesn't really permit that we do that here, but I encourage you to try it just for fun. If you do, I'll give you 5,000 bonus points, like the "Challenging Stage" on *Galaga*. (Are any of you even old enough to remember *Galaga*?) See my first book, "Cheating the LSAT", for a few examples of the "Worlds" approach in action.

Like Question 1 in the first game, we're presented with five complete outcomes and asked to identify the *one* that could be true. As I noted earlier, the surest/easiest/fastest way to approach this question is to take the rules, one at a time, and use them as weapons to eliminate answer choices. Like this:

• *Rule 1*: **T before W.** This eliminates C. All other answers survive.
• *Rule 2*: **L must be first or last.** This eliminates E. All other answers survive.
• *Rule 3*: **W and Z can't be last.** This eliminates A. We're down to just B and D.
• *Rule 4*: **P between O and L.** This eliminates D.

The only surviving answer is B, and we've tested all the rules. So we know we understand all the rules, and B is the answer. We should be feeling very optimistic about the game at this point.

## QUESTION 7:

**Which one of the following must be true?**

A) At least two of the members dive from the plane after Larue.
B) At least two of the members dive from the plane after Ohba.
C) At least two of the members dive from the plane after Pei.
D) At least two of the members dive from the plane after Treviño.
E) At least two of the members dive from the plane after Weiss.

Here, we are asked to identify a scenario that must (always) be true. This means that the four incorrect answers *could* be false. Because it's a "must be" question, it should be easier to positively identify the correct answer than to eliminate the incorrect answers. (The correct answer should jump out at us as the one that has to be true, in other words.) Let's see:

A) I sure don't think so. Couldn't L go last?
B) Why does this have to be true? Couldn't O go last?
C) We know that P can't go sixth, but why couldn't it go fifth? We're still waiting to see something attractive here.
D) Bingo. We actually predicted this one in advance, while doing our main diagram. The latest T can go is fourth, because W has to go after T but W can't go last. So W and one other guy have to go after T. This is our answer.
E) Well, W can't go last so at least *one* team member has to go after W. But W can go fifth, which would make this answer untrue.

Our answer is D.

## QUESTION 8:

If Larue dives from the plane last, then each of the following could be true EXCEPT:

A) Treviño dives from the plane fourth.
B) Weiss dives from the plane fourth.
C) Ohba dives from the plane fifth.
D) Pei dives from the plane fifth.
E) Zacny dives from the plane fifth.

We're given a new rule here, a rule that applies only to Question 8. So right next to Question 8 on my test page (in the top margin, perhaps?), I'd make a diagram that looks like this:

```
___ ___ ___ ___  L
 W               T
 P
```

If L goes last, then O will have to be before P in order to satisfy Rule 4. Since the last spot is filled, and we have to leave space for P between O and L, we can infer that O can't go fifth:

```
___ ___ ___ ___  L
 W               T
 P               Ø

        O ... P
        T ... W
```

(Note that if you did the "two worlds" approach that I contemplated in the sidebar, you'd already have made this diagram.) Let's check to see if we've already answered the question. "Could be true EXCEPT" just means, "must be false." So this is another "must be" question, and the correct answer will hopefully jump out at us as the one that won't work. Let's see:

A) I think T fourth and W fifth would be okay.
B) I think W fourth would be okay... T would still have a few places to go (1-3).
C) Bingo. We predicted this in our special diagram for this question. Sometimes the LSAT is just plain easy.
D) Nah, P would love to go fifth, because that would give O lots of room (1-4) ahead of it.
E) Sure, there's no reason why Z couldn't go fifth here. Our answer is C.

## QUESTION 9:

**If Zacny dives from the plane immediately after Weiss, then which one of the following must be false?**

A) Larue dives from the plane first.
B) Treviño dives from the plane third.
C) Zacny dives from the plane third.
D) Pei dives from the plane fourth.
E) Zacny dives from the plane fourth.

Again we're given a new rule, so again we have to make a new diagram. The new rule, by itself, looks like this:

W Z

This means that Z can't go first. And since Z can't go last (Rule 3), it means that W now can't go fifth:

And that, in turn, means that the latest T could go is third (with W fourth and Z fifth):

We're asked to identify an answer that must be false. Let's see if one of them jumps out at us.

A) I think L first would be fine. L - P - T - W - Z - O, for example.
B) I think T third would be fine. Matter of fact, the example I gave for answer A has T in the third spot.
C) If Z is third, then W has to be second and T has to be first. If T is first, then L has to be last (because L has to go first or last). So then O in the fourth spot and P in the fifth spot (to keep P between O and L). There's only one way to do it, but this does work.
D) Hmm. If P goes fourth, then that mucks up the middle of the order, where the WZ block needs to go. If P is fourth, WZ can't go fifth-sixth because Rule Three says Z can't go last. If WZ go second-third, then T has to go first. But this opening sequence, T – W – Z – P, has already made it impossible to keep P between L and O. This is the trickiest question so far in this game, but D simply won't work. So this is going to be our answer.
E) I think Z can go fourth. L – T – W – Z – P – O, for example.

Our answer is D.

## QUESTION 10:

If Treviño dives from the plane immediately after Larue, then each of the following could be true EXCEPT:

A) Ohba dives from the plane third.
B) Weiss dives from the plane third.
C) Zacny dives from the plane third.
D) Pei dives from the plane fourth.
E) Weiss dives from the plane fourth.

One more new rule, so one more new diagram. If T goes immediately after L, and L must go either first or last (Rule 2), then L has to go first. Like this:

$$\underline{L} \quad \underline{T} \quad \underline{\phantom{x}} \quad \underline{\phantom{x}} \quad \underline{\phantom{x}} \quad \underline{\phantom{x}}$$

W
Z
P̸

Because of Rule 4, if L is first then P has to go before O:

P ... O

And that, in turn, means that O can't go third:

$$\underline{L} \quad \underline{T} \quad \underline{\phantom{x}} \quad \underline{\phantom{x}} \quad \underline{\phantom{x}} \quad \underline{\phantom{x}}$$

Ø                    W
Z
P̸

Let's see if that sorts it out. We're asked, for the third time in a row, to find an answer choice that must be false.

A) There we have it. We predicted that O can't go third, so this is our answer.
B) This would work. L – T – W – P – Z – O, for example.
C) This would work. L – T – Z – W – P - O, for example.
D) This would work. L – T – Z – P – W – O, for example.
E) This would work. L – T – P – W – Z – O, for example.

Our answer is A.

Like Game One, I'd definitely call Game Two an easy game. I anticipate the next two will be a bit (or even a lot) harder.

# Game Three

A company's six vehicles—a hatchback, a limousine, a pickup, a roadster, a sedan, and a van—are serviced during a certain week—Monday through Saturday—one vehicle per day. The following conditions must apply:

- At least one of the vehicles is serviced later in the week than the hatchback.
- The roadster is serviced later in the week than the van and earlier in the week than the hatchback.
- Either the pickup and the van are serviced on consecutive days, or the pickup and the sedan are serviced on consecutive days, but not both.
- The sedan is serviced earlier in the week than the pickup or earlier in the week than the limousine, but not both.

## Game Three Setup (Questions 11-17)

Didn't I tell you the patterns would start to repeat themselves? I honestly didn't expect it to happen this soon, but here we are. This game, on its surface, looks extremely similar to the previous game. We have six vehicles that have to be put *in order*. Every vehicle must go exactly once. There are no ties. We'll see how it turns out, but I expect us to crush a game like this. (Like we did the last one.)

Let's start by laying out our days:

$$\text{—} \quad \text{—} \quad \text{—} \quad \text{—} \quad \text{—} \quad \text{—}$$
$$\text{M} \quad \text{T} \quad \text{W} \quad \text{Th} \quad \text{F} \quad \text{S}$$

Now we'll work our way through the rules. The first rule says at least one vehicle has to be after the hatchback. We can jot that down like this:

$$\text{H} \ldots \text{—}$$

Next, we learn that the roadster is after the van but before the hatchback. Let's immediately combine this rule with Rule 1, like so:

$$\text{V} \ldots \text{R} \ldots \text{H} \ldots \text{—}$$

I can't overstate the importance of that last step. *The rules are more powerful in combination than they are alone.* For example: Without combining rules one and two, it might appear (based solely on Rule 2) that the roadster could go on Friday. But since the hatchback has a space behind it (Rule 1) and the roadster has to go before the hatchback (Rule 2) we can now see that the roadster *cannot* go on Friday. Similarly, the van can't go on Thursday... we wouldn't be able to see that without examining the two rules *together*. Get in the habit of automatically connecting rules that contain common variables. Here's the layout, including all the who-can't-go-where implications from the first two rules:

$$
\begin{array}{cccccc}
\text{—} & \text{—} & \text{—} & \text{—} & \text{—} & \text{—} \\
\text{M} & \text{T} & \text{W} & \text{Th} & \text{F} & \text{S} \\
\cancel{R} & \cancel{H} & & \cancel{V} & \cancel{V} & \cancel{V} \\
\cancel{H} & & & \cancel{R} & \cancel{R} & \cancel{R} \\
& & & & & \cancel{H}
\end{array}
$$

The next rule presents an option. *Either* P is next to V (in either order), or P is next to S (in either order) but not both. I'm going to translate this into two outcomes. If it's true that P is next to V, then P can't be next to S:

$$\boxed{\widehat{PV}} \longleftrightarrow \boxed{\widehat{PS}}$$

Alternatively, if P is next to S, then P can't be next to V:

$$\widehat{PS} \longleftrightarrow \widehat{PV}$$

The next rule also requires a bit of translation. S is before P or before L, but not both. This simply means that S is *in between* P and L (note that this is exactly like Rule 4 in the previous game), like this:

$$P/L \dots S \dots L/P$$

That last rule leads to two inferences about S: it can't go first or last.

And now, I'm noticing that both the first and last spots (especially the last spot) are pretty bound up. Who can go first? Well, it can't be H, R, or S... so it has to be P, L, or V. And who can go last? If it can't be V, R, H, or S, then it can only be L or P. I might as well add that to the diagram:

I'd love to be able to combine Rules 3 and 4 with the Rule 1/2 combo, but unfortunately I don't think we can. I don't see any obvious next step as far as inferences go, so let's see if we can tackle the questions.

11

## QUESTION 11:

**Which one of the following could be the order in which the vehicles are serviced, from Monday through Saturday?**

A) the hatchback, the pickup, the sedan, the limousine, the van, the roadster
B) the pickup, the sedan, the van, the roadster, the hatchback, the limousine
C) the pickup, the van, the sedan, the roadster, the limousine, the hatchback
D) the van, the roadster, the pickup, the hatchback, the sedan, the limousine
E) the van, the sedan, the pickup, the roadster, the hatchback, the limousine

Like the first question in Games One and Two, I'm going to do this one via process of elimination. I'll use the rules, one at a time, to kill off as many answer choices as I can. When I'm done with all the rules, there should only be one answer choice left standing.

• *Rule 1*: **H can't go last.** This gets rid of C. Easy, right?
• *Rule 2*: **V before R before H.** This gets rid of A. We're down to B, D, and E.
• *Rule 3*: **Either PV touch (in either order) or PS touch (in either order) but not both.** This gets rid of D, because neither PV nor PS are touching. We're down to B and E.
• *Rule 4*: **Sedan between L and P.** This gets rid of E.

We've tested all the rules, and B is the only answer to pass all the tests. So B is our answer.

12

## QUESTION 12:

**Which one of the following CANNOT be the vehicle serviced on Thursday?**

A) the hatchback
B) the limousine
C) the pickup
D) the sedan
E) the van

We predicted this question well in advance, by combining Rule 1 and Rule 2 together. The van can't go on Thursday, because it has to go before R, and H, and at least one other vehicle. Our answer is E. Too easy. There's really no need to evaluate the other answer choices here, since we know for certain that V can't go Thursday.

## QUESTION 13:

If neither the pickup nor the limousine is serviced on Monday, then which one of the following must be true?

A) The hatchback and the limousine are serviced on consecutive days.
B) The hatchback and the sedan are serviced on consecutive days.
C) The van is serviced on Monday.
D) The limousine is serviced on Saturday.
E) The pickup is serviced on Saturday.

This question gives us a new bit of information, so we have to first make a new diagram and add the new information to it. Of course, all the old rules still apply. We already knew that only P, L, and V were eligible to go on Monday. So... if, uh, well... if H, R, S ,P, and L are all out for Monday, then I guess there's only one guy left, right? V is gonna have to go first. Like this:

$$
\begin{array}{c c c c c}
\underline{V} & \underline{\phantom{xx}} & \underline{\phantom{xx}} & \underline{\phantom{xx}} & \underline{L/P} \\
\cancel{R} & \cancel{H} & \cancel{V} & \cancel{V} & \cancel{V} \\
\cancel{H} & & & \cancel{R} & \cancel{R} \\
\cancel{S} & & & & \cancel{H} \\
& & & & \cancel{S}
\end{array}
$$

The question asks us to identify something that must be true, based on the above. Let's see:

A) I see no reason why this has to be true. I'm not going to waste too much time thinking about it until I've evaluated all the other answer choices.
B) Nah, same explanation as A.
C) Yup. We've already written this into our diagram for this question. So this is our answer, guaranteed.
D) No, L could go other places.
E) No, P could go other places.

Our answer is C.

14

## QUESTION 14:

If the limousine is not serviced on Saturday, then each of the following could be true EXCEPT:

A) The limousine is serviced on Monday.
B) The roadster is serviced on Tuesday.
C) The hatchback is serviced on Wednesday.
D) The roadster is serviced on Wednesday.
E) The sedan is serviced on Wednesday.

Déjà vu! If V, R, H, S, and L are all out for Saturday, and P is the only vehicle left, then P has to go on Saturday. Like this:

```
L/V  __  __  __  __   P
 R̶   H̶        V̶  V̶   V̶
 H̶             R̶   R̶
 S̶                 H̶
                    S̶
```

And now, we can go one more step. Remember that either PV or PS have to touch. If P is last, then there's no way for P to touch V (because V has a lot of guys that have to go after it). Therefore, P must touch S. Which means S has to go on Friday:

```
L/V  __  __  __   S    P
 R̶   H̶        V̶   V̶   V̶
 H̶             R̶   R̶
 S̶                 H̶
                    S̶
```

Intuition (gained through doing a *lot* of logic games) tells me that that might be enough to answer the question. We're asked to find an answer that must be false: "Could be true EXCEPT" = "find the one that must be false." Let's see:

A) I see no reason why this can't be true.
B) I see no reason why this can't be true either.
C) Sure, no problem.
D) No problem.
E) Yeah, this is it. The sedan, as diagrammed above, has to go on Friday in this scenario.

Our answer is E.

## QUESTION 15:

If the sedan is serviced earlier in the week than the pickup, then which one of the following could be true?

A) The limousine is serviced on Wednesday.
B) The sedan is serviced on Wednesday.
C) The van is serviced on Wednesday.
D) The hatchback is serviced on Friday.
E) The limousine is serviced on Saturday.

Again a new rule, and again a new diagram. Here, if S has to go before P, then L has to go before S in order to keep S between L and P. Like this:

L ... S ... P

But wait. We predicted, when we first started, that only L and P were available to go last. If that's true, and it's not L, then it must be P:

| L/V | _ | _ | _ | _ | P |
|-----|---|---|---|---|---|
| R̶ | H̶ | | V̶ | V̶ | V̶ |
| H̶ | | | | R̶ | R̶ |
| S̶ | | | | | H̶ |
| P̶ | | | | | S̶ |
| | | | | | L̶ |

And that, in turn, triggers the rule that says either PS or PV have to touch. Since V has to go early in the order, if P goes Saturday then S has to go Friday. This is just like the previous question.

| L/V | _ | _ | _ | S | P |
|-----|---|---|---|---|---|
| R̶ | H̶ | | V̶ | V̶ | V̶ |
| H̶ | | | | R̶ | R̶ |
| S̶ | | | | | H̶ |
| P̶ | | | | | S̶ |
| | | | | | L̶ |

We're asked to find something that "could" be true. It'll probably be easiest to knock out the four answer choices that must be false. Let's do it.

A) I don't see why not. I'm hoping B-E will all be obviously impossible, so I can happily choose A.
B) Nope, S has to go Friday.
C) Nope, V has to go either Monday or Tuesday, in order to save room behind it for R and H.
D) No, S is already in the Friday spot.
E) No, P is already in the Saturday spot.

Our answer is A.

## "Must Be" Trumps "Could Be"

Make special note of the technique here, because it will save you some time and increase your accuracy. This question is a "could be true," but I made no effort to actually prove that our eventual answer, A, actually works. If I know, for certain, that B-E all must be false, and if I don't see any reason why A must be false, then I am safe in assuming that A has gotta work. It's a lot harder to prove a "could be" than it is to prove a "must be." So A is our answer here through a very easy process of elimination.

## QUESTION 16:

If the limousine is serviced on Saturday, then which one of the following must be true?

A) The pickup is serviced earlier in the week than the roadster.
B) The pickup is serviced earlier in the week than the sedan.
C) The sedan is serviced earlier in the week than the roadster.
D) The hatchback and the limousine are serviced on consecutive days.
E) The roadster and the hatchback are serviced on consecutive days.

Wow, the Saturday spot is sure getting a lot of action. We kind of anticipated this, when we predicted that either P or L has to go last.

If L has to go last, then P has to go before S in order to keep S between P and L. So the rule looks like this:

P ... S ... L

If that's true, then P can't go Friday or Saturday, and L can't go Monday or Tuesday.

```
P/V  ___  ___  ___   L
 R    H    V    V     V
 H    L         R     R
 S              P     H
 L                    S
                      P
```

We're asked to find something that must be true. Let's see.

A) No, I don't see why this would have to be true. (V - R - P - S - H - L would work.)
B) Well yeah, duh, that's what we already said. This is a one-rule sort of question. If you understood the last rule to mean "S between L and P," then as soon as L goes last you know P is before S. This will be our answer.
C) No, this could be false. (V - R - P - S - H - L would work.)
D) No, this could be false. (V - R - P - H - S - L would work.)
E) No, this could be false. (See examples for A, C, and D.)

Our answer is B.

## QUESTION 17:

**Which one of the following could be the list of the vehicles serviced on Tuesday, Wednesday, and Friday, listed in that order?**

A) the pickup, the hatchback, the limousine
B) the pickup, the roadster, the hatchback
C) the sedan, the limousine, the hatchback
D) the van, the limousine, the hatchback
E) the van, the roadster, the limousine

We're asked to identify a partial list of vehicles, on a weird combination of days: Tuesday, Wednesday, and Friday. (Big note: Thursday is skipped.) Usually, incomplete list questions like this tend to be significantly more difficult than the other questions in a game. For that reason, and since it's the last question in the game, I wouldn't be mad at you if you just skipped this one and proceeded to the next game. But we've had a very easy time of this game, so I think we'll be able to figure this one out. I don't think there's any way to answer in advance, so let's just check out the answer choices and try to eliminate the four that won't work.

A) This won't work because either P or L must go on Saturday.
B) I don't immediately see why this won't work. V-P-R-S-H-L would satisfy this answer choice and, I believe, all the rules. So this is probably our answer. But let's knock out the must-be-false answers, just to be sure.
C) I don't think I'd be able to make P touch either V or S if I did this. If S and L are on Tuesday-Wednesday, and H is on Friday, then V will have to go Monday and R will have to go on Thursday in order to keep V before R before H. That leaves only P for the Saturday spot, which isn't touching either V or S. This is out.
D) This would force R into the Thursday spot, in order to keep V before R before H. But it leaves only the first and last spots for S, which can't go first or last because it has to stay between P and L. So this is out too.
E) This would force H into the Thursday spot, because it has to go after V and R but can't go last. So again we're left with just the first and last spot for S, which won't work... just like D, above.

So our answer is B.

I gotta say it... this has been an easy Goddamned section of games so far. There's simply been nothing out of the ordinary. Questions 5 and 17 were difficult, but there have been absolutely no surprises. Everything we've seen before has happened previously on multiple released LSATs. If you do enough practice, eventually you will start to see the patterns recur over, and over, and over. Still, almost every test throws in at least one twist. So I'm expecting Game Four to be a doozy.

# Game Four

A street entertainer has six boxes stacked one on top of the other and numbered consecutively 1 through 6, from the lowest box up to the highest. Each box contains a single ball, and each ball is one of three colors—green, red, or white. Onlookers are to guess the color of each ball in each box, given that the following conditions hold:

- There are more red balls than white balls.
- There is a box containing a green ball that is lower in the stack than any box that contains a red ball.
- There is a white ball in a box that is immediately below a box that contains a green ball.

### Game Four Setup (Questions 18-23)

Ooh, yeah—that's more like it. The first three games were extremely familiar, but this one is a different beast. Most tests have at least one game that doesn't fit so neatly into the known patterns. It's probably very difficult for the LSAC to continually come up with new games, so most of their ideas are repeats, and yet in every test they manage to come up with one or two interesting twists.

Ideally, you'll have gotten almost all the questions on the previous three games right before tackling this one. I'm sure we can handle it, but it would be a real tragedy to have made silly mistakes on those earlier, easier games because we were rushing to get to this later, harder one. If we're going to run out of time and guess on this game, so be it! Make sure you get as many of the easy points as possible.

Here we have to do *two* main operations: First, we have to figure out how many of each color ball the entertainer has. Green, red, and white are available, but we don't know exactly how many of each. Second, we have to figure out the order of those balls, from bottom to top.

Having read through all the rules, I'm going to discuss them slightly out of order. The first thing I notice is that the first and third rules both mention white. Rule 1: More red balls than white balls. One aspect of Rule 3: There has to be at least one white ball. In combination, these two rules imply that there are at least two red balls:

$$R, R, W, \_\_, \_\_, \_\_,$$

What color can those other three balls be? Well, another aspect of Rule 3 is that there must be at least one green ball.

$$R, R, W, G, \_\_, \_\_,$$

So we really only have two unknowns. Hmm. Can they both be white? No, because that would leave three white and only two red... there must be more red than white. Can one of them be white? Yes... but only if the other unknown was red. So one way to do it is this:

$$R, R, W, G, W, R$$

Otherwise, the unknowns cannot be white, and must be either red or green:

$$R, R, W, G, R/G, R/G$$

Now let's think about the ordering for a bit. The second and third rule both restrict the possible arrangement. Rule 2 says that there has to be at least one green ball that is lower than *all* the red balls. Another way of thinking about that is that none of the reds can be below the lowest green. Here's how I'd write that rule:

$$R^{all}$$
$$\vdots$$
$$G^{\geq 1}$$

One implication of this rule is that a red ball cannot possibly be on the bottom of the stack:

```
6 ___
5 ___
4 ___
3 ___
2 ___
1 ___  R̶
```

(The lowest a red ball could possibly go is second, and then only if a green ball was on the very bottom.)

Finally, the last rule says that there has to be a white immediately below a green somewhere in the stack. This does *not* mean that these are the only whites and greens, but at least once there has to be a green ball immediately above a white ball. Like this:

Aaaand... I'm stuck. I don't immediately see any more implications of the inferences I've made. I think we're going to have to do a lot of testing to answer each question. Here we go:

# 18

## QUESTION 18:

If there are exactly two white balls, then which one of the following boxes could contain a green ball?

A) box 1
B) box 3
C) box 4
D) box 5
E) box 6

I contemplated the "two whites" scenario above. Since there are more reds than whites, and at least one green, that means we've got three reds, two whites, and one green to deal with here.

If we have just one green, then one of the whites must be immediately below it. And *all* of the reds have to be above it. So our picture looks like this:

The only floater in this scenario is one of the whites. We're asked to identify a box that could contain a green ball. The answer can only be second or third, since there is one ball that must go below our green, and three balls that must go above it. Like this:

| | | | | |
|---|---|---|---|---|
| 6 __ | ⎫ | | 6 R | |
| 5 __ | ⎬ R, R, R, W | | 5 R | |
| 4 __ | | | 4 R | |
| 3 __ | ⎭ | OR | 3 G | |
| 2 G | | | 2 W | |
| 1 W | | | 1 W | |

The answer must be box 2 or box 3. Since only box 3 is listed among the answer choices, B is our answer.

## QUESTION 19:

If there are green balls in boxes 5 and 6, then which one of the following could be true?

A) There are red balls in boxes 1 and 4.
B) There are red balls in boxes 2 and 4.
C) There is a white ball in box 1.
D) There is a white ball in box 2.
E) There is a white ball in box 3.

The first thing to do here is incorporate the new information into our diagram:

6 G
5 G
4 __
3 __
2 __
1 __

Hmm. This seems problematic. Remember, there has to be at least one green *below* all the reds. Greens in box 5 and 6 do not help us meet that requirement. So there's going to have to be at least one more green, somewhere near the bottom.

And if there are three greens, then that means the remaining balls must be two reds and one white, because that's the only way to meet the requirement of more reds than whites. So I think there's really only a couple ways to do this:

**G, G, G, R, R, W**

| 6 G | 6 G |
| 5 G | 5 G |
| 4 R | 4 W |
| 3 R | 3 R |
| 2 G | 2 R |
| 1 W | 1 G |

Scenario 19.1          Scenario 19.2

I just don't see any other way to meet all the rules simultaneously. If I'm right, then the question should be pretty easy to answer.

A) No, there can never be a red ball in box 1, because at least one green has to go below all the reds. (We already predicted this in our opening discussion of the game.)
B) There can be a red ball in box 4 (scenario 19.1) or box 2 (scenario 19.2), but I don't think there can be a red in boxes 4 and 2 simultaneously.
C) Yes, I think this is possible. See scenario 19.1.
D) No, I don't see this in either scenario.
E) No, I don't see this in either scenario.

Our answer is C.

# 20

## QUESTION 20:

The ball in which one of the following boxes must be the same color as at least one of the other balls?

A) box 2
B) box 3
C) box 4
D) box 5
E) box 6

This is a unique question. Worded another way, it's asking, "Which box can't contain the only ball of its color?" In other words, if there is only one green or one white ball, which box can that ball *not* be in? (We can exclude red from our analysis here, because there can never be just one red ball.)

It's worth noticing, right off the bat, that Question 19 lays out a couple scenarios where there is only one white ball. These are *not* the only scenarios in which there is only one white ball, because there were additional restrictions on Question 19 (green balls in boxes 5 and 6). Still, the work we did for Question 19 is useful here to eliminate answer choices. In scenario 19.1, the lone white ball was in box 1. So if box 1 was listed as an answer choice for Question 20, it could not be the answer. (Unfortunately, it's not even listed.) But in scenario 19.2, the lone white ball was in box 4. So it's possible for box 4 to contain a ball that doesn't match any other balls, and C cannot be the answer for Question 20.

But at that point, I feel kinda stuck. We're probably going to end up testing the other answer choices until we find one that won't work. The question is... should we test them in order? Or can we come up with a prime suspect to haul in for questioning first?

My prime suspect here is box 6, at the very top. The reason for my suspicion is that the reds in this game tend to want to go higher in the order, and the greens and whites are required to go lower. Let's see if my suspicion is justified.

If box 6 contained the *only* white ball, it would be impossible to satisfy Rule 3 (there's a white ball somewhere immediately below a green ball). And if box 6 contained the *only* green ball, it would be impossible to satisfy Rule 2 (there's a green ball below all of the red balls). Obviously box 6 can't contain the only red ball, since there have to be at least two red balls.

So just like that, our answer is E.

## Trust your gut

Question 20 is tough, but we made short work of it by testing a prime suspect first. It certainly would have been possible to answer the question through brute force—we could have tested each answer choice, one at a time, until we found one that wouldn't work. Unfortunately, the correct answer here turns out to be E, so we would have done an awful lot of work to reach the correct answer. I'm very glad we were able to find a shortcut.

I know this might seem like magic right now. But if you do enough practice, eventually you'll start to develop this sort of intuition. *The patterns repeat themselves.* Don't be afraid of an answer because it feels "too obvious." On the LSAT, the suspect that seems guilty usually is. Intuition isn't enough to choose a final answer—but it's certainly enough to investigate a suspected answer first.

## QUESTION 21:

**Which one of the following must be true?**

A) There is a green ball in a box that is lower than box 4.
B) There is a green ball in a box that is higher than box 4.
C) There is a red ball in a box that is lower than box 4.
D) There is a red ball in a box that is higher than box 4.
E) There is a white ball in a box that is lower than box 4.

We're not given any new information here, so our only choice is to evaluate the answer choices one at a time. Unlike Question 20, there's not even any reason to suspect one answer over the others. So we'll just start at the top and ask, "Does this always have to be true? Or could it be false?"

A) Wow, right off the bat—this will end up as our correct answer. How could we possibly avoid having a green ball lower than box 4? Remember, there have to be at least two red balls, and at least one green ball has to go below all of the reds. So if we put reds in 5 and 6, and a lone green in box 4... that would leave three whites in boxes 1, 2, and 3? Nah... that's more whites than reds, which violates Rule 1. There's no way to avoid putting a green ball somewhere below box 4. So this answer is a "must be true." Let's just make sure that we can make B-E false, so we can be 100% confident in A.
B) Nah, there's no reason to even suspect that this would have to be true. Reds love to go at the top—it's more than possible to put nothing but reds in the top two boxes. There's nothing stopping us from putting reds in the top *four* boxes, actually. (Green in box 2, white in box 1... no problem.)
C) Why would reds have to go lower? No way.
D) It's true that reds like to go higher, but Question 19 proved that it's possible to avoid putting reds in boxes 5 and 6.
E) Scenario 19.2 proves that this doesn't always have to be true.

Our answer is A.

22

## QUESTION 22:

If there are red balls in boxes 2 and 3, then which one of the following could be true?

A) There is a red ball in box 1.
B) There is a white ball in box 1.
C) There is a green ball in box 4.
D) There is a red ball in box 5.
E) There is a white ball in box 6.

New information, new diagram. Like this:

```
6  __
5  __
4  __
3  R̲
2  R̲
1  __
```

Okay, now we just need to consider the new information in light of the old rules. The first thing that jumps out is the rule requiring at least one green to be below all the reds. If reds are in 2 and 3, this means that box 1 must be green:

```
6  __
5  __
4  __
3  R̲
2  R̲
1  G̲
```

That takes care of Rule 2. Next, let's think about Rule 3. We haven't yet satisfied this rule... we need to put a white immediately below a green. We've only got three boxes to play with, so there are only two ways to do it:

```
6  G̲          6  __
5  W̲          5  G̲
4  __          4  W̲
3  R̲          3  R̲
2  R̲          2  R̲
1  G̲          1  G̲
```

Scenario 22.1          Scenario 22.2

Finally, Rule 1 says we have to have more reds than whites. So the missing spots have to be red or green.

| | Scenario 22.1 | | Scenario 22.2 |
|---|---|---|---|
| 6 | G | 6 | R/G |
| 5 | W | 5 | G |
| 4 | R/G | 4 | W |
| 3 | R | 3 | R |
| 2 | R | 2 | R |
| 1 | G | 1 | G |

I'm almost positive this will be enough to answer the question. We're asked to find an answer that "could be true." If there's only one answer that will work, that means there are four answers that will *not* work. As I've discussed earlier in this chapter, it's usually easier to eliminate four *must be* falses than it is to prove that a *could be* true will really work. So let's try to knock out four answer choices here.

A) No, box 1 has to be green.
B) No, box 1 has to be green.
C) I think this will work (see scenario 22.1). But I'll just eliminate D and E, rather than try to prove this is acceptable.
D) Nah... box 5 has to be either green or white.
E) Nope. This wouldn't work in either scenario. Our answer is C.

# QUESTION 23:

If boxes 2, 3, and 4 all contain balls that are the same color as each other, then which one of the following must be true?

A) Exactly two of the boxes contain a green ball.
B) Exactly three of the boxes contain a green ball.
C) Exactly three of the boxes contain a red ball.
D) Exactly one of the boxes contains a white ball.
E) Exactly two of the boxes contain a white ball.

First question here: If boxes 2, 3, and 4 are all the same color, what color might that be? Can't be white, right? (We predicted, way back at the top, that there's a two-white maximum.) So this can only happen with green or red. Let's just sketch out those two possibilities real quick:

```
6 __        6 __
5 __        5 __
4  R        4  G
3  R        3  G
2  R        2  G
1 __        1 __
```
Scenario 23.1        Scenario 23.2

In order to satisfy Rule 2, box 1 will have to contain green in scenario 23.1:

```
6 __
5 __
4  R
3  R
2  R
1  G
```
Scenario 23.1

And then, in order to satisfy Rule 3, box 6 will have to contain green and box 5 will have to contain white. So Scenario 23.1 is complete:

```
6  G
5  W
4  R
3  R
2  R
1  G
```
Scenario 23.1

On to scenario 23.2. We haven't used any reds or whites yet, and reds have to out-number whites. So two of the remaining boxes are red, and one is white. Reds can't go in box one, so that's white. Sweet, this also satisfies Rule 3. To satisfy Rule 1, boxes 5 and 6 must both be red. It's another complete scenario:

6    R

5    R

4    G

3    G

2    G

1    W

Scenario 23.2

From here, this question will be easy. We're asked to identify a statement that must be true. We have two active scenarios here, so the correct answer must be true in both of those scenarios. (Otherwise, it doesn't always have to be true.) Let's see:

A)    No, scenario 23.2 has three green balls.
B)    No, scenario 23.1 has two green balls.
C)    No, scenario 23.2 has two red balls.
D)    Yes, this is true in both scenarios.
E)    No, this is false in both scenarios.

Our answer is D.

Game Four is manageable, but it's definitely tougher and more time-consuming than the earlier games. (It's an unfamiliar pattern, and many questions required a lot of testing of answer choices.) Make sure you master the first three games before you worry too much about this one—that goes for everyone, no matter what your current level of scoring. The key to completing a logic game section in 35 minutes is *domination of the earlier games*. Even an expert will take a while to solve this final game. The key is to kick ass on the earlier games so that you have plenty of time to grind out the fourth game. The worst mistake you could ever make is to rush through the earlier, easier games—making silly mistakes—in order to reach this much more difficult game. Most students would be thrilled with 18-19 points on a section of Logic Games, and that can easily be achieved without even attempting Game Four. Focus on accuracy and the easier games first. Eventually, speed will come through mastery.

# SECTION
# THREE

# Reading Comprehension

## (or: Exposing the Main Point)

Despite what the LSAT prep behemoths will try to tell you—or, more accurately, try to *sell* you—the big secret to the Reading Comprehension is that there *is* no secret. I'm actually shocked by the expensive books and boring lessons being hawked on this topic. It's called *Reading Comprehension,* which necessarily implies a fairly straightforward, two-step process:

1) Read.
2) Comprehend.

This ain't rocket science, but the behemoths sure as hell make it out to be. If you've already been suckered into buying a book or class on it, I'm sure you've found a dizzying array of underlining, highlighting, note-taking, arrow-drawing, and diagramming techniques that supposedly enhance your comprehension. But you've probably learned, as I have over my years as an LSAT instructor, that all this bullshit actually tends to make people comprehend the passages *less*, not more. You're not being graded on how well you can annotate the passage—this isn't an art project! Of course, if these complicated techniques actually *have* helped you kick ass on the Reading Comprehension, then by all means stick with them. But since you're reading this chapter, I'm going to guess that whatever you're doing isn't working out all *that* well. Right? So my first recommendation is simply to abandon whatever nonsense you may have been tainted with in the past. I think it's counterproductive for most students, and you're not going to find any of that stuff in this book.

Instead, you'll find me hammering away on one big concept: The main point is more than half the battle. If you can force yourself to stay awake, and be sure to *just get the big picture* out of each passage, you'll be well on your way to answering most of the questions. To expose the main point in any passage, there *is* one magic phrase I want you to learn. It doesn't justify an entire book on reading comprehension, but it's incredibly powerful nonetheless. That phrase is *"Why are you wasting my time with this?"*

# Passage One (Questions 1-7)

In Alaska, tradition is a powerful legal concept, appearing in a wide variety of legal contexts relating to natural-resource and public-lands activities. Both state and federal laws in the United States assign
(5) privileges and exemptions to individuals engaged in "traditional" activities using otherwise off-limits land and resources. But in spite of its prevalence in statutory law, the term "tradition" is rarely defined. Instead, there seems to be a presumption that its
(10) meaning is obvious. Failure to define "tradition" clearly in written law has given rise to problematic and inconsistent legal results.

One of the most prevalent ideas associated with the term "tradition" in the law is that tradition is based
(15) on long-standing practice, where "long-standing" refers not only to the passage of time but also to the continuity and regularity of a practice. But two recent court cases involving indigenous use of sea otter pelts illustrate the problems that can arise in the application
(20) of this sense of "traditional."

The hunting of sea otters was initially prohibited by the Fur Seal Treaty of 1910. The Marine Mammal Protection Act (MMPA) of 1972 continued the prohibition, but it also included an Alaska Native
(25) exemption, which allowed takings of protected animals for use in creating authentic native articles by means of "traditional native handicrafts." The U.S. Fish and Wildlife Service (FWS) subsequently issued regulations defining authentic native articles as those

(30) "commonly produced" before 1972, when the MMPA took effect. Not covered by the exemption, according to the FWS, were items produced from sea otter pelts, because Alaska Natives had not produced such handicrafts "within living memory."

(35) In 1986, FWS agents seized articles of clothing made from sea otter pelts from Marina Katelnikoff, an Aleut. She sued, but the district court upheld the FWS regulations. Then in 1991 Katelnikoff joined a similar suit brought by Boyd Dickinson, a Tlingit from whom
(40) articles of clothing made from sea otter pelts had also been seized. After hearing testimony establishing that Alaska Natives had made many uses of sea otters before the occupation of the territory by Russia in the late 1700s, the court reconsidered what constituted a
(45) traditional item under the statute. The court now held that the FWS's regulations were based on a "strained interpretation" of the word "traditional," and that the reference to "living memory" imposed an excessively restrictive time frame. The court stated, "The fact that
(50) Alaskan natives were prevented, by circumstances beyond their control, from exercising a tradition for a given period of time does not mean that it has been lost forever or that it has become any less a 'tradition.' It defies common sense to define 'traditional' in such
(55) a way that only those traditions that were exercised during a comparatively short period in history could qualify as 'traditional.'"

*Why are you wasting my time with this, Goddamn it?* At the end of the first paragraph, I honestly couldn't care less about this topic. But I'm going to fake interest in hopes of eventually achieving interest—fake it 'til you make it—and the trick I use for faking it is to ask the speaker to please, for the love of God, get to the fucking point already.

At the end of the first paragraph, it seems to me that the author is here to waste my time with a boring treatise on the importance of "tradition" in Alaskan law, and the problems/inconsistencies associated with the failure to define "tradition" clearly in written law. I'm obviously not trying to memorize every word here... I'm just trying to make the author get to her point.

At the end of the second paragraph, the author is still wasting my time on the importance of "tradition" in Alaskan law. One meaning of "tradition," it seems, has something to do with "long-standing practice" in terms of continuity and regularity. And the author hints that two recent cases—involving sea otter pelts—have illustrated the definitional problems hinted at in the first paragraph. This paragraph pisses me off more than the first paragraph, because it's more introductory fluff. Where is the actual conflict? This passage would have been a lot more interesting if it had started out with the conflict, rather than twenty lines of "There's a conflict!" pregame chatter. (Hey Jim Nantz and Nick Faldo! If the players are already on the golf course, then stop talking and *show the Goddamned golf.* Do you really think we tuned in to hear you idiots rambling? Or did we maybe want to watch Tiger?) Here's hoping paragraph three will show us the *fight,* already.

At the end of the third paragraph... Jesus Christ. I was hoping for blood—or at the very least a lawsuit—and instead all we got was a bunch of government regulations. At this point, the only thing we've learned is that there's been a fight over whether sea otter pelts are "traditional"—apparently the U.S. Fish and Wildlife Service says no, because such pelts hadn't been created "within living memory." I'm guessing that in paragraph four we'll learn something about Alaskan Natives who disagree with this ruling, hoping to cash in on the MMPA exemption by skinning themselves some baby otters. Let's see.

Finally some fucking action! At the beginning of paragraph four, we finally see a human being—Marina Katelnikoff, a bona fide Aleut—and we finally see something happen—Marina's bloody baby otter pelts suddenly get "seized" by the FWS. I think The Rock probably plays the role of the FWS here, storming Marina's igloo, guns blazing, to bust the notorious otter murderer. And then, *Law and Order* style, Agent Rock wins his first court case against Marina. Victory!

Yeah, except then Marina joins up with the sleazy-sounding "Boyd Dickinson," and Agent Rock ends up losing after all. A district court says that the FWS was wrong in using their "in living memory" definition to define "tradition." Instead, the district court notes that in the late 1700s, Alaskan Natives had used sea otter pelts, and that's "traditional" enough for them.

It's not a great movie. It's a shitty movie, as a matter of fact. But I think we've grasped the main point. Why is the author wasting our time with this? Well, she wanted to tell us that "tradition" is important in Alaskan law but very hard to define, and it's been fought about in Alaskan courts. Recently, Native Alaskans have defeated the government (in at least one case dealing with bloody otters) and won a definition of "traditional" that is pretty broad in scope: all you have to do is find a record of natives doing something sometime in history, even all the way back in the 1700s, and you get to call that activity "traditional."

Do I give a shit? No, I most certainly do not. But I think we get the big picture. Which means we can answer the questions. Let's do it.

## Be an asshole

I'm taking a very confrontational attitude as I read. I'm interrupting the author, and I'm asking very pointed questions, and, frankly, I'm being a dick. And I'm doing all that *on purpose.* I've found that being an asshole forces me to pay attention to the argument. In real life I'd just politely tune out the author's blathering, but for the next 35 minutes I *have* to pay attention. When I put a chip on my shoulder and ask the author "why are you wasting my time with this?" I put myself in a position where I'm obligated to listen for the response.

# QUESTION 1:

**Which one of the following most accurately expresses the main point of the passage?**

A)  Two cases involving the use of sea otter pelts by Alaska Natives illustrate the difficulties surrounding the application of the legal concept of tradition in Alaska.

B)  Two court decisions have challenged the notion that for an activity to be considered "traditional," it must be shown to be a long-standing activity that has been regularly and continually practiced.

C)  Two court cases involving the use of sea otter pelts by Alaska Natives exemplify the wave of lawsuits that are now occurring in response to changes in natural-resource and public-lands regulations.

D)  Definitions of certain legal terms long taken for granted are being reviewed in light of new evidence that has come from historical sources relating to Alaska Native culture.

E)  Alaskan state laws and U.S. federal laws are being challenged by Alaska Natives because the laws are not sufficiently sensitive to indigenous peoples' concerns.

When we're asked, point blank, to identify the main point of a passage, we should be able to do a damn good job of predicting the answer in advance. It is, after all, the most important (or only) thing we were looking for as we read the passage. If we can't say what the main point was, then we're simply not doing it right. We are reading too fast perhaps, or not paying close enough attention. But I think we can do it. As we discussed above, the main point is something like "tradition is important in Alaska, but hard to define, and the government wants to define it one way, but at least one Alaskan court disagrees." Let's see.

A)  Pretty damn close to our prediction. We should be happy with this if we can eliminate B-E.

B)  No, the Rock won his first case, and then lost the second. So the first case didn't "challenge" the "regular" and "continuous" definitions—only the second decision did.

C)  Wait up. Who said anything about a "wave of lawsuits that are now occurring in response to changes in natural-resource and public-lands regulations"?! We were only told about two lawsuits, and they were specifically about a certain definition of "tradition" in regard to seal otter murdering... not a whole broad slew of attacks on natural-resource and public-lands regulations in general. This is way too broad of an answer... the passage was about something much narrower than this.

D)  This is also too broad. "Tradition" is the only term that's really discussed here, not a whole range of long-standing legal terms.

E)  Nah. The problem with this answer choice is that it's far too favorable to the Alaskan Natives. The author never said the law should be "more sensitive" to the needs of the natives. The author remained very dispassionate, which is part of the reason why the passage was so horrifically boring. She could have wanted the natives to win, but she just as easily could have wanted Agent Rock to win.

Our answer is A, because it does the best job of describing what this boring passage was all about.

2

## QUESTION 2:

The court in the 1991 case referred to the FWS's interpretation of the term "traditional" as "strained" (line 46) because, in the court's view, the interpretation

A) ignored the ways in which Alaska Natives have historically understood the term "traditional"
B) was not consonant with any dictionary definition of "traditional"
C) was inconsistent with what the term "traditional" is normally understood to mean
D) led the FWS to use the word "traditional" to describe a practice that should not have been described as such
E) failed to specify which handicrafts qualified to be designated as "traditional"

This question basically says, "Why did Agent Rock lose his second case?" I think this answer should be reasonably predictable as well, if we were paying attention to the movie. I think a good answer would be, "The district court said the FWS's interpretation of 'traditional' was strained because it required a practice to have been carried on 'in living memory' in order to qualify as 'traditional.' The court ruled against that definition, and found that a practice that hadn't happened since the 1700s could qualify."

A) This definitely isn't what we're looking for. And I don't think the Alaskan Natives' own understanding of "tradition" has anything to do with it. We're talking about a legal definition of the term, not a cultural one.
B) I don't see what the dictionary has to do with it. Again, we're dealing with a *legal* definition.
C) Well, yeah, the court did invoke "common sense" in line 54. This doesn't match our prediction, but it *does* match something that the court actually said. So it's in the running as the best answer so far, and we'll have to take it if D and E don't offer anything better.
D) This answer gets it backward. The FWS was calling otter-murdering *non*traditional. It's the court that decided to call otter-murdering "traditional." This is out.
E) I think the regulation did fail to define exactly what crafts were "traditional" and which were not, but that's not why the court called the regulations "strained." The court objected to the "in living memory" definition, not the lack of specific craft designations.

Our answer has to be C, because it's the only answer that's really supported by the passage.

## QUESTION 3:

According to the passage, the court's decision in the 1991 case was based on which one of the following?

A) a narrow interpretation of the term "long-standing"
B) a common-sense interpretation of the phrase "within living memory"
C) strict adherence to the intent of FWS regulations
D) a new interpretation of the Fur Seal Treaty of 1910
E) testimony establishing certain historical facts

This is a lot like Question 2, in that it's asking for something we know about the second case—the one in which Agent Rock lost, the one in which the Natives were allowed to continue slaughtering. Shouldn't be too tough. All we need to do is pick an answer that is non-speculative and well-supported by the facts presented in the passage.

A) No, the court decided to *broadly* interpret the term "long-standing" to include a practice that actually hadn't been happening much since the 1700s.
B) No, the court entirely *dismissed* the "within living memory" standard. The court defined "traditional" to include a practice that had *not* occurred within the life-time of anyone on the planet.
C) The court overturned the FWS, so I don't see how they were "strictly adhering" to the FWS regs.
D) Wasn't the case about the FWS regs, not the 1910 treaty? This one just doesn't feel right to me... I don't remember the court talking about the treaty.
E) Yes. The court *did* hear testimony—see line 41—and ended up basing its decision on facts established by that testimony. This is our answer.

## QUESTION 4:

The passage most strongly suggests that the court in the 1986 case believed that "traditional" should be defined in a way that

A) reflects a compromise between the competing concerns surrounding the issue at hand
B) emphasizes the continuity and regularity of practices to which the term is applied
C) reflects the term's usage in everyday discourse
D) encourages the term's application to recently developed, as well as age-old, activities
E) reflects the concerns of the people engaging in what they consider to be traditional activities

Okay, this question is asking about the earlier case—the one that Agent Rock won. How was "traditional" defined in that case? I'm not sure we were specifically told. But since the Rock won, I think "traditional" must have been defined narrowly. The Natives would have lost under the "in living memory" standard. So that's my prediction.

A) What the fuck does this even mean? We shouldn't waste our time trying to parse this one unless and until we've eliminated all the other answers.
B) Yes, I think this is probably right. "In living memory" was an interpretation of the "continuity" and "regularity" standard. The Natives would lose if the court emphasized this standard, because the otter-murdering had *not* been continuously or regularly practiced since the 1700s. I like this answer.
C) Maybe the 1991 court used this standard—it did mention common sense—but I don't think the 1986 court did.
D) The 1991 court definitely applied "traditional" to "age-old" activities. But the 1986 court clearly did not.
E) Nah, the Alaskan Natives *lost* the 1986 case. The 1986 court definitely didn't care what the Natives "considered" to be traditional.

Our answer is B.

## QUESTION 5:

**Which one of the following is most strongly suggested by the passage?**

A) **Between 1910 and 1972, Alaska Natives were prohibited from hunting sea otters.**
B) **Traditional items made from sea otter pelts were specifically mentioned in the Alaska Native exemption of the MMPA.**
C) **In the late 1700s, Russian hunters pressured the Russian government to bar Alaska Natives from hunting sea otters.**
D) **By 1972, the sea otter population in Alaska had returned to the levels at which it had been prior to the late 1700s.**
E) **Prior to the late 1700s, sea otters were the marine animal most often hunted by Alaska Natives.**

There's no way to predict this one, since we're not given any new information or asked a specific question about the passage. All we have to do here is pick the answer that has the best evidentiary support found in the passage. Ideally, we'll be able to put our finger on a specific line and say, "Right *here*—this is where the passage provides support for this answer."

A) Lines 21 through 25 specifically support the idea that Alaskan Natives—along with everyone else—were prohibited from otter-bloodying from 1910 to 1972. We should be happy to pick this, but let's make sure nothing else sounds good before we do.
B) No, I think the whole problem, as presented by the passage, is that specific traditional items were *not* specified in the rules and regulations.
C) I do not recall Russian hunters ever being mentioned in the passage. If I had seen a Russian hunter, I would have pictured Dolph Lundgren in my movie. Since I didn't see Dolph, there's no way I can pick this answer. (The man is an incredible badass, by the way—if you ever want to feel utterly inferior, I recommend reading up on him. His Wikipedia entry alone will break you.)
D) Huh? Were sea otter populations ever mentioned?
E) Since no other animals were mentioned, I don't see how the passage could have concluded that sea otters were the animal "most often hunted."

We have to go with the answer that has the clearest support from the passage. Our answer is A.

## QUESTION 6:

The author's reference to the Fur Seal Treaty (line 22) primarily serves to

A) establish the earliest point in time at which fur seals were considered to be on the brink of extinction
B) indicate that several animals in addition to sea otters were covered by various regulatory exemptions issued over the years
C) demonstrate that there is a well-known legal precedent for prohibiting the hunting of protected animals
D) suggest that the sea otter population was imperiled by Russian seal hunters and not by Alaska Natives
E) help explain the evolution of Alaska Natives' legal rights with respect to handicrafts defined as "traditional"

The Fur Seal Treaty was mentioned as the beginning, in 1910, of the prohibitions against otter-bloodying. We should pick an answer that says that.

A) Nah, I doubt it. Species probably get close to extinction long before anybody actually does anything about it.
B) I don't see how "several additional animals" had anything to do with the passage.
C) Hmm. Does the passage actually say that the Treaty was "well-known"? This feels like a trap to me.
D) Nah, the Treaty had nothing to do with Dolph Lundgren. And yes, I know that Dolph Lundgren is not actually Russian. Did you know that "after serving his mandatory two years in the Swedish Marine Corps at the Amphibious Ranger School, he enrolled at the Royal Institute of Technology in Stockholm and graduated with a degree in chemical engineering"? Well, did you? (Thanks Wikipedia.)
E) Yeah, I suppose so. The treaty was the first prohibition of otter-murdering, but the prohibition began to "evolve" in 1972 when the term "traditional" was included in the MMPA. I don't love this answer, but I hate all the others.

Since we can at least make a case for E, it's gotta be our answer.

## QUESTION 7:

The ruling in the 1991 case would be most relevant as a precedent for deciding in a future case that which one of the following is a "traditional" Alaska Native handicraft?

A) A handicraft no longer practiced but shown by archaeological evidence to have been common among indigenous peoples several millennia ago
B) A handicraft that commonly involves taking the pelts of more than one species that has been designated as endangered
C) A handicraft that was once common but was discontinued when herd animals necessary for its practice abandoned their local habitat due to industrial development
D) A handicraft about which only a very few indigenous craftspeople were historically in possession of any knowledge
E) A handicraft about which young Alaska Natives know little because, while it was once common, few elder Alaska Natives still practice it

The 1991 case held that the definition of "traditional" can encompass activities that haven't occurred for centuries—a definition very favorable to the Alaskan Natives. Let's see if that definition would apply to any of the answer choices.

A) Hmm. Several millennia? I don't even know how long that is, but it sounds longer than the 1991 court might have anticipated. "Archaeological evidence?" Seems like a stretch. We could pick this if all the other answer choices really sucked, but I bet we find something better.
B) I don't think the 1991 court made any ruling about handicrafts that contain the carcasses of multiple endangered species. I don't see how this can be the answer.
C) This is the best answer so far. The 1991 court upheld as "traditional" a practice that had been discontinued due to factors beyond the native tribes' control. That seems to match the facts in this answer choice.
D) Nah, I think the handicraft had to at least have been commonly produced by a group of Natives at *some* point in order to be called "traditional" by the court's definition. This answer choice seems to imply a standard that is broader than what the 1991 court intended.
E) No, the 1991 court actually doesn't care whether anybody living has knowledge of a handicraft. The ruling encompassed a craft that hadn't been seen much since the 1700s, and was discontinued due to circumstances beyond the Native Alaskans' control.

Our answer is C, because it best matches the circumstances of the 1991 ruling.

Well, that passage more or less sucked. But I really wasn't expecting it to be any better. In any section of Reading Comprehension, I'm hoping to find one or two passages that catch my genuine interest. I tried to fake it on Passage One, in hopes that my acting would lead to actual excitement. Fantasizing about Dolph Lundgren and the Rock did help a little, but I can't say that I was anywhere near fully titillated. Still, we got all the questions right. Let's count it as a small victory, and hope that the second passage is a bit sexier.

# Passage Two (Questions 8-15)

The literary development of Kate Chopin, author of *The Awakening* (1899), took her through several phases of nineteenth-century women's fiction. Born in 1850, Chopin grew up with the sentimental novels that
(5) formed the bulk of the fiction of the mid–nineteenth century. In these works, authors employed elevated, romantic language to portray female characters whose sole concern was to establish their social positions through courtship and marriage. Later, when she
(10) started writing her own fiction, Chopin took as her models the works of a group of women writers known as the local colorists.

After 1865, what had traditionally been regarded as "women's culture" began to dissolve as women
(15) entered higher education, the professions, and the political world in greater numbers. The local colorists, who published stories about regional life in the 1870s and 1880s, were attracted to the new worlds opening up to women, and felt free to move within these worlds
(20) as artists. Like anthropologists, the local colorists observed culture and character with almost scientific detachment. However, as "women's culture" continued to disappear, the local colorists began to mourn its demise by investing its images with mythic significance.
(25) In their stories, the garden became a paradisal sanctuary; the house became an emblem of female nurturing; and the artifacts of domesticity became virtual totemic objects.

Unlike the local colorists, Chopin devoted herself
(30) to telling stories of loneliness, isolation, and frustration. But she used the conventions of the local colorists to solve a specific narrative problem: how to deal with extreme psychological states without resorting to the excesses of the sentimental novels she read as a youth.
(35) By reporting narrative events as if they were part of a region's "local color," Chopin could tell rather shocking or even melodramatic tales in an uninflected manner.

Chopin did not share the local colorists' growing nostalgia for the past, however, and by the 1890s she
(40) was looking beyond them to the more ambitious models offered by a movement known as the New Women. In the form as well as the content of their work, the New Women writers pursued freedom and innovation. They modified the form of the sentimental
(45) novel to make room for interludes of fantasy and parable, especially episodes in which women dream of an entirely different world than the one they inhabit. Instead of the crisply plotted short stories that had been the primary genre of the local colorists, the New
(50) Women writers experimented with impressionistic methods in an effort to explore hitherto unrecorded aspects of female consciousness. In *The Awakening*, Chopin embraced this impressionistic approach more fully to produce 39 numbered sections of uneven
(55) length unified less by their style or content than by their sustained focus on faithfully rendering the workings of the protagonist's mind.

*Oh, dear God.* At the end of the first paragraph, I can almost guarantee that this passage is going to bore the shit out of me. I have zero interest in nineteenth-century fiction, and even less interest in *analysis* of nineteenth-century fiction. *Yeah, well, get over it. Why is the author wasting your time?* Fine. At the end of the first paragraph, the author has cornered us with a story about Kate Chopin and "several phases" of the author's development. Apparently Chopin grew up reading "sentimental" novels about women chasing men and social status, and later modeled her own writing on "local colorists." We have no idea what "local colorists" are, but it seems like we're about to find out. I'll stop my whining now, and take it like a man.

*Why are you wasting my time with this?* The second paragraph isn't wasting our time too egregiously after all—there's a lot of information here. (Detailed facts are a hell of a lot more interesting than the conclusory fluff that we got in the beginning of Passage One.) First, paragraph two gives us a quick look at what the local colorists actually did: They published regional stories about women moving out of traditional roles and into higher education, the professions, and politics. Second, the author seems to hint at a positive opinion of the local colorists, sharing the complimentary observation that the colorists were "like anthropologists" in their "almost scientific detachment." But at the end of the second paragraph, we learn that the local colorists ended up glorifying the days of so-called "women's culture." The colorists had started out as detached observers, but ended up putting the old days on a pedestal. It seems as if the author doesn't love the local colorists that much after all.

At the beginning of the third paragraph, we learn that Chopin herself was "unlike" the local colorists, even as she modeled herself on those writers. How is that possible? At the end of line 30, we're looking at a mystery! In real life, I do not give two shits about this mystery. But since I'm making the best of it here, slogging through another LSAT Reading Comprehension passage, I'm going to pretend I care. How did Chopin take the local colorists as her model, but end up producing a product that was unlike the colorists'?

She did it by using the colorists' original method: detached reporting. She presented events as part of "local color" without emotional attachment, even when those stories were shocking or melodramatic. At this point, I think the author's main idea is something about how amazing Chopin is. Let's see where the fourth paragraph goes.

Yep, in the fourth paragraph, our hero Chopin moves entirely past the "nostalgia" of the local colorists, and joins the "more ambitious" New Women. Now she's pursuing freedom and innovation. She's "modifying the form" of the sentimental novel and spicing things up with fantasy. She's "experimenting" with impressionism and exploring "hitherto unrecorded aspects of female consciousness." It's devolved into gushing at this point—it's a love letter to Chopin. The last sentence, somewhat disconnected from the rest of the passage, is about one of Chopin's works in particular, *The Awakening*, which the author says is impressionistic, yet "faithfully renders the workings of the protagonist's mind."

OK. Let me share a little secret with you: I am not about to rush to the local library to pick myself up a copy of *The Awakening*, or any other book by Chopin. I would pour bleach into my own eyeballs before reading that stuff. But I *did* get the main point of the passage here: The author thinks Chopin is interesting. Revolutionary, even. Someone worth talking about. Someone who developed over time, growing and innovating. The author was here to waste our time about how Chopin is someone we should know about. Fine. Let's see if we can answer these questions and get out of here.

## QUESTION 8:

Which one of the following statements most accurately summarizes the content of the passage?

A) Although Chopin drew a great deal of the material for *The Awakening* from the concerns of the New Women, she adapted them, using the techniques of the local colorists, to recapture the atmosphere of the novels she had read in her youth.

B) Avoiding the sentimental excesses of novels she read in her youth, and influenced first by the conventions of the local colorists and then by the innovative methods of the New Women, Chopin developed the literary style she used in *The Awakening*.

C) With its stylistic shifts, variety of content, and attention to the internal psychology of its characters, Chopin's *The Awakening* was unlike any work of fiction written during the nineteenth century.

D) In *The Awakening*, Chopin rebelled against the stylistic restraint of the local colorists, choosing instead to tell her story in elevated, romantic language that would more accurately convey her protagonist's loneliness and frustration.

E) Because she felt a kinship with the subject matter but not the stylistic conventions of the local colorists, Chopin turned to the New Women as models for the style she was struggling to develop in *The Awakening*.

Well, we just summarized the passage ("Chopin is interesting, *etc.*") so this shouldn't be too tough.

A) This answer is absolute nonsense. If you read the passage carefully *at all*, then you could not have picked this answer. First, the passage didn't mention anything specific about where Chopin got her material for *The Awakening*. Second, she never "adapted the concerns" of the New Women. Nor did she try to "recapture" the romantic novels of her youth. This might be the worst answer in the history of the LSAT.

B) Yes, yes, yes. This answer directly parallels Chopin's development as described by the passage. She avoided sentiment, she was influenced by the local colorists, then the New Women, and this all culminated in *The Awakening*. I can't imagine a much better answer than this.

C) Nah. The passage wasn't really about *The Awakening*. It was about Chopin's development. So B is much better than C.

D) Same explanation as C.

E) Similar to C and D... the passage was really about Chopin's development, not the genesis of *The Awakening*. I do think this is the second-best answer, but I like B a lot better because it sums up Chopin's development nicely. Our answer is B.

## QUESTION 9:

With which one of the following statements about the local colorists would Chopin have been most likely to agree?

A) Their idealization of settings and objects formerly associated with "women's culture" was misguided.

B) Their tendency to observe character dispassionately caused their fiction to have little emotional impact.

C) Their chief contribution to literature lay in their status as inspiration for the New Women.

D) Their focus on regional life prevented them from addressing the new realms opening up to women.

E) Their conventions prevented them from portraying extreme psychological states with scientific detachment.

This question is asking us what the author thought *Chopin* thought about the local colorists. Since the author likes Chopin so much, the author and Chopin probably think the same thing: They like the dispassionate reportage style. But they didn't like how the local colorists eventually romanticized the era of "women's culture"—Chopin wrote shocking melodrama rather than fruity descriptions of the good old days of home and hearth and motherhood and all that bullshit. I think we've got it.

A) Well, we just said that Chopin and the author didn't like the "romanticizing" of women's culture, which is damn close to "idealization." This seems awful good.
B) Nah, Chopin *liked* (and adopted) the dispassionate style.
C) I don't think the passage says anything about the local colorists "inspiring" the New Women. For all we know, the New Women never even heard of the local colorists.
D) No, in paragraph two we have a description of the local colorists explicitly reporting on the new realms that were opening up to women. Like B, this answer says the exact opposite of what the passage said.
E) No, the local colorists *did* have "almost scientific detachment"—at least initially. Eventually they got all sappy and fell into romanticizing, but the passage doesn't say this was caused by "their conventions." It doesn't even say *what* the cause was.

The best answer is A, because it matches our prediction and is very well supported by the passage.

## QUESTION 10:

10

**According to the passage, which one of the following conventions did Chopin adopt from other nineteenth-century women writers?**

A) elevated, romantic language
B) mythic images of "women's culture"
C) detached narrative stance
D) strong plot lines
E) lonely, isolated protagonists

Fairly easy question here. Pick the one that Chopin learned, and took, from the influences mentioned in the passage.

A) No, Chopin avoided romance.
B) No, Chopin avoided mythicizing "women's culture."
C) Yes—as we've previously discussed, Chopin adopted the detached narrative stance of the local colorists.
D) I don't think we're told specifically whether Chopin had strong plot lines, but we know that she was influenced by the New Women, who avoided "crisply plotted short stories" and instead turned to impressionism. Chopin herself used impressionism in *The Awakening*, which seems to suggest Chopin might not have had strong plot lines.
E) Chopin did have lonely protagonists, but she didn't get this from any of the influences mentioned. We're told she was "unlike" the local colorists in this regard.

Our answer is C, because it has clear support from the passage.

11

## QUESTION 11:

**As it is used by the author in line 14 of the passage, "women's culture" most probably refers to a culture that was expressed primarily through women's**

A) domestic experiences
B) regional customs
C) artistic productions
D) educational achievements
E) political activities

My understanding of "women's culture" as mentioned in the beginning of the passage has something to do with women trying to advance their social status via men, marriage, and family. Hopefully we'll find an answer that looks something like that.

A) "Domestic" is awful close to "men, marriage, and family." I think we can be happy with this if all the other answers miss the mark. (As a matter of fact, it even says "domesticity" in line 27.)
B) I don't know what regional customs have to do with "women's culture" as described in the passage. We have to like A much better.
C) Nah, I'm pretty sure this is the opposite of what was meant by "women's culture" in the passage. Women weren't supposed to create or achieve back in those days... they were supposed to be barefoot and pregnant.
D) Same explanation as C.
E) Same explanation as C and D.

Our answer is A.

12

## QUESTION 12:

**The author of the passage describes the sentimental novels of the mid–nineteenth century in lines 3–9 primarily in order to**

A) argue that Chopin's style represents an attempt to mimic these novels
B) explain why Chopin later rejected the work of the local colorists
C) establish the background against which Chopin's fiction developed
D) illustrate the excesses to which Chopin believed nostalgic tendencies would lead
E) prove that women's literature was already flourishing by the time Chopin began to write

The very beginning of the passage started by describing the romance bullshit that Chopin read as a little girl. Let's see if that's enough to get it done.

A) No, Chopin definitely didn't try to "mimic" the romance bullshit.
B) I'm not sure we were ever told "why" Chopin ever did what she did. The author took us through Chopin's development, but never inside Chopin's head. I don't love this answer.
C) Well, yeah. The first paragraph was background. This is the best answer so far.
D) Again, we never really went inside Chopin's head. I don't see how this can be it.
E) Nah, the romantic bullshit presented in the first paragraph was definitely not meant to "prove" that women's literature was already flourishing. The opposite is true, if anything.

Let's go with C, since it best matches our prediction of "It's what she read as a little girl."

## QUESTION 13:

**The passage suggests that one of the differences between *The Awakening* and the work of the New Women was that *The Awakening***

A)  attempted to explore aspects of female consciousness
B)  described the dream world of female characters
C)  employed impressionism more consistently throughout
D)  relied more on fantasy to suggest psychological states
E)  displayed greater unity of style and content

The very last paragraph says that *The Awakening* "embraced the impressionistic approach more fully" than did her influences, the New Women. I think the correct answer simply has to be something like that, because we really weren't told much else about *The Awakening*.

A)  The book did this, but I think the New Women did this also. We're asked to identify a difference, but this seems to be a similarity.
B)  Again, this is a similarity.
C)  This is close to our prediction of "fuller use of impressionism." Looking back at the last paragraph of the passage, I notice that the New Women used "interludes" of fantasy and parable, whereas *The Awakening* seems to have used it in every single section. (Which sounds boring as hell to me, btw.) Anyway, I think this answer is well-supported by the passage, so I like it a lot.
D)  I think this might be too specific. Were we told that *The Awakening* used *fantasy*, specifically? We know it was impressionistic, but we were told that fantasy and parable are two types of impressionism. And we aren't told which of those Chopin preferred, if any, or if she employed some other sort of impressionism. This feels like a trap.
E)  No, we're actually told that *The Awakening* wasn't unified in style or content.

Our answer is C.

## QUESTION 14:

The primary purpose of the passage is to

A) educate readers of *The Awakening* about aspects of Chopin's life that are reflected in the novel
B) discuss the relationship between Chopin's artistic development and changes in nineteenth-century women's fiction
C) trace the evolution of nineteenth-century women's fiction using Chopin as a typical example
D) counter a claim that Chopin's fiction was influenced by external social circumstances
E) weigh the value of Chopin's novels and stories against those of other writers of her time

Like Question 8, this is another "Hey, did you catch the main point? Were you awake?" question. There are always at least a couple of these accompanying every single passage. *Why did the author waste our time?* Well, what she really wants to say is something like "Chopin is interesting, and her development was interesting." Let's see if that's an answer choice:

A) No, the passage says nothing about Chopin's own life being incorporated into her work.
B) Sure, this is pretty good. The passage talked about a couple of different movements in women's literature, and how those movements were reflected in Chopin's own development. This ain't bad.
C) No, Chopin is definitely not presented as "typical."
D) Huh? This would be the answer if the passage had said, "Some people think XYZ about Chopin, but they are wrong." The passage simply didn't do that.
E) Nope, no other writers are mentioned.

Our answer is B, because it's the only one that's anywhere close to answering the question "Why are you wasting my time with this?" This is a super-easy question, if you're approaching the Reading Comprehension in the right way.

## QUESTION 15:

**The work of the New Women, as it is characterized in the passage, gives the most support for which one of the following generalizations?**

A) Works of fiction written in a passionate, engaged style are more apt to effect changes in social customs than are works written in a scientific, detached style.

B) Even writers who advocate social change can end up regretting the change once it has occurred.

C) Changes in social customs inevitably lead to changes in literary techniques as writers attempt to make sense of the new social realities.

D) Innovations in fictional technique grow out of writers' attempts to describe aspects of reality that have been neglected in previous works.

E) Writers can most accurately depict extreme psychological states by using an uninflected manner.

The only thing I really remember about the New Women is that they experimented with impressionism in the form of interludes of fantasy and parable. I hope that's enough to get us out of here.

A) Nah, the passage didn't talk about any effects of women's literature on social customs.

B) This answer might describe the local colorists, who "mourned the demise" of women's culture by romanticizing domesticity. But it doesn't describe the New Women.

C) No, there was nothing in the passage about how changes in culture inevitably change literature.

D) Yep. Lines 49-52 say "the New Women writers experimented with impressionistic methods in an effort to explore hitherto unrecorded aspects of female consciousness." If you "generalize" that, you'd get a statement that looks a lot like D.

E) The local colorists used the uninflected manner, not the New Women. (At least we weren't told the New Women did this.)

Our answer is D.

Another terrible passage, but the questions were pretty manageable if you managed to stay awake. Halfway done!

# Passage Three (Questions 16-21)

Until the 1950s, most scientists believed that the geology of the ocean floor had remained essentially unchanged for many millions of years. But this idea became insupportable as new discoveries were made.
(5) First, scientists noticed that the ocean floor exhibited odd magnetic variations. Though unexpected, this was not entirely surprising, because it was known that basalt—the volcanic rock making up much of the ocean floor—contains magnetite, a strongly magnetic
(10) mineral that was already known to locally distort compass readings on land. This distortion is due to the fact that although some basalt has so-called "normal" polarity—that is, the magnetite in it has the same polarity as the earth's present magnetic field—other
(15) basalt has reversed polarity, an alignment opposite that of the present field. This occurs because in magma (molten rock), grains of magnetite—behaving like little compass needles—align themselves with the earth's magnetic field, which has reversed at various
(20) times throughout history. When magma cools to form solid basalt, the alignment of the magnetite grains is "locked in," recording the earth's polarity at the time of cooling.

As more of the ocean floor was mapped, the
(25) magnetic variations revealed recognizable patterns, particularly in the area around the other great oceanic discovery of the 1950s: the global mid-ocean ridge, an immense submarine mountain range that winds its way around the earth much like the seams of a baseball.
(30) Alternating stripes of rock with differing polarities are laid out in rows on either side of the mid-ocean ridge: one stripe with normal polarity and the next with reversed polarity. Scientists theorized that mid-ocean ridges mark structurally weak zones where the ocean
(35) floor is being pulled apart along the ridge crest. New magma from deep within the earth rises easily through these weak zones and eventually erupts along the crest of the ridges to create new oceanic crust. Over millions of years, this process, called ocean floor spreading,
(40) built the mid-ocean ridge.

This theory was supported by several lines of evidence. First, at or near the ridge crest, the rocks are very young, and they become progressively older away from the crest. Further, the youngest rocks all
(45) have normal polarity. Finally, because geophysicists had already determined the ages of continental volcanic rocks and, by measuring the magnetic orientation of these same rocks, had assigned ages to the earth's recent magnetic reversals, they were able to compare
(50) these known ages of magnetic reversals with the ocean floor's magnetic striping pattern, enabling scientists to show that, if we assume that the ocean floor moved away from the spreading center at a rate of several centimeters per year, there is a remarkable correlation
(55) between the ages of the earth's magnetic reversals and the striping pattern.

*What the fuck is this nerd blathering about?* Uhh, something about magnetism? The nerd seems to want to waste our time with a bunch of technical stuff about how scientists have discovered, fairly recently, that the ocean floor has changed geologically over the past many millions of years, when they had previously thought the ocean floor was unchanged. The reason they were able to discover this, according to the nerd, has something to do with magnetism. Basically, the ocean floor is mostly made up of "basalt," which is a volcanic rock containing "magnetite," which is strongly magnetic. While the basalt is molten (*i.e.* fluid), the grains of magnetite tend to want to align themselves with the earth's polarity, which changes over time. But the grains get frozen into their current position when the magma cools, so scientists can later look at the varying polarity of the magnetite to see how the earth's polarity changed over time.

Please don't be tricked into thinking that I actually understand jack shit about the science here. All I'm trying to do is follow along as best I can with the nerd's story, and figure out why he's wasting our time. At the end of the first paragraph, I've got something like "scientists have discovered, by looking at magnetite, that the ocean floor has changed over the past millions of years." The nerd has not yet told us *how* he believes the ocean floor is changing. All we have so far is his opinion that it has changed, with no detail about what that change looks like.

The second paragraph looks at a giant mountain range underneath the ocean: the "mid-ocean ridge." Scientists have noticed rock with stripes of differing polarities on either side of the ridge. These stripes have caused them to theorize that the ocean floor is actually spreading. New rock is created at the middle of the ridge, and the polarity of the earth is recorded at the time the rock is created. Later, more rock is added with a different polarity, causing the polarity stripes. So in the second paragraph the author has shared a theory about how the ocean has changed: Scientists believe its floor is spreading.

The third paragraph provides several pieces of support for the ocean-spreading theory:

1) The rocks are younger at the middle of the mid-ocean crest.

2) The youngest rocks all have "normal" polarity, which presumably means polarity that matches the current polarity of the earth.

3) Geophysicists have compared what they already knew about the earth's polarity switches over time, and these polarity switches match the polarity of the stripes on the ocean floor, which supports the ocean spreading theory.

*Okay dude, so why are you wasting my time with this?* It seems as if the nerd has come here to tell us about a new theory—the ocean floor is spreading!—that the nerd believes is correct.

It's funny. Although the science is bewildering (the earth's polarity changes over time? You mean the North Pole becomes the South Pole? WTF?), I think I have a better handle on this passage than I had on either of the previous passages. Don't be afraid of the science! The point isn't to understand the exact details, the point is to *grasp the author's main idea*. The author's main idea here is this: "There's this new theory that the ocean floor is spreading, and that theory is probably right." That's enough to tackle the questions.

16

## QUESTION 16:

**Which one of the following most accurately expresses the main idea of the passage?**

A) In the 1950s, scientists refined their theories concerning the process by which the ocean floor was formed many millions of years ago.
B) The discovery of basalt's magnetic properties in the 1950s led scientists to formulate a new theory to account for the magnetic striping on the ocean floor.
C) In the 1950s, two significant discoveries led to the transformation of scientific views about the geology of the oceans.
D) Local distortions to compass readings are caused, scientists have discovered, by magma that rises through weak zones in the ocean floor to create new oceanic crust.
E) The discovery of the ocean floor's magnetic variations convinced scientists of the need to map the entire ocean floor, which in turn led to the discovery of the global mid-ocean ridge.

No problem, a main point question. I'd love an answer that said, "The new theory that the ocean floor is spreading is probably correct."

A) I don't think so. The point was that "the ocean floor is currently changing," whereas this implies that the ocean floor was "created" long ago rather than being in a continual process of creation.
B) I don't think so. I'm looking for "The ocean floor is currently changing." This answer is part of the story, but it doesn't capture the most important part.
C) This answer provides a bit more detail than my prediction, but it does basically do what we were looking for. "The transformation of scientific views" matches our prediction of "new theory." And "geology of the oceans" matches "ocean floor is spreading." I didn't predict the "two significant discoveries" part, but that's supported by the discovery mentioned in paragraph one (odd magnetic variations) and the discovery mentioned in paragraph two (patterns in the magnetic variations). Looks pretty good.
D) The purpose of the passage wasn't to explain why magnetic variations occur. The purpose of the passage was to talk about a new theory *prompted* by those variations. Close but no cigar. C was better.
E) Nah, this isn't what happened. The passage just doesn't say, "scientists decided to map the entire ocean floor *because of* the variations."

Our answer is C, because it's closest to our prediction and best embodies the reason why the nerd came here to waste our time.

17

## QUESTION 17:

**The author characterizes the correlation mentioned in the last sentence of the passage as "remarkable" in order to suggest that the correlation**

A) indicates that ocean floor spreading occurs at an extremely slow rate
B) explains the existence of the global mid-ocean ridge
C) demonstrates that the earth's magnetic field is considerably stronger than previously believed
D) provides strong confirmation of the ocean floor spreading theory
E) reveals that the earth's magnetic reversals have occurred at very regular intervals

The purpose of the third paragraph was to provide support for the ocean-spreading theory. The correlation mentioned in the last sentence does exactly that. The author notes the "remarkable" similarity between what scientists know about the earth's polarity changes over time and what's been observed in the ocean floor patterns for the purpose of claiming that the ocean-floor-spreading theory is correct. That ought to do it.

A) Not quite. The author wasn't trying to prove that the spreading is happening slowly. The author was trying to prove that the spreading is happening, period. I don't think this can be it.
B) No, the purpose of the passage, or the passage's last sentence, was not to explain the existence of the mid-ocean ridge. It was to prove that ocean spreading is happening.
C) Nah, not even close.
D) Boom. This matches our prediction perfectly.
E) No, there's nothing mentioned about "very regular intervals."

Our answer is D.

## QUESTION 18:

18

According to the passage, which one of the following is true of magnetite grains?

A) In the youngest basalt, they are aligned with the earth's current polarity.
B) In magma, most but not all of them align themselves with the earth's magnetic field.
C) They are not found in other types of rock besides basalt.
D) They are about the size of typical grains of sand.
E) They are too small to be visible to the naked eye.

The only thing I know about magnetite is that it is very magnetic, and aligns itself with the earth's polarity as long as it is in molten rock. Once the rock cools, the magnetite particles are stuck in position.

A) Well yeah, probably. Assuming that the newest rock was created while the earth's polarity is what it currently is, the magnetite in the youngest rock would match the current polarity of the earth. We should be happy with this answer.
B) Why would we suspect this? The passage doesn't say there are any non-conforming particles of magnetite. This seems speculative.
C) The passage never says this. Magnetite could be found in *every* type of rock, for all we know.
D) Nah, the size of the particles was never mentioned.
E) Same explanation as D.

Our answer is A.

## QUESTION 19:

If the time intervals between the earth's magnetic field reversals fluctuate greatly, then, based on the passage, which one of the following is most likely to be true?

A) Compass readings are most likely to be distorted near the peaks of the mid-ocean ridge.
B) It is this fluctuation that causes the ridge to wind around the earth like the seams on a baseball.
C) Some of the magnetic stripes of basalt on the ocean floor are much wider than others.
D) Continental rock is a more reliable indicator of the earth's magnetic field reversals than is oceanic rock.
E) Within any given magnetic stripe on the ocean floor, the age of the basalt does not vary.

Well, I'm obviously not a geophysicist. But based on my understanding of the passage, if the time periods between the earth's polarity changes fluctuate greatly, then the stripes in the ocean floor (which are caused by those polarity changes) ought to also fluctuate greatly. (Some stripes might be very narrow, perhaps, while others are very wide?) Let's see if that's what they're looking for.

A) This isn't what we're looking for. I suspect the answer has to be something about the stripes here, because it just seems commonsensical.
B) No, the passage mentioned "seams on a baseball" as a descriptive flourish but did not attempt to explain *why* this happens.
C) Boom again. I love it when we can exactly predict the correct answers.
D) Not what I'm looking for, and I already have C, so I can't spend too much time thinking about this one.
E) Same explanation as D. Here, we have positively identified the correct answer. All other answer choices are incorrect by definition, because we already know which one is right. It's awful nice when this happens.

Our answer is C.

## QUESTION 20:

Which one of the following would, if true, most help to support the ocean floor spreading theory?

A) There are types of rock other than basalt that are known to distort compass readings.
B) The ages of the earth's magnetic reversals have been verified by means other than examining magnetite grains in rock.
C) Pieces of basalt similar to the type found on the mid-ocean ridge have been found on the continents.
D) Along its length, the peak of the mid-ocean ridge varies greatly in height above the ocean floor.
E) Basalt is the only type of volcanic rock found in portions of the ocean floor nearest to the continents.

The third paragraph already provided three pieces of evidence for the ocean-spreading theory, so the case is looking pretty good. But a case can always get stronger, so we're going to see if we can pick an answer that provides another, or stronger, reason to believe that the ocean floor is spreading.

A) I don't see how this helps our case.
B) This could be it. It's always good to verify your data via other experimental means. Since the stripes on the ocean floor matched what scientists thought they knew about historical polarity fluctuations, it would be great to add in "And by the way, what the scientists knew about polarity fluctuations has been verified by other means." I can't argue with this answer choice.
C) Irrelevant.
D) This doesn't help our case.
E) This doesn't help our case either.

Our answer is B, because I can see how I'd like to include it in my argument if I was trying to prove that the ocean-spreading theory is correct.

## QUESTION 21:

21

**Which one of the following is most strongly supported by the passage?**

A) Submarine basalt found near the continents is likely to be some of the oldest rock on the ocean floor.
B) The older a sample of basalt is, the more times it has reversed its polarity.
C) Compass readings are more likely to become distorted at sea than on land.
D) The magnetic fields surrounding magnetite grains gradually weaken over millions of years on the ocean floor.
E) Any rock that exhibits present-day magnetic polarity was formed after the latest reversal of the earth's magnetic field.

There's no way to predict this one in advance, because we're not asked a detailed question. All we have to do is pick the answer that seems most obvious, (and least speculative) based on the passage.

A) Possibly. The ocean-spreading theory posits a "spreading center" which would imply the newest rocks are being created at the middle of the ocean and the rocks get older the further you get from the mid-ocean ridge. Does "near the continents" mean "farthest away from the mid-ocean ridge?" Seems likely, right? I bet this turns out to be the correct answer.
B) Nah, the polarity stops reversing once the rock cools. It doesn't keep reversing over time.
C) This is simply speculative. The passage never says whether the readings are more accurate in one location or the other.
D) Also speculative. This is just not discussed in the passage.
E) Definitely not. There are stripes of polarity on the ocean floor. Some of them were created several polarity-reversals ago, but happen to match today's polarity.

Our answer is A, because it's the only one that the passage gives us reason to believe is true.

Call me a nerd, but I actually enjoyed that passage. I suppose it might have just seemed relatively more palatable in comparison to the shit appetizers that preceded it. In any case, I feel very good about our answers. Let's wrap it up.

# Passage Four (Questions 22-27)

**Passage A**

Central to the historian's profession and scholarship has been the ideal of objectivity. The assumptions upon which this ideal rests include a commitment to the reality of the past, a sharp separation
(5) between fact and value, and above all, a distinction between history and fiction.

According to this ideal, historical facts are prior to and independent of interpretation: the value of an interpretation should be judged by how well it accounts
(10) for the facts; if an interpretation is contradicted by facts, it should be abandoned. The fact that successive generations of historians have ascribed different meanings to past events does not mean, as relativist historians claim, that the events themselves lack fixed
(15) or absolute meanings.

Objective historians see their role as that of a neutral judge, one who must never become an advocate or, worse, propagandist. Their conclusions should display the judicial qualities of balance and
(20) evenhandedness. As with the judiciary, these qualities require insulation from political considerations, and avoidance of partisanship or bias. Thus objective historians must purge themselves of external loyalties; their primary allegiance is to objective historical truth
(25) and to colleagues who share a commitment to its discovery.

**Passage B**

The very possibility of historical scholarship as an enterprise distinct from propaganda requires of its practitioners that self-discipline that enables them to
(30) do such things as abandon wishful thinking, assimilate bad news, and discard pleasing interpretations that fail elementary tests of evidence and logic.

Yet objectivity, for the historian, should not be confused with neutrality. Objectivity is perfectly
(35) compatible with strong political commitment. The objective thinker does not value detachment as an end in itself but only as an indispensable means of achieving deeper understanding. In historical scholarship, the ideal of objectivity is most compellingly embodied in
(40) the *powerful argument*—one that reveals by its every twist and turn its respectful appreciation of the alternative arguments it rejects. Such a text attains power precisely because its author has managed to suspend momentarily his or her own perceptions so as
(45) to anticipate and take into account objections and alternative constructions—not those of straw men, but those that truly issue from the rival's position, understood as sensitively and stated as eloquently as the rival could desire. To mount a telling attack on a
(50) position, one must first inhabit it. Those so habituated to their customary intellectual abode that they cannot even explore others can never be persuasive to anyone but fellow habitués.

Such arguments are often more faithful to the
(55) complexity of historical interpretation—more faithful even to the irreducible plurality of human perspectives—than texts that abjure position-taking altogether. The powerful argument is the highest fruit of the kind of thinking I would call objective, and in it neutrality
(60) plays no part. Authentic objectivity bears no resemblance to the television newscaster's mechanical gesture of allocating the same number of seconds to both sides of a question, editorially splitting the difference between them, irrespective of their perceived merits.

You'll notice that there are two shorter passages here (Passage A and Passage B) instead of the usual single, longer passage. This is the so-called "comparative reading" passage, which first appeared on the LSAT in June 2007. The big prep companies fell all over each other when this change was announced—any time students are worried, the behemoths are there to hawk their expensive magic techniques. Please don't buy the snake oil. It's still called Reading Comprehension, so the same two-step process applies: 1) Read, and 2) Comprehend. No shit, right? To maximize your comprehension, simply ask each speaker "why are you wasting my time with this?" Take your time. Remember that speed comes from accuracy, not the other way around.

*Okay then, Passage A, why are* you *wasting my time with this?* At the end of the first paragraph, Passage A seems to be telling us that historians need to be objective. Objectivity, according to Passage A, means a commitment to reality. Historians should avoid value judgments, and instead focus on facts. Fiction should be avoided above all. Great! I feel very comfortable with this paragraph.

The second paragraph proposes an alternative view of history that Passage A rejects: the idea that historical events themselves have changing meanings. The author believes that when an interpretation of history can't account for particular facts, it should be abandoned. The author does *not* believe that different historical interpretations of an event mean that the event *itself* changed. The author believes in a single, objective, factual truth that exists independent of whatever bullshit interpretations scholars write about it.

In the third paragraph, the author indulges further in his love affair with "objective historians." It gets a bit annoying here. He's comparing these historians to the judiciary, and he's ascribing almost godlike powers of balance and evenhandedness and avoidance of bias. Wow. The speaker *really* likes historians who are objective. That's the main point of Passage A: objective historians are awesome.

*Passage B, you're up. Why are* you *here to waste our time?* At the end of the first paragraph, Passage B seems to be echoing Passage A. He's here to talk about historians who are "self-disciplined" and reality-based. But the beginning of the second paragraph of Passage B breaks from Passage A in one regard: where Passage A had said that unbiased history required "insulation from political considerations, and avoidance of partisanship," Passage B says, "Objectivity is perfectly compatible with strong political commitment." Oh, really? Why does Passage B think this? That's a point that seems to beg explanation.

*Hey, Passage B, how can you believe that a historian can simultaneously be objective and still strongly committed politically? Explain yourself.* At the end of Passage B, the author says that historians should think objectively *in order to equip themselves to create the most powerful possible argument.* In other words, objectivity is valued by Passage B not as an end in itself, but as a weapon for better debate. Political partisanship is OK, but to be a truly effective political partisan you must be able to put yourself into your opponent's shoes. Don't fall for a simplistic "straw man" understanding of your opponent's position. Instead, craft your opponent's argument as you would craft it yourself. This will help you truly understand the other side of the debate, and thereby allow you to shore up the weaknesses in your own position. I think I've got it.

The third paragraph makes one further point that I really happen to agree with. Today's American TV journalism, which is allegedly "objective" because it devotes equal time to idiots from both parties, is not doing anyone a service. For the news to be truly valuable, it should deeply analyze both sides of an issue, then use facts and logic to present a thoughtful opinion. One "conservative" and one "liberal" yelling at each other is lazy production, and doesn't actually teach us anything. Passage B says this applies to historical scholarship as well.

Let's sum it up before diving in to the questions. Passage A really *really* loves "objective historians," and provides some guidelines for ensuring objectivity. Passage B agrees in principle, but offers a more nuanced view of what objectivity means. Passage A thinks historians should avoid partisanship at all costs; Passage B thinks historians should employ objectivity in order to arrive at smarter, more powerful viewpoints. That's all I got—I definitely didn't attempt to memorize or recap every single detail from both arguments. But you could take the test booklet away from me and I could tell you the basic thesis of each mini-passage. That's all we're going to need.

## 22

### QUESTION 22:

Both passages are concerned with answering which one of the following questions?

A) What are the most serious flaws found in recent historical scholarship?
B) What must historians do in order to avoid bias in their scholarship?
C) How did the ideal of objectivity first develop?
D) Is the scholarship produced by relativist historians sound?
E) Why do the prevailing interpretations of past events change from one era to the next?

Both passages are all about objective history. That's all we can predict before evaluating the answer choices.

A) Hmm. Did Passage A ever talk about "serious flaws" of recent historical scholarship? Did Passage B? I really don't think this was the focus of either speaker.
B) Passage A goes on and on about this, and Passage B definitely mentions it in the first paragraph. We've gotta like this answer because it's supported in both passages.
C) Nah, I don't remember either speaker discussing the "origins of objectivity."
D) Passage A seems to take a shot at relativist historians, but Passage B never mentions them. Answer B is still our leader.
E) Neither speaker takes up this issue.

Our answer is B, because it describes the issue that both speakers were most clearly talking about.

## 23

### QUESTION 23:

Both passages identify which one of the following as a requirement for historical research?

A) the historian's willingness to borrow methods of analysis from other disciplines when evaluating evidence
B) the historian's willingness to employ methodologies favored by proponents of competing views when evaluating evidence
C) the historian's willingness to relinquish favored interpretations in light of the discovery of facts inconsistent with them
D) the historian's willingness to answer in detail all possible objections that might be made against his or her interpretation
E) the historian's willingness to accord respectful consideration to rival interpretations

Both passages see objectivity as a requirement for historical scholarship. I hope there's an answer that says exactly that.

A) Huh? I don't remember either speaker mentioning this.

B) Passage B definitely thinks historians should look at the various positions held by competing advocates. But I'm not sure Passage A would agree with this; Passage A seems to think that historians should remain in their ivory towers and not sully themselves in such a way. I doubt this is the answer.

C) Yes. Passage A says, "If an interpretation is contradicted by facts, it should be abandoned." Passage B says historians should "discard pleasing interpretations that fail elementary tests of evidence and logic." This answer is very well supported by the two passages... it's almost certain to end up as our choice. Let's quickly scan D and E just to be sure.

D) I don't think Passage A touches this issue at all. No way.

E) Again, I don't think Passage A says anything about "respectful consideration" of competing viewpoints.

Our answer is C, because it has clear support from both passages.

## QUESTION 24:

24

**The author of passage B and the kind of objective historian described in passage A would be most likely to disagree over whether**

A) detachment aids the historian in achieving an objective view of past events

B) an objective historical account can include a strong political commitment

C) historians today are less objective than they were previously

D) propaganda is an essential tool of historical scholarship

E) historians of different eras have arrived at differing interpretations of the same historical events

As we discussed above, the two passages seem to disagree over whether it's possible to be simultaneously political and objective.

A) I think this could be it. Passage A worships detached objectivity for its own sake. Passage B thinks objectivity is a tool that should be used to arrive at a stronger political argument. I don't think Passage B is a fan of "detachment" itself—not necessarily, anyway. I will happily pick this answer if nothing else seems good.

B) Oh, well, that's even better. This matches my prediction perfectly. I suppose A is wrong because Passage B does prefer objectivity, which is a concept closely related to "detachment." But B is so good that I'm not going to waste too much more time thinking about A. The two speakers very clearly disagree on the politics issue.

C) I don't think either speaker talks about the evolution of historical scholarship.

D) I think both speakers *agree* that propaganda should be avoided. This isn't a point of disagreement.

E) Passage A definitely thinks this happened, but Passage B doesn't ever say otherwise.

Our answer is B, because we know for sure that this is something the two authors are fighting about.

25

## QUESTION 25:

**Which one of the following most accurately describes an attitude toward objectivity present in each passage?**

A) Objectivity is a goal that few historians can claim to achieve.
B) Objectivity is essential to the practice of historical scholarship.
C) Objectivity cannot be achieved unless historians set aside political allegiances.
D) Historians are not good judges of their own objectivity.
E) Historians who value objectivity are becoming less common.

Another main point question. As we've been saying repeatedly, both passages like objectivity a lot. Passage A loves it for its own sake, while Passage B sees it as a tool for more effective partisanship.

A) I don't think either speaker takes a position on how many historians are actually objective.
B) Yes. Both passages think objectivity is important.
C) Passage A says yes to this, but Passage B says no.
D) Neither speaker takes a position on this issue.
E) Nah, same explanation as A.

Our answer is B. This question was way too easy—all we had to do here was get the 40,000-foot view of each speaker's main point. That's not hard as long as you don't fall asleep.

26

## QUESTION 26:

**Both passages mention propaganda primarily in order to**

A) refute a claim made by proponents of a rival approach to historical scholarship
B) suggest that scholars in fields other than history tend to be more biased than historians
C) point to a type of scholarship that has recently been discredited
D) identify one extreme to which historians may tend
E) draw contrasts with other kinds of persuasive writing

Both passages hate propaganda.

A) I don't recall either passage mentioning a claim being made by any proponent of a "rival approach to historical scholarship." For this to be the answer, both speakers would have had to say something like "People who believe XYZ have been shown to be wrong... because of propaganda." This is just nonsense, really.
B) Does either speaker talk about other fields? I certainly don't remember them doing that.
C) Does either speaker talk about a type of scholarship being "recently discredited"? I don't remember that happening.
D) This is the best answer so far. Both speakers mention propaganda as something that historians can fall into, and should avoid. It's not a stretch to consider propaganda as "extreme." We should be happy with this answer if E sucks.
E) Nah, neither speaker discusses "other kinds of persuasive writing."

Our answer is D.

## QUESTION 27:

The argument described in passage A and the argument made by the author of passage B are both advanced by

A) citing historical scholarship that fails to achieve objectivity
B) showing how certain recent developments in historical scholarship have undermined the credibility of the profession
C) summarizing opposing arguments in order to point out their flaws
D) suggesting that historians should adopt standards used by professionals in certain other fields
E) identifying what are seen as obstacles to achieving objectivity

This question is asking us to identify a method of reasoning used by both passages. Let's just pick the answer that seems to best match the techniques actually used by the two speakers.

A) Passage A took a shot at historical "relativists," but I'm not sure Passage B took any shots at any other schools of historical scholarship. I don't think this is it.
B) Did either passage discuss "recent developments"? I don't really remember them doing that.
C) No, I don't think the two passages were saying, "Other people believe XYZ, but actually ABC is true." We're still looking for an answer that describes something both speakers did.
D) Passage B did mention another field—journalism—but for the purpose of slamming it, not for the purpose of saying historians should be like journalists. Still looking!
E) Yes, this happened. Passage A mentioned "political considerations" as one possible obstacle to objectivity. Passage B mentioned "wishful thinking," among other things. That's enough to make this our answer.

The one question you have to ask to get through this section is *"Why are you wasting my time with this?"* It was enough to answer almost every single question on this last passage. It's almost too easy.

# SECTION
# FOUR

# Logical Reasoning

## (Or: Even More Bullshit)

Same approach as Section One... you're an old hand at calling bullshit by now. Take it easy on your friends and family with this approach, okay? But on the LSAT Logical Reasoning, don't hold back.

# QUESTION 1:

**Commentator:** In last week's wreck involving one of Acme Engines' older locomotives, the engineer lost control of the train when his knee accidentally struck a fuel shut-down switch. Acme claims it is not liable because it never realized that the knee-level switches were a safety hazard. When asked why it relocated knee-level switches in its newer locomotives, Acme said engineers had complained that they were simply inconvenient. However, it is unlikely that Acme would have spent the $500,000 it took to relocate switches in the newer locomotives merely because of inconvenience. Thus, Acme Engines should be held liable for last week's wreck.

The point that Acme Engines spent $500,000 relocating knee-level switches in its newer locomotives is offered in the commentator's argument as

A) proof that the engineer is not at all responsible for the train wreck
B) a reason for believing that the wreck would have occurred even if Acme Engines had remodeled their older locomotives
C) an explanation of why the train wreck occurred
D) evidence that knee-level switches are not in fact hazardous
E) an indication that Acme Engines had been aware of the potential dangers of knee-level switches before the wreck occurred

The argument goes basically like this: Fact: The train company went to great expense to relocate a certain switch. Fact: They *claim* they did it because their engineers thought the switch was inconvenient. (Commentator's opinion: This seems unlikely given the great expense.) Fact: A switch on an older locomotive recently caused an accident. Conclusion: The train company should be held liable for the wreck.

In terms of logic only, this argument is bullshit because it assumes, without providing evidence, that just because a company might have known that one of its switches was dangerous, it is therefore liable for any damage caused by that switch. Important note here: You may certainly *agree* with the commentator, based on your own sense of justice. It's okay if you feel that the commentator's assumption is valid—I won't argue. But you must recognize that the assumption exists. We don't get to make the law! If the law says "a company that seems to know that one of its products is dangerous is liable for whatever damage is caused," then the plaintiff will win. But if the law says "a company that seems to know that one of its products is dangerous cannot be held liable for whatever damage is caused," then the defendant will win. If we notice that the commentator has made an *assumption*, then we've done our job.

We haven't even looked at the actual question yet, but that's OK. Because we *argued*, we have an extremely strong grasp on what the commentator was saying. The question asks us to identify the argumentative purpose of highlighting the fact that the train company paid so much money to relocate its switches. Why did the commentator do this? Well, this piece of evidence was meant to show that the company knew the switches were dangerous. Let's see if we can find an answer that matches up with that prediction.

A) No, the commentator was trying to prove that the train company should be held liable. That's not necessarily the same thing as saying the engineer is "not at all responsible." (More than one party can be held liable for an accident, right?) This feels like a trap.
B) No, the commentator was definitely not trying to prove that the remodeled engines would have the exact same safety problem. (Quite the opposite, actually.)
C) The commentator says the train wreck occurred because of the badly designed old switch. But the fact that the train company spent so much money relocating the switch on later models isn't used to prove this point. This fact was presented to support the idea that the train company knew the switches were dangerous.
D) No, this is the opposite of what the commentator believes.
E) Yep. This matches our prediction quite nicely—so this is our answer.

## QUESTION 2:

Artist: Almost everyone in this country really wants to be an artist even though they may have to work other jobs to pay the rent. After all, just about everyone I know hopes to someday be able to make a living as a painter, musician, or poet even if they currently work as dishwashers or discount store clerks.

The reasoning in the artist's argument is flawed in that the argument

A) contains a premise that presupposes the truth of the conclusion
B) presumes that what is true of each person in a country is also true of the country's population as a whole
C) defends a view solely on the grounds that the view is widely held
D) bases its conclusion on a sample that is unlikely to accurately represent people in the country as a whole
E) fails to make a needed distinction between wanting to be an artist and making a living as an artist

Comical. The artist is full of shit because he is saying "all the folks I know personally feel a certain way, therefore *everyone in the country* feels that way." Unless this guy knows everyone in the country, or a random sampling of everyone in the country, he's an idiot.

With that, we *own* this question. We're asked to identify a flaw, and the flaw is "you do not know everyone in the country."

A) Nah. This would be the answer if the argument had said, "Every word in the Bible is true because it says so in the Bible."
B) No, this would be the answer if the argument had said, "Every American owns one toothbrush, therefore the population of America owns one toothbrush."
C) Nope. This would be the answer if the argument had said, "God is widely believed to exist, therefore God exists."
D) Yeah. Taking a sample that exists solely of your buddies does not represent the entire country. This is it.
E) No, the argument doesn't do this. It specifically addresses the fact that wannabe artists end up washing dishes.

Our answer is D.

## QUESTION 3:

The QWERTY keyboard became the standard keyboard with the invention of the typewriter and remains the standard for typing devices today. If an alternative known as the Dvorak keyboard were today's standard, typists would type significantly faster. Nevertheless, it is not practical to switch to the Dvorak keyboard because the cost to society of switching, in terms of time, money, and frustration, would be greater than the benefits that would be ultimately gained from faster typing.

The example above best illustrates which one of the following propositions?

A) Often it is not worthwhile to move to a process that improves speed if it comes at the expense of accuracy.
B) People usually settle on a standard because that standard is more efficient than any alternatives.
C) People often remain with an entrenched standard rather than move to a more efficient alternative simply because they dislike change.
D) The emotional cost associated with change is a factor that sometimes outweighs financial considerations.
E) The fact that a standard is already in wide use can be a crucial factor in making it a more practical choice than an alternative.

Depending on what degree of nerd belt you own, you may have actually experimented with a Dvorak keyboard at some point. It's an objectively superior layout designed for speed. The problem is that we're all so used to QWERTY. When I set my keyboard on Dvorak one especially nerdy day, the experiment only lasted about five minutes. I'm not about to unlearn all the typing drills that Ms. Dryden put me through in my freshman year of high school, and relearn an entirely new system. No thanks. So even though the QWERTY keyboard was actually designed to slow typists down—true story—I'll probably use QWERTY for my entire life. Anyway, that's what this argument is all about. And unlike most LSAT arguments, I actually buy it. I'm not calling bullshit, because the whole thing makes pretty good sense to me.

We're asked to find a proposition that is "best illustrated" by the Dvorak vs. QWERTY example. Shouldn't be too difficult. Just pick the best match.

A) No, switching to Dvorak wouldn't in the long run cause a decrease in accuracy. The problem, as articulated by the argument, is that the pain of switching over is too great. I'd prefer to type slower my entire life than spend time learning a whole new system.
B) If this were the case, then we would have settled on Dvorak, not QWERTY. This isn't what the argument is talking about.
C) This answer started off really good, but then it closed with "simply because they dislike change." Is that really what the argument was about? I think not. I was totally willing to change to Dvorak until I realized that the change would be difficult and time-consuming. It's not change itself that people fear—it's the *cost* of the change. This answer feels like a trap to me.
D) Emotional cost? Nah, it was the time and effort that concerned me. This can't be it.
E) It's boring, but it's the right answer. The example presented in the argument *does* illustrate a standard (the QWERTY keyboard) that is already in wide use, and the wide usage is a big factor in making that standard a more practical choice than an alternative (Dvorak). This is our answer.

## QUESTION 4:

Sam: Mountain lions, a protected species, are preying on bighorn sheep, another protected species. We must let nature take its course and hope the bighorns survive.

Meli: Nonsense. We must do what we can to ensure the survival of the bighorn, even if that means limiting the mountain lion population.

**Which one of the following is a point of disagreement between Meli and Sam?**

A) Humans should not intervene to protect bighorn sheep from mountain lions.
B) The preservation of a species as a whole is more important than the loss of a few individuals.
C) The preservation of a predatory species is easier to ensure than the preservation of the species preyed upon.
D) Any measures to limit the mountain lion population would likely push the species to extinction.
E) If the population of mountain lions is not limited, the bighorn sheep species will not survive.

Sam's evidence is "mountain lions are preying on bighorn sheep" and "bighorn sheep and mountain lions are both protected species." I'm willing to accept all that, but what's up with Sam's conclusion? Sam concludes, out of the blue, that "we must let nature take its course." Where's Sam's justification for that assertion? Is there a law that says we can't intervene?

Meli calls Sam's argument "nonsense." OK, I was already pissed at Sam for making an unwarranted conclusion, and now I'm *also* pissed at Meli for making such a bold accusation. (Generally, it's a good idea to get pissed at anyone who is popping off on the LSAT.) Okay, big talker... *why* it nonsense? Unfortunately, Meli is just as full of shit as Sam. Without presenting any evidence, Meli concludes that we have to do whatever we can to save the bighorn, even at the expense of the mountain lion. Says who?

They're both idiots. They're definitely arguing. Our task is to figure out what the idiots are arguing about. Are they arguing about facts? Or are they arguing about conclusions?

I think it's the latter. Meli doesn't even address Sam's facts. She seems to accept that mountain lions are eating bighorns, and that both are endangered species. She disagrees with Sam's interpretation, or conclusion, on what those facts lead to. Sam says, "These facts mean we should do nothing." Meli says, "These facts mean we should do something." So they've reached precisely opposite conclusions on the exact same facts.

A) This looks good to me. Meli has explicitly said no to this answer choice, and Sam has explicitly said yes to it. So this answer is exactly what they're arguing about.
B) No, neither Sam nor Meli even address this issue. If either of them fails (or they both fail) to address an answer choice, then that can't be what they're arguing about.
C) Difficulty of intervention isn't the issue here. Neither Sam nor Meli takes any position on how hard or easy it would be to save either species.
D) Sam takes no position on whether or not an intervention would push mountain lions toward extinction. That's enough to prove that this isn't the answer. (And furthermore, I don't think Meli took a position on this issue either. She mentions limiting the population, but that's not the same as extinction.)
E) Sam says, "We should hope the bighorns survive," so it seems as if Sam isn't sure whether or not the mountain lions are going to cause a bighorn extinction. Meli thinks we should do something, which suggests but does not necessarily prove that she believes that the bighorn is guaranteed to go extinct if we don't intervene. Maybe she just hates mountain lions. Because one speaker clearly says "yes," and one speaker clearly says "no," to the statement presented in A, that's our answer.

## QUESTION 5:

**Parent:** Pushing very young children into rigorous study in an effort to make our nation more competitive does more harm than good. Curricula for these young students must address their special developmental needs, and while rigorous work in secondary school makes sense, the same approach in the early years of primary school produces only short-term gains and may cause young children to burn out on schoolwork. Using very young students as pawns in the race to make the nation economically competitive is unfair and may ultimately work against us.

**Which one of the following can be inferred from the parent's statements?**

A)  For our nation to be competitive, our secondary school curriculum must include more rigorous study than it now does.
B)  The developmental needs of secondary school students are not now being addressed in our high schools.
C)  Our country can be competitive only if the developmental needs of all our students can be met.
D)  A curriculum of rigorous study does not adequately address the developmental needs of primary school students.
E)  Unless our nation encourages more rigorous study in the early years of primary school, we cannot be economically competitive.

Seems like the parent doesn't want his special snowflake forced to, you know, *do any actual work* while in school. Instead of "pushing very young children into rigorous study," the parent says we should "address their special developmental needs." Unfortunately, the parent doesn't tell us what the hell those special developmental needs *are*. All I'm hearing here is "Oh *no*... we definitely can't make them *study rigorously. God forbid!*" I'm not hearing any solutions. Where's the "Here's my plan, including details on what we should actually do"?

We're asked to find something that "can be inferred from the parent's statements." This means, "Which one must be true, according to the parent's argument?" We can look for two different types of answers here. One could be something that the parent has actually said. Another is something that has been necessarily implied by the parent—something that the parent might not have actually said, but something that has to be true in order for the parent's statements to make sense. I don't think we can really predict this one in advance. We just have to pick the statement that has the best support from the parent's statements.

A)  No, I don't think so. This parent says rigorous work in secondary school "makes sense" but doesn't go so far as to say that it is necessary if we want to be competitive. (Generally, this parent seems *against* rigorous work.) This can't be it.
B)  The parent doesn't mention the developmental needs of secondary school students. Snowflake is a "very young child." No way.
C)  This answer has the same problem as B. The parent did not say that we have to address the developmental needs of *all* our students. The parent is concerned with addressing the developmental needs of very young children. Not all of our children are very young. This is out.
D)  The parent didn't actually say this, but his argument doesn't make much sense without it. The parent's big point is, "We can't give young kids a rigorous curriculum because of Snowflake's developmental needs!" If a rigorous curriculum *does* meet Snowflake's developmental needs, then the parent would be a raving lunatic. So I think this answer choice can be "properly inferred" from the parent's statements. If everything the parent says is true, then D also has to be true.
E)  This is the exact opposite of what the parent believes.

Our answer is D.

## QUESTION 6:

A transit company's bus drivers are evaluated by supervisors riding with each driver. Drivers complain that this affects their performance, but because the supervisor's presence affects every driver's performance, those drivers performing best with a supervisor aboard will likely also be the best drivers under normal conditions.

Which one of the following is an assumption on which the argument depends?

A) There is no effective way of evaluating the bus drivers' performance without having supervisors ride with them.
B) The supervisors are excellent judges of a bus driver's performance.
C) For most bus drivers, the presence of a supervisor makes their performance slightly worse than it otherwise would be.
D) The bus drivers are each affected in roughly the same way and to the same extent by the presence of the supervisor.
E) The bus drivers themselves are able to deliver accurate assessments of their driving performance.

This argument isn't terrible. It's basically "If you're good under extra pressure, you're probably good under normal conditions as well." That's not patently unreasonable. But by the same logic you could say "Nathan beat Tiger Woods at golf in an experiment involving an air horn blast at the top of every single backswing. Because Nathan beat Tiger under these stressful circumstances, Nathan will probably beat Tiger at the Masters this year." Sorry, it wouldn't work that way.

We're asked to find an assumption on which the argument depends. That's a Necessary Assumption question. We're asked to find a critical component of the argument that was assumed, rather than stated. Which answer choice, if untrue, would cause the argument to fail?

A) No, I don't think the speaker assumed that the current plan of supervisor ride-along evaluations is the only way to do it. All the speaker really said here was, "This plan should work."

B) If this answer said, "The supervisors are not completely inept at judging driver performance," then I would consider that a necessary component of the argument. But I think "excellent" is a step too far. Couldn't the plan still work if the supervisors were only "good" or "fair" at evaluating driver performance?

## "No, because..."

Improv comedians try to respond with "yes, and..." to anything said on stage. The point is to be spontaneous and go with the flow. This attitude would make you a hit at any party, but on the LSAT you should do the exact opposite. The LSAT's arguments are godawful, and your job is to articulate why. So get in the habit of responding with hostility to everything you read. Shoot back immediately with "No, that's bullshit because..."

If you find yourself nodding along as you read, agreeing with the speaker, nine times out of ten you're doing it wrong.

C) I think this could be it. The argument explicitly states that drivers complain about the supervisors' presence, and that the supervisors' presence affects every driver's performance. But what if the supervisors' presence makes some drivers perform better? What about the guy who comes to work drunk every day, but sobers up when the supervisor rides shotgun? If observation makes some drivers better, but other drivers worse, it isn't the best way to identify the best drivers, is it? This is a pretty good answer, because it protects against that scenario. But let's see if we can eliminate D and E.

D) Oooh... this is better. This answer does the exact same thing that I initially thought C did. In retrospect, C is too specific. The assumption isn't necessarily that supervisor observation makes most drivers worse, but that the supervisor observation affects the drivers in the same way. This is subtle, but imagine if the supervisor performance made all drivers slightly better. If that's true, then C would be false but the plan would still do a good job of identifying the best drivers. On the other hand, if the supervisor observation causes different reactions in different drivers, then the plan is garbage. So D is a necessary component of the argument: if D is false, the argument fails.

E) No, self-evaluations are totally irrelevant.

Our answer is D. The trap, C, almost got me. Good thing I always read all five answers before making a final choice (I've been burned before).

7

## QUESTION 7:

Economic growth accelerates business demand for the development of new technologies. Businesses supplying these new technologies are relatively few, while those wishing to buy them are many. Yet an acceleration of technological change can cause suppliers as well as buyers of new technologies to fail.

**Which one of the following is most strongly supported by the information above?**

A) Businesses supplying new technologies are more likely to prosper in times of accelerated technological change than other businesses.
B) Businesses that supply new technologies may not always benefit from economic growth.
C) The development of new technologies may accelerate economic growth in general.
D) Businesses that adopt new technologies are most likely to prosper in a period of general economic growth.
E) Economic growth increases business failures.

I'm not sure this makes any sense. Economic growth stimulates demand for new technologies. Few businesses supply these technologies, but many businesses want to buy. Sounds pretty good for the businesses supplying the technologies, right? You don't need to be a Ph.D. economist to understand that low supply and high demand tend to lead to high prices. So I was expecting the conclusion here to say, "this tends to be awesome for the few companies supplying these technologies, even if it's not so good for the companies that have to pay up the ass for those same technologies." But that's not what it says. Instead, it says an acceleration of technological change can "cause suppliers as well as buyers of these new technologies to fail." Huh? Puzzling.

We're asked to find something "strongly supported" by the puzzling facts. It's a tough one to predict in advance, because the facts don't really add up to anything concrete. No matter. On a question like this, all we need to do is pick an answer that has direct support from the facts provided. We'll avoid anything speculative, and pick the one that seems most obvious according to the evidence on the page.

## Boring is beautiful

On a question that asks, "Which one of the following must be true" or "is most supported by the information above," you should avoid trying to get cute or clever. Just pick the answer that has clear support from the facts on the page. Avoid anything speculative, and pick the most obvious one. The answer we choose here is not earth-shattering. Doesn't matter—it's supported by the facts, so it's the credited answer.

A) See, this is where I *thought* the argument was going to go: blowout parties in the rooftop pool at The Standard hotel for the tech companies, even if the other companies don't fare so well. But that's *not* where the argument went, so this can't be the answer.
B) Uh, yeah, well... this seems to be what the facts say, right? Tech companies can fail, even as economic growth spurs technological change. This answer is obvious—boring even—according to the facts on the page. We're not going to write home about it, but it's the correct answer.
C) This isn't supported by the facts. The facts *do* say that economic growth can accelerate change, but the facts do *not* say that the cause and effect can work the other way. Smoking causes cancer... does that mean that cancer causes smoking? Nah.
D) The facts simply don't mention whether it's good or bad for a company to adopt new technologies. All we know is demand for tech is increased. What happens after tech adoption is unclear. This answer doesn't have support from the passage.
E) We know businesses *can* fail during economic growth, but that doesn't mean failure is more likely during economic growth than other times.

Our answer is B, because it's the only one that has support from the given evidence.

## QUESTION 8:

Energy analyst: During this record-breaking heat wave, air conditioner use has overloaded the region's electrical power grid, resulting in frequent power blackouts throughout the region. For this reason, residents have been asked to cut back voluntarily on air conditioner use in their homes. But even if this request is heeded, blackouts will probably occur unless the heat wave abates.

Which one of the following, if true, most helps to resolve the apparent discrepancy in the information above?

A) Air-conditioning is not the only significant drain on the electrical system in the area.
B) Most air-conditioning in the region is used to cool businesses and factories.
C) Most air-conditioning systems could be made more energy efficient by implementing simple design modifications.
D) Residents of the region are not likely to reduce their air conditioner use voluntarily during particularly hot weather.
E) The heat wave is expected to abate in the near future.

The conclusion surprised me here. I was expecting to hear this: "We've asked folks to shut down their air conditioners during this heat wave in order to prevent blackouts. But individuals are probably going to say 'fuck THAT' and keep their air conditioners on, cause it's hot as hell outside. So we'll probably still have blackouts." That makes sense.

Instead, we got, "Even if people *do* shut off their air conditioners, we'll still have blackouts during the heat wave." Wait... *why*? There's a mystery here: asking residents to cut back on the AC isn't going to be enough, *even if they comply*. The question asks us to "resolve" that mystery. In other words, find an answer choice that would make the mysterious set of facts make sense. How can it simultaneously be true that people would cut back on their AC, but the blackouts would still happen during the heat wave? Is there some other power drain happening?

My guess is something about businesses, schools, industry perhaps... something like "Snow cone factories kick into high gear during heat waves, and use 90% of the region's power when operating at full capacity" would be perfect. If that's true, then we'd have an explanation of how the voluntary residential cutbacks wouldn't keep the blackouts from happening. Obviously the correct answer isn't going to be about snow cones, specifically. (If it is, I'm hopping the next flight to Las Vegas.) But that's the *type* of answer we need: something that explains how the mystery can make sense.

A) This isn't a very complete explanation—it doesn't actually say, specifically, what the other electrical drain would be—but it does say, "There are other power drains besides residences," which is the gist of our prediction above, after all. I don't love it, but we could definitely choose it if nothing else is good.
B) Okay, I think this is a more complete explanation. It specifically points to air conditioning at other places besides residences. Now that I look back at A, I notice that it doesn't even tie closely enough to the heat wave. (If AC isn't the most significant drain, then why would the blackouts be happening during the heat wave?) We have to like B better than A, because it echoes our "AC at industry and factories" above.
C) It's *nice* that air-conditioning systems could be made more energy efficient. We can all get behind that. Nice as that is—I'm warm and fuzzy, are you?—it's totally irrelevant to explaining why the residential cutbacks won't stop the blackouts. This is out.
D) This is a trap, because the conclusion is qualified by the phrase, "Even if the request is heeded." Of course we all know that people won't *actually* comply... that's beside the energy analyst's point. The point was *"even if they do* comply, we're still screwed." So this doesn't solve our mystery.
E) This would be great! Heat waves suck balls. But this doesn't explain why the blackouts will continue happening during the heat wave.

Our answer is B, because it's the best solution to the mystery we were assigned to solve.

## QUESTION 9:

Long-term and short-term relaxation training are two common forms of treatment for individuals experiencing problematic levels of anxiety. Yet studies show that on average, regardless of which form of treatment one receives, symptoms of anxiety decrease to a normal level within the short-term-training time period. Thus, for most people the generally more expensive long-term training is unwarranted.

**Which one of the following, if true, most weakens the argument?**

A) A decrease in symptoms of anxiety often occurs even with no treatment or intervention by a mental health professional.
B) Short-term relaxation training conducted by a more experienced practitioner can be more expensive than long-term training conducted by a less experienced practitioner.
C) Recipients of long-term training are much less likely than recipients of short-term training to have recurrences of problematic levels of anxiety.
D) The fact that an individual thinks that a treatment will reduce his or her anxiety tends, in and of itself, to reduce the individual's anxiety.
E) Short-term relaxation training involves the teaching of a wider variety of anxiety-combating relaxation techniques than does long-term training.

## Wrong, Yet Right

The prediction I make here has absolutely nothing to do with the correct answer—but I'm still glad I made the prediction. Having an answer in mind makes it much easier to get past answer choices like A and B, which simply don't get the job done. *The point isn't always to precisely predict the answer.* Sometimes the point is to predict *an* answer that you'd be happy with, to create a benchmark for the answer choices. Here, answer C meets or exceeds my benchmark, so I had no problem choosing it.

The reasoning is fine here if you're happy having a "normal level" of anxiety. The given facts do prove that for most people, short-term relaxation training will reduce anxiety to a normal level, and that, therefore, long-term training is unnecessary for most people. *But why would you want any anxiety at all?* We're asked to weaken the argument, so my prediction here is "most people would prefer to have no anxiety at all" or "even normal levels of anxiety are unacceptable for most people." Either of these would crush the argument.

A) This is terrific news for anxiety sufferers: Hey! Your anxiety might go away by itself! But that doesn't weaken the idea that long-term training is unnecessary—it actually strengthens that conclusion. So this can't be the answer.
B) Again, this misses the mark. What does price have to do with whether long-term training is necessary? No way.
C) Oooh. This did not match our prediction, but it's another good attack. I'm a bit mad at myself for not thinking of this! Maybe a crash course in relaxation can reduce anxiety *temporarily*, but with a super-high rate of relapse. In that case, wouldn't some anxiety sufferers consider the longer-term cure "necessary" if it had a dramatically lower risk of recidivism? If this is true, then the argument is in trouble. I like this answer a lot.
D) Placebo effect? I'm not sure that's relevant. It doesn't matter *how* the two cures worked—they both worked, and the point is that the long-term treatment is therefore unnecessary. This answer does absolutely nothing to the argument.
E) This would strengthen the idea that long-term relaxation training sucks.

Our answer is C, because it's a great attack on the argument. The other answers just don't measure up.

## QUESTION 10:

**Editorial: Many critics of consumerism insist that advertising persuades people that they need certain consumer goods when they merely desire them. However, this accusation rests on a fuzzy distinction, that between wants and needs. In life, it is often impossible to determine whether something is merely desirable or whether it is essential to one's happiness.**

**Which one of the following most accurately expresses the conclusion drawn in the editorial's argument?**

A) The claim that advertising persuades people that they need things that they merely want rests on a fuzzy distinction.
B) Many critics of consumerism insist that advertising attempts to blur people's ability to distinguish between wants and needs.
C) There is nothing wrong with advertising that tries to persuade people that they need certain consumer goods.
D) Many critics of consumerism fail to realize that certain things are essential to human happiness.
E) Critics of consumerism often use fuzzy distinctions to support their claims.

Despite my best efforts to disagree with everything anyone says to me on the LSAT, I can't help but go along with this one. Obviously I don't need my iPhone—for survival. But I'd be significantly less happy without it. How else would I listen to The Chronic while playing Plants vs. Zombies? It's not strictly necessary to keep me breathing, but I still consider it essential for my happiness.

Fortunately, we're not asked to strengthen this argument, or weaken it, or identify an assumption or flaw. We simply must identify the main conclusion of the argument. It basically boils down to "Critics of consumerism are wrong," for two reasons. First, when anybody says "So-and-so is wrong," that's almost always their conclusion. Second, the rest of the argument supports that statement. Fact: I don't need my iPhone to breathe, but I do need it to satisfy my addiction to rap and video games. "Need" can have more than one meaning. THEREFORE, critics of consumerism are wrong when they say, "Advertising persuades people to believe they 'need' things they don't." Sweet. Armed with a strong prediction—"Critics of consumerism are wrong"—we can dive into the answer choices.

A) Saying someone's argument "rests on a fuzzy distinction" captures the idea that they are wrong. That matches our prediction. The answer goes a little further than our prediction did, but as long as it does this accurately—as long as it matches the argument that the editorial actually made—it can still be the correct answer. The argument did talk about a fuzzy distinction—the problem of "want" vs. "need." So this would make a solid answer.
B) This is true—this correctly captures what the critics believe. And that was presented in the argument. But the point of the argument was "These guys are wrong." This answer choice contains no such accusation. It's part of the argument, but it's not the conclusion of the argument. So it can't be the answer.
C) This goes a step too far. The editorial didn't conclude with "Therefore, the advertising is fine by me." For all we know, the editorialist is a more vehement critic of consumerism than the critics he is criticizing! (Say that five times fast.) It's possible to say someone's argument sucks and still agree with their conclusion. This answer is a trap.
D) No, this is inaccurate. The editorial attacks the critics on one particular issue—the idea that "need" can be interpreted in different ways. This answer paints with a much broader brush. The editorial did not say, "Hey, you guys are ignoring the possibility that some things are necessary for happiness." It's subtle, but A was a more precise description of the argument.
E) Nah. The word "often" here is completely unsupported by the argument.

Our answer is A.

### Think in CAPS

To figure out what the conclusion of an argument is, try inserting a big THEREFORE between the pieces of the argument. If your statement makes sense, then whatever came after the THEREFORE was probably the conclusion. If it sounds funny, try rearranging—change the order of the elements and put the THEREFORE in front of some other part of the argument. When it sounds right, you've probably figured out the conclusion.

This is a nifty trick, but you'll need to learn to do it in your head. Your LSAT proctor probably won't look kindly on doing this aloud.

# QUESTION 11:

People who browse the web for medical information often cannot discriminate between scientifically valid information and quackery. Much of the quackery is particularly appealing to readers with no medical background because it is usually written more clearly than scientific papers. Thus, people who rely on the web when attempting to diagnose their medical conditions are likely to do themselves more harm than good.

Which one of the following is an assumption the argument requires?

A) People who browse the web for medical information typically do so in an attempt to diagnose their medical conditions.
B) People who attempt to diagnose their medical conditions are likely to do themselves more harm than good unless they rely exclusively on scientifically valid information.
C) People who have sufficient medical knowledge to discriminate between scientifically valid information and quackery will do themselves no harm if they rely on the web when attempting to diagnose their medical conditions.
D) Many people who browse the web assume that information is not scientifically valid unless it is clearly written.
E) People attempting to diagnose their medical conditions will do themselves more harm than good only if they rely on quackery instead of scientifically valid information.

The logic goes like this: Laymen who search the web for a cure can't tell the difference between real science and complete bullshit. Also, pseudo-medical bullshit appeals to laymen because it uses one-syllable language that the laymen find easier to understand than the fancy college-boy language used in actual medical papers. Therefore, people "are likely to do more harm than good" by searching on the web.

It's not a terrible argument. But it has a flaw: there's a difference between buying the bullshit, and the bullshit doing actual harm. First, can the bullshit itself cause harm? Sure, some nonsense herbal remedy might not work, but what's the harm in a little cilantro? Second, what kind of diseases are we talking about here? If an herbal toenail fungus remedy utterly fails to work, can we say that the patient is thereby harmed? Or are we talking about cancer, where reliance on cilantro will do serious harm if it causes you to forego the chemotherapy that would save your life?

Both of those objections point out assumptions made by the argument: herbal remedies can cause harm, and/or herbal remedies can cause patients to forego treatment that actually works.

A) Nah. The argument doesn't assume that when people browse medical information, they are typically trying to diagnose themselves. Maybe they've already been diagnosed, and they're just trying to learn more. Or maybe, just for fun, they're reading up on whatever STD the skanks of Jersey Shore have been swapping around this week. The argument doesn't care why most people are browsing—it's just trying to warn against all the bullshit that's out there.
B) I like this one. It says, "If people rely at all on the bullshit, they are going to cause themselves more harm than good." I think this was the missing link in the argument—the connection to harm needed tightening. We could live with this.
C) This 1) is irrelevant, since the argument was about people who can't discriminate between bullshit and science, and 2) weakens the idea that bullshit will cause harm, not strengthen it. So this is a tragically terrible answer.
D) The argument doesn't care about web browsers generally—it's concerned with people who are searching for medical advice. This answer simply misses the point.
E) The word "only" makes this answer wrong. The phrase "only if" creates a necessary condition. This answer says, "If people cause themselves harm, then we know they relied on quackery." That's the reverse of what the argument implied.

B gets it right: "If people rely on quackery, we know they will be harmed." So B is our answer.

## QUESTION 12:

When adults toss balls to very young children they generally try to toss them as slowly as possible to compensate for the children's developing coordination. But recent studies show that despite their developing coordination, children actually have an easier time catching balls that are thrown at a faster speed.

Which one of the following, if true, most helps to explain why very young children find it easier to catch balls that are thrown at a faster speed?

A) Balls thrown at a faster speed, unlike balls thrown at a slower speed, trigger regions in the brain that control the tracking of objects for self-defense.
B) Balls that are tossed more slowly tend to have a higher arc that makes it less likely that the ball will be obscured by the body of the adult tossing it.
C) Adults generally find it easier to catch balls that are thrown slowly than balls that are thrown at a faster speed.
D) Children are able to toss balls back to the adults with more accuracy when they throw fast than when they throw the ball back more slowly.
E) There is a limit to how fast the balls can be tossed to the children before the children start to have more difficulty in catching them.

If you want to teach a toddler to catch, chuck a quick one right at his face. What could possibly go wrong?

Like Question 8 above, there's a mystery here. *Why would it be easier for toddlers to catch balls thrown with some speed than balls that are thrown as slowly as possible?* The correct answer must provide an explanation for this mystery. I'm not sure we can predict it exactly, but one possible explanation would be something like "Kids can't moderate their motor reactions—they react *too* quickly, moving their hands *past* the point where they need to be to catch a slowly-thrown ball." If that's true, it would explain why they suck at catching slowly-thrown balls, but do better if we throw it a bit faster. Let's see if that's it.

A) Oh, okay. This is a decent explanation. Basically, it's, "Slowly-thrown balls don't register as an incoming threat, so the kids can't use their self-defense mechanisms to catch it. But a faster ball looks like an incoming threat—a striking cobra to the eyeball, perhaps?—so kids will instinctively react to it." This doesn't precisely match our prediction, but like our prediction it would *explain* why kids are better at catching fastballs than softballs. So I bet this is it. (The same thing happened to us on Question 9, didn't it?—our prediction there guided us to the correct *type* of answer.)
B) If this is true, then slow balls would be easier to catch, not harder. So this doesn't explain why kids struggle more with slower balls.
C) This is certainly true in real life, but it doesn't explain why the exact opposite is true for kids.
D) The return throw is totally irrelevant. This is a catastrophically bad answer, because it doesn't even attempt to explain why toddlers are better at *catching* fastballs than slow ones.
E) This is undoubtedly true in real life. If we hired Roger Clemens to fire 100-MPH fastballs at the kids' faces, they'd catch quite a few in their teeth, and none in their hands. But this certainly doesn't explain why they *do* catch "faster" balls better than balls thrown "as slowly as possible."

Our answer is A, because it's the only good explanation for the stated phenomenon.

13

## QUESTION 13:

Like a genetic profile, a functional magnetic-resonance image (fMRI) of the brain can contain information that a patient wishes to keep private. An fMRI of a brain also contains enough information about a patient's skull to create a recognizable image of that patient's face. A genetic profile can be linked to a patient only by referring to labels or records.

The statements above, if true, most strongly support which one of the following?

A) It is not important that medical providers apply labels to fMRIs of patients' brains.
B) An fMRI has the potential to compromise patient privacy in circumstances in which a genetic profile would not.
C) In most cases patients cannot be reasonably sure that the information in a genetic profile will be kept private.
D) Most of the information contained in an fMRI of a person's brain is also contained in that person's genetic profile.
E) Patients are more concerned about threats to privacy posed by fMRIs than they are about those posed by genetic profiles.

What are they getting at here? Fact: An fMRI can contain sensitive information (like a genetic profile). Fact: An fMRI contains enough information to create a recognizable image of the patient's face. Fact: Genetic profiles can be linked to a patient only by referring to labels or records. *Hmm.*

We're asked to find something "strongly supported" by the given facts. So we just have to pick the answer that has the best evidence on the page.

The only thing that I'm *sure* that all the evidence adds up to is that there is a *difference* between genetic profiles and fMRIs—genetic profiles don't contain information that can be personally identified, but fMRIs do contain information that could tie them to their owner (via facial recognition.) I don't care what the answers say—I haven't looked at them yet. That's what the *facts* say.

And if *that* is true, then it seems like a patient who gives a shit about privacy should be especially careful with fMRIs—even more careful than that patient would be with a genetic profile—since fMRIs contain private information *and* potentially personally identifying information. I'm less sure about this last statement, because it's also possible that genetic profiles have much more sensitive information in them than do fMRIs, which would mean that disclosure, even if less likely, would have worse consequences. (But at that point, we're probably overthinking it.)

If both of our predictions are listed in the answer choices, we'd obviously prefer "There is a difference between genetic profiles and fMRIs" to "We should be more careful with fMRIs than genetic profiles" because we know the first thing *for sure*, while the second is a bit speculative. (The first prediction is *more strongly supported* than the second.)

A) Nah. It's possible to identify fMRIs by creating a facial image of the subject and then going "Heyyyyyy, that's our old buddy Randall! I'd recognize his bearded mug anywhere!" But this is surely not the most effective, or certain, way to keep track of these things. I'm pretty sure doctors would go ahead and label the things.
B) Well, yeah. I think so. In the circumstance where the record didn't have a name or ID on it, the fMRI could still be attached to an individual, whereas a genetic profile could not. In *that situation*, it is certain that the fMRI would be more likely to compromise privacy than the genetic profile would be. We have to like this answer. It's basically our "there's a difference" prediction above.
C) No way. Who said anything about "most cases"? Maybe doctors are great at keeping genetic profiles private. Maybe they are stored separately from the labels and records, in titanium safes, at the bottom of the ocean, guarded by ninja octopuses. Who knows? We just weren't told.
D) We were given absolutely no reason to believe that this would be true. Terrible answer.
E) This is somewhat speculative... it's more like our second prediction above, where B is more like our first prediction. Of the two, I prefer the more certain, and less speculative, one.

Our answer is B.

## QUESTION 14:

Council member: I recommend that the abandoned shoe factory be used as a municipal emergency shelter. Some council members assert that the courthouse would be a better shelter site, but they have provided no evidence of this. Thus, the shoe factory would be a better shelter site.

A questionable technique used in the council member's argument is that of

A) asserting that a lack of evidence against a view is proof that the view is correct

B) accepting a claim simply because advocates of an opposing claim have not adequately defended their view

C) attacking the proponents of the courthouse rather than addressing their argument

D) attempting to persuade its audience by appealing to their fear

E) attacking an argument that is not held by any actual council member

Wow, no problem here. I've seen this argument a million times, in various incarnations—it's an extremely common flaw. The logic is basically, "You haven't proven your case, *therefore my case is proven.*" It's like saying that, based on the fact that atheists can't *prove* there's no God, Jesus must definitely be watching us all from heaven. The problem with that logic is that it could be used to prove absolutely *anything.* "Atheists can't prove there is no God, therefore *Allah* must definitely be watching." "Atheists can't prove there is no God, therefore Xenu/astrology/Ronald McDonald/ whatever-the-fuck-you-want must definitely be watching." Sorry, it's a crock. And I've heard it many times before.

A) Close, but not quite. The argument wasn't "You haven't *disproven my case,* therefore I'm right." The argument was "You haven't *proven your case,* therefore I'm right." Those two things are very similar, and we could pick this answer if there isn't something better, but we can't fall in love with it.

B) Yep. This one says, "You haven't proven *your* case, so my case is proven." That's exactly what we're looking for, so we have to like it better than A.

C) This would be the answer if the argument had said, "Proponents of the courthouse plan like to wear women's underwear, therefore the shoe factory is a better choice."

D) This would be the answer if the argument had said, "If we go with the courthouse plan, cannibal rapist Oakland Raiders fans will run free in our streets, therefore we should use the shoe factory."

E) This would be the answer if the argument had said, "Councilman Jones believes that Ronald McDonald is the president of the United States, so we should use the shoe factory."

Our answer is B.

15

## QUESTION 15:

It was misleading for James to tell the Core Curriculum Committee that the chair of the Anthropology Department had endorsed his proposal. The chair of the Anthropology Department had told James that his proposal had her endorsement, but only if the draft proposal she saw included all the recommendations James would ultimately make to the Core Curriculum Committee.

**The argument relies on which one of the following assumptions?**

A) If the chair of the Anthropology Department did not endorse James's proposed recommendations, the Core Curriculum Committee would be unlikely to implement them.

B) The chair of the Anthropology Department would have been opposed to any recommendations James proposed to the Core Curriculum Committee other than those she had seen.

C) James thought that the Core Curriculum Committee would implement the proposed recommendations only if they believed that the recommendations had been endorsed by the chair of the Anthropology Department.

D) James thought that the chair of the Anthropology Department would have endorsed all of the recommendations that he proposed to the Core Curriculum Committee.

E) The draft proposal that the chair of the Anthropology Department had seen did not include all of the recommendations in James's proposal to the Core Curriculum Committee.

Any time I see an accusation (you're wrong, you're misguided, you're misleading) I strongly suspect that the accusation is the conclusion of the argument. This is no exception. The conclusion is, "It was misleading for James to tell the Core Curriculum Committee that the chair of the Anthropology Department had endorsed his proposal." Here's the evidence: The chair of the Anthropology Department *did* tell James that the draft proposal he showed her had approval, but on one condition: James couldn't add anything to the draft proposal he had showed her when making recommendations to the Committee.

Okay, so what do we think? Was James right to tell the Core Curriculum Committee that the Anthropology Department approved of his proposal? Think about it for a second. I'll wait.

If you said yes, *or* no, then you're wrong. The best answer is "We don't have enough information." The answer in law school is almost always, "we don't have enough information, because _____."

We need to know whether or not James *added* anything to the proposal when he presented it to the Committee. If he *did* add to the proposal, then he is a lying sonofabitch for telling the Committee he had Anthropology's approval. Simple as that.

Since the argument accuses James of misleading the Committee, it *assumes* that James added something to the proposal. That must be our answer here.

A) Not what we're looking for. Likelihood of implementation is irrelevant. The only thing we can care about here is whether or not James misled the committee.

B) This is a close miss. We don't know if the chair would disagree with whatever James might add to the proposal, just that she approved only the proposal she saw. She might have even approved of James' changes if she had been given the opportunity to see them.

C) Same explanation as A. Likelihood of implementation is just irrelevant.

D) Nah. We don't care what was going on in James' head. Did he make changes to the proposal, or didn't he?

E) There we go. The argument has assumed that James said things to the Committee that he didn't run by Anthropology. This answer is a Necessary Assumption, because if it is untrue it ruins the argument. If this answer is untrue, it becomes "The draft the chair saw included all the recommendations made to the Core Committee." If that's true, then James did not mislead the Committee. This is our answer.

## QUESTION 16:

Travaillier Corporation has recently hired employees with experience in the bus tour industry, and its executives have also been negotiating with charter bus companies that subcontract with bus tour companies. But Travaillier has traditionally focused on serving consumers who travel primarily by air, and marketing surveys show that Travaillier's traditional consumers have not changed their vacation preferences. Therefore, Travaillier must be attempting to enlarge its consumer base by attracting new customers.

Which one of the following, if true, would most weaken the argument?

A) In the past, Travaillier has found it very difficult to change its customers' vacation preferences.
B) Several travel companies other than Travaillier have recently tried and failed to expand into the bus tour business.
C) At least one of Travaillier's new employees not only has experience in the bus tour industry but has also designed air travel vacation packages.
D) Some of Travaillier's competitors have increased profits by concentrating their attention on their customers who spend the most on vacations.
E) The industry consultants employed by Travaillier typically recommend that companies expand by introducing their current customers to new products and services.

The evidence strongly suggests that Travaillier is planning a move into bus tours. They have hired experienced bus tour employees. They are negotiating with charter bus subcontractors. Neither of these facts is *conclusive* by itself, but together they make it a pretty good bet that Travaillier means to start offering bus tours.

But the speaker is puzzled by this move, for two reasons. 1) Travaillier has traditionally focused on serving air travelers. 2) Travaillier's traditional consumers have not changed their vacation preferences. So Travaillier *seems* to be moving into bus tours, but Travaillier's existing customers probably aren't interested in bus tours. The argument takes all this evidence and concludes that Travaillier must be shooting for new customers.

That's not a terrible line of reasoning. It's far from proven, but it does seem reasonably supported by the evidence. If I were to argue with the conclusion, I'd focus on the word "must." Are we *sure* that they *must* be reaching for new customers? How do we know that they're not trying to convince air travelers that bus travel is also a good idea? I'd like the conclusion better if it said Travaillier *might* be shooting for new customers, or even *probably* shooting for new customers.

We've been asked to weaken the argument, so we need to pick an answer that suggests Travaillier is trying to convert its existing air customers to bus tours, or is trying to do anything else besides attract new customers.

A) This would actually strengthen the idea that Travaillier is shooting for new customers, rather than trying to convert its existing customers to bus tours. We're looking for a weakener, so this one is out.
B) It's really not relevant what other companies have done. The only issue here is Travaillier's intentions. Just because other companies have tried something and failed does not mean that Travaillier can't also intend to try the same thing.
C) I just can't see how this would weaken the idea that Travaillier is reaching for new customers. I can't even make a reasonable case for this answer choice. No way.
D) Again, what *other* companies are doing just isn't relevant. Terrible answer.
E) OK, this is the best answer. It's not a perfect answer, by any means—Travaillier's executives could always tell the consultants to fuck off, and shoot for new customers despite the advice the consultants typically give. Or the consultants could advise Travaillier differently from how they usually advise a company. But yeah, if the consultants Travaillier is using usually recommend that a company try to convert its current customers to new services, then there is *at least one reason* to believe that Travaillier is *not* shooting for new customers. All the other answers sucked horrifically, so this one is the only conceivable choice. Best of a bad lot—our answer is E.

# QUESTION 17:

Educator: Traditional classroom education is ineffective because education in such an environment is not truly a social process and only social processes can develop students' insights. In the traditional classroom, the teacher acts from outside the group and interaction between teachers and students is rigid and artificial.

The educator's conclusion follows logically if which one of the following is assumed?

A) Development of insight takes place only if genuine education also occurs.
B) Classroom education is effective if the interaction between teachers and students is neither rigid nor artificial.
C) All social processes involve interaction that is neither rigid nor artificial.
D) Education is not effective unless it leads to the development of insight.
E) The teacher does not act from outside the group in a nontraditional classroom.

Here's another example of what I was talking about on Question 15: The word "ineffective" probably indicates the conclusion of the argument, because it's an accusation. If you're gonna talk shit, you better back it up. And the rest of the argument here gives evidence for the accusation. One: Traditional classroom education is not social, and only social processes can develop insight. Two: Traditional classroom teachers act from outside the group. Three: Interaction between teachers and students is rigid and artificial in the traditional classroom.

We're asked to make the conclusion (traditional classroom education is ineffective) "follow logically" from the evidence. This should be fairly easy. I see three ways to do what we need to do—we have three premises, and if we connect any one of them to the conclusion, then the conclusion is proven. Like this:

- **Insight is required for effective education.** We know that traditional classroom education is not social, and therefore does not develop insight. So if insight is necessary for effective education, then traditional classroom education can't be effective.
- **Teachers who act from outside the group cannot be effective.** We know that traditional classroom teachers act from outside the group. So if it's impossible for acting outside the group to be effective, then traditional classroom education can't be effective.
- **Rigid, artificial interaction between teacher and students cannot be effective.** We know that interaction between teachers and students in the traditional classroom is rigid and artificial. So if it's impossible for rigid, artificial interaction to be effective, then traditional classroom education can't be effective.

Any one of the above would make a perfect answer—any one of them would *prove* the conclusion we are asked to prove, and would therefore be 100% positive to be our answer. Let's see if we can find one of them in the given choices:

A) This gets it backward. If it said, "Development of insight occurs if genuine education also occurs," this would match our first prediction. But that's not what it says. (The word "only" makes it wrong. See the sidebar about "If" and "Only if" for an explanation.) We needed "Development of insight is *necessary*" but this one says, "Development of insight is *sufficient*."
B) This is also very close, but wrong—this time, the *lack* of the word "only" makes it wrong. If it said, "Classroom education is effective *only* if the interaction between teachers and students is neither rigid nor artificial," then it would match our third prediction above. But that's not what it says. We needed "lack of rigidity and artificiality is *necessary*" but this one says, "lack of rigidity and artificiality is *sufficient*."
C) This one crosses premises in a way that doesn't connect to the conclusion. We need a connection to the conclusion, and this isn't it.
D) Yep. This one makes the development of insight *necessary* for effective education. This matches our first prediction, and we can be almost certain that it's our answer. But let's quickly eliminate E anyway, just to be sure.
E) This does nothing to prove that traditional classroom education is ineffective. Who gives a shit what happens in *non*traditional classrooms? That's beside the point.

Our answer is D.

# "If," "Only If" and "If and Only If"

You may want to sit down for this sidebar.

Imagine you invited me to a party. I could be a polite guest and simply say "Yes, I'll be there," or "I'm sorry, I have a prior obligation." Either of those responses would make it easy for you–you'd know for sure whether or not you should plan on me. But I could also be a pain in the ass and put a *condition* on my attendance. I could say, "I'll go *if* Miguel Angel Jimenez goes." Or I could say, "I'll go *only if* Miguel Angel Jimenez goes." In real life, those two statements might sound like the same thing–you'd try to figure out whether Miguel is coming, and then you'd know whether or not I'll be there. But on the LSAT, it's more complicated than that. The two statements *do not* mean the same thing on the LSAT–they mean subtly, yet concretely, different things. The purpose of this box is to explain that difference, because it's a critical concept.

If I say "I'll go if Miguel goes," what I'm telling you is that Miguel is a *sufficient condition* for my attendance. If Miguel is there, that's *sufficient* information for you to know that I will also be there. Memorize this: *The word "if," on the LSAT, indicates a sufficient condition.* So "I'll go if Miguel goes" looks like this:

M → N

This does not, of course, mean that if I go Miguel must also go. The arrow only goes one way! What it *does* mean is that if I'm not there, Miguel can't be there:

N̶ → M̶

Now, I need you to carefully consider what this actually means:

- It's okay for Miguel and Nathan to both be at the party.
- It's okay for neither Miguel nor Nathan to be at the party.
- It's okay for Nathan to be there without Miguel. (I said I'd go if Miguel goes, but I didn't say I wouldn't go without him!)
- It's *NOT* okay for Miguel to be there without Nathan. (I said I'd be there if Miguel was there. So if Miguel is there and I'm absent, then I've broken my promise to you.)

This might all seem obvious so far. But the next step is where your mind will be blown, so please pay careful attention.

If I say "I'll go *only if* Miguel goes" (or "I'll *only* go if Miguel goes"), I'm no longer telling you that Miguel is a sufficient condition for my attendance, like I was in the discussion above. Rather, I'm telling you that Miguel is a *necessary* condition: If I'm there, then Miguel is also going to be there. Memorize this: *"Only" indicates a*

*necessary condition.* So "I'll go only if Miguel goes" looks like this:

N → M

This does not mean that if Miguel goes I must also go. The arrow only goes one way! What it *does* mean is that if Miguel is not there, I can't be there:

M̶ → N̶

(This is called contrapositive. If you're having trouble following the discussion, it really might help to check out my blog posts on sufficient and necessary conditions. Visit www.foxlsat.com)

Now, I need you to carefully consider what this actually means:

- It's okay for Miguel and Nathan to both be at the party.
- It's okay for neither Miguel nor Nathan to be at the party.
- It's okay for Miguel to be there without Nathan. (I said I'd *only* go if Miguel goes, but that doesn't preclude me from skipping the party even if he's there!)
- It's *NOT* okay for Nathan to be there without Miguel. (I said I'd *only* be there if Miguel was there, so if Miguel is absent and I'm there, I've broken my promise to you.)

To recap:
- *In both scenarios, it's okay for both Miguel and Nathan to be at the party.*
  *In both scenarios, it's okay for both Miguel and Nathan to be absent from the party.*
- *In the "I'll be there if Miguel is there" scenario, it's okay for Nathan to be there without Miguel, but it is not okay for Miguel to be there without Nathan.*
- *In the "I'll only be there if Miguel is there" scenario, it's okay for Miguel to be there without Nathan, but it's not okay for Nathan to be there without Miguel.*
- *Please note the difference between the last two outcomes. This is a departure from how people tend to talk in everyday life, so it's something that you might just need to memorize for the LSAT.*

Now let's tackle this statement:

"I'll go to your party IF AND ONLY IF Miguel goes."

You might need to memorize this. "If and only if" means that BOTH rules ("I'll go IF Miguel goes," and "I'll go ONLY IF Miguel goes") are simultaneously in effect. What this means is that Miguel is both a sufficient condition AND a necessary condition for my attendance.

*-continued on the next page*

-continued from the previous page

As we discussed before:
- "I'll go IF Miguel goes" indicates that Miguel is a sufficient condition for my attendance. If Miguel is there, then I'm definitely going to be there.
- "I'll go ONLY if Miguel goes" indicates that Miguel is a necessary condition for my attendance. If Miguel is not there, then I'm definitely not going to be there.
- "I'll go IF AND ONLY IF Miguel goes" indicates that both of these rules are in effect. So you'll either see both of us at your party or neither of us at your party – you definitely won't see either of us there alone.

To diagram this statement, you can do one of two things. First, you could simply put both rules in effect:

M → N (I'll go if Miguel goes.)
N̶ → M̶ (Contrapositive)

N → M (I'll go only if Miguel goes.)
M̶ → N̶ (Contrapositive)

If you write all that, you'll have correctly captured all the implications of the "if and only if" rule.

Or, you can simply make the arrow go both ways. Note that "If and only if" is the ONLY time you can allow the arrow to go both ways. The diagram would look like this:

M ↔ N (I'll go if and only if Miguel goes.)
N̶ ↔ M̶ (Contrapositive)

Fortunately for people with bad memories like mine, there aren't that many things to memorize. Once you've got these basics down, it'll just be a matter of practice. Please send an email or pick up the phone if you have any questions!

## 18 QUESTION 18:

The probability of avoiding heart disease is increased if one avoids fat in one's diet. Furthermore, one is less likely to eat fat if one avoids eating dairy foods. Thus the probability of maintaining good health is increased by avoiding dairy foods.

The reasoning in the argument is most vulnerable to criticism on which one of the following grounds?

A) The argument ignores the possibility that, even though a practice may have potentially negative consequences, its elimination may also have negative consequences.
B) The argument fails to consider the possibility that there are more ways than one of decreasing the risk of a certain type of occurrence.
C) The argument presumes, without providing justification, that factors that carry increased risks of negative consequences ought to be eliminated.
D) The argument fails to show that the evidence appealed to is relevant to the conclusion asserted.
E) The argument fails to consider that what is probable will not necessarily occur.

The facts were only about heart disease, but the conclusion was about the much broader "good health." I think I can make a similarly bad argument: The more calories one eats, the more likely one will be obese. The more obese one is, the shorter one's expected lifespan is. So, therefore, we definitely know for sure that *complete avoidance of all calories in any form is the best way to extend one's life.*

Well, that's obviously dumb, right? Obesity isn't the *only* killer—surely starvation would work even quicker. With that example, I bet we've already gotten to the heart of the correct answer.

We're asked to find a reason why the argument is vulnerable to criticism. My prediction is, "this argument is bullshit because dairy foods might be good for you (or even necessary for survival) in a ton of other ways besides avoiding heart disease." Let's see.

A) We gotta love it. It matches our predicted "dairy might be good for you in other ways," and it also matches our starvation example. We should be thrilled to pick this answer. Let's just make sure B through E are all off the mark.
B) Nah. This would be the answer if the argument had said, "Therefore avoidance of dairy is the *only* way to reduce the risk of heart disease." The argument didn't do that. (The very next thing this gal said could very well have been, "Furthermore, avoiding meat is even better for avoiding heart disease." She didn't say that, but she *could* have.) This answer choice accuses the speaker of saying something she didn't actually say.

C) Well first of all, it's not necessarily wrong to assume that we should "avoid in-creased risks of negative consequences." Is it? I certainly do look both ways before I cross the street—and I don't think I'm being unreasonable by doing so. And second, more importantly, the argument didn't actually tell anyone what they *should* do. All it said was, "Avoiding dairy increases the probability of good health." So again, this answer choice accuses the speaker of something she didn't actually do.

D) No way, this isn't even a logical flaw. It's obvious that "heart disease" is *relevant* to "health." That's a common-sense assumption. You're not allowed to make a lot of logical leaps on the LSAT, but that's a safe one. It would actually be stupid to assume that heart disease is *not* relevant to health.

E) The argument doesn't say, "Avoidance of dairy will guarantee you live to 100." The argument acknowledges the uncertain nature of the evidence when it says "probability of maintaining good health."

Our answer is A.

# QUESTION 19:

19

**Professor: One cannot frame an accurate conception of one's physical environment on the basis of a single momentary perception, since each such glimpse occurs from only one particular perspective. Similarly, any history book gives only a distorted view of the past, since it reflects the biases and prejudices of its author.**

**The professor's argument proceeds by**

A) **attempting to show that one piece of reasoning is incorrect by comparing it with another, presumably flawed, piece of reasoning**

B) **developing a case for one particular conclusion by arguing that if that conclusion were false, absurd consequences would follow**

C) **making a case for the conclusion of one argument by showing that argument's resemblance to another, presumably cogent, argument**

D) **arguing that because something has a certain group of characteristics, it must also have another, closely related, characteristic**

E) **arguing that a type of human cognition is unreliable in one instance because it has been shown to be unreliable under similar circumstances**

Arguing always helps. My argument here is, "What the hell does your analogy about momentary perception have to do with a *history book*? Are the two even remotely the same thing? The fact that I can't instantly learn everything about a crowded room with a momentary glimpse does *not* prove that a history author can't, with years of work, produce a careful and unbiased work. Your argument sucks."

We're asked to identify the method of argumentation used by the professor. My prediction is "The professor has used a bullshit analogy." This is a common argumenta-tive technique on the LSAT. As a matter of fact, on Section 1, Question 17 of this test the same exact thing happened.

A) No, there's no parallel piece of reasoning given in the argument. This would be the answer if the professor had said, "George was wrong when he confused correla-tion with causation, therefore Phil, who used the same reasoning, is also wrong."

B) No, the professor didn't do this. This would be the answer if the professor had said, "Noah's Ark can't possibly have happened, because if it *did* happen, then every human on Earth—black, white, and otherwise—is the product of Noah's incestuous family. That would be absurd."

C) Best answer so far. This basically means, "used an analogy," which is what we were looking for.

D) Nah. This would be the answer if the argument had said, "Because Joe listens to Rush Limbaugh and votes Republican, he must be white."

E) Nope. This would be the answer if the argument had said, "Eyewitness testimony has been shown to be unreliable in countless studies, therefore eyewitness testi-mony can't be relied upon in this case."

Our answer is C.

## QUESTION 20:

To date, most of the proposals that have been endorsed by the Citizens League have been passed by the city council. Thus, any future proposal that is endorsed by the Citizens League will probably be passed as well.

**The pattern of reasoning in which one of the following arguments is most similar to that in the argument above?**

A) Most of the Vasani grants that have been awarded in previous years have gone to academic biologists. Thus, if most of the Vasani grants awarded next year are awarded to academics, most of these will probably be biologists.

B) Most of the individual trees growing on the coastal islands in this area are deciduous. Therefore, most of the tree species on these islands are probably deciduous varieties.

C) Most of the editors who have worked for the local newspaper have not been sympathetic to local farmers. Thus, if the newspaper hires someone who is sympathetic to local farmers, they will probably not be hired as an editor.

D) Most of the entries that were received after the deadline for last year's photography contest were rejected by the judges' committee. Thus, the people whose entries were received after the deadline last year will probably send them in well before the deadline this year.

E) Most of the stone artifacts that have been found at the archaeological site have been domestic tools. Thus, if the next artifact found at the site is made of stone, it will probably be a domestic tool.

This argument isn't patently flawed, but it does make the assumption that something that has happened most of the time in the past will probably continue to happen in the future. That's not totally ridiculous, but it's not exactly proven either. (Note that if the argument had omitted the word "probably" from its conclusion, then the statement *would* be ridiculous, and I would be far more pissed off here. But since the argument hedges, rather than making an absolute prediction, I'll save the outrage.) We're asked to find a similar pattern of reasoning, so we're looking for something that uses the same past-performance-*probably*-predicts-future-results logic.

A) My argument in favor of this answer is that it does use the past-performance-probably-predicts-future-results line of reasoning. That's enough to make it our correct answer, if none of the other choices are remotely close. But my argument *against* this answer is that the conclusion didn't sound exactly correct. I wanted it to say, "Thus, next year's Vasani grant will probably be awarded to an academic biologist," rather than "If it's awarded to an academic, it will be a biologist." That's a subtle distinction, but it's probably important. We're on Question #20, after all. This feels like it's probably a cleverly-written incorrect answer to me.

B) There's no prediction about the future here. And this argument introduces a flaw (if a group of individuals has a certain characteristic, then the whole has the same characteristic) that wasn't present in the given argument. I liked A better, so this is out.

C) Same explanation as A. It does make a prediction based on past results, but again I don't love the conclusion. I wanted it to say, "Thus, the next editor will probably not be sympathetic to local farmers." Instead, we go "Thus, the next newspaper hire, if sympathetic, probably won't be editor." Because A and C are objectionable for the same reason, I bet they both turn out to be wrong.

D) This started out really well, but it needed to conclude with, "Most entries received after this year's deadline will probably be rejected" in order to be correct. The prediction here is "Those people will probably learn their lesson," when it was supposed to be "What happened in the past will probably keep happening." This is out.

E) I think this is the best answer. Most stone artifacts located at this site have been domestic tools. So the next stone artifact that's found will probably also be a domestic tool. I had problems with all the other answers, and E just feels like a better match. So let's pick E and move on. We might miss one of these occasionally, but I'd rather take that risk than waste ten minutes on a single question, especially a difficult one late in the section. Trust your gut!

## QUESTION 21:

**Chemist: The molecules of a certain weed-killer are always present in two forms, one the mirror image of the other. One form of the molecule kills weeds, while the other has no effect on them. As a result, the effectiveness of the weed-killer in a given situation is heavily influenced by which of the two forms is more concentrated in the soil, which in turn varies widely because local soil conditions will usually favor the breakdown of one form or the other. Thus, much of the data on the effects of this weed-killer are probably misleading.**

**Which one of the following, if true, most strengthens the chemist's argument?**

A) **In general, if the molecules of a weed-killer are always present in two forms, then it is likely that weeds are killed by one of those two forms but unaffected by the other.**
B) **Almost all of the data on the effects of the weed-killer are drawn from laboratory studies in which both forms of the weed-killer's molecules are equally concentrated in the soil and equally likely to break down in that soil.**
C) **Of the two forms of the weed-killer's molecules, the one that kills weeds is found in most local soil conditions to be the more concentrated form.**
D) **The data on the effects of the weed-killer are drawn from studies of the weed-killer under a variety of soil conditions similar to those in which the weed-killer is normally applied.**
E) **Data on the weed-killer's effects that rely solely on the examination of the effects of only one of the two forms of the weed-killer's molecules will almost certainly be misleading.**

The conclusion here seems like a big leap. I understand that this certain weed-killer has two molecules—mirrors of each other—one which kills weeds, and one which does not. And I understand that soil conditions can vary, which can lead to the break-down of either the effective weed-killing molecule or the ineffective weed-killing molecule. So I understand that soil conditions can make this weed-killer more or less effective. But what I don't understand is why "much of the data" on this weed-killer would be misleading. Don't scientists usually account for things like this? Did the guys who were counting up the dead (or alive) weeds just say, "Well, we know that soil conditions can change the efficacy of this weed-killer, so we should *probably* collect a soil sample while we're at it, but, ah, fuck it. It's Beer-Thirty"?

   We must strengthen the argument, so the correct answer must be along the lines of what I just said. "The data was collected without regard to soil type."

A) This is simply not what I'm looking for. I wouldn't even bother trying to figure out what it means until I see what else is on offer.
B) At first I thought this might actually weaken the argument, because it basically says, "The soil that was tested was a neutral soil that doesn't favor or disfavor the weed-killing molecule." But that's *exactly* why this answer strengthens the argument: Under these conditions, the weed-killer works in a consistently medium-strength sort of way. But that's not how it's really going to work in practice—in practice, it's going to sometimes work like gangbusters (favorable soil conditions), and sometimes it's going to be worthless (unfavorable soil conditions). The lazy-ass scientists needed to test the weed-killer under a *variety* of conditions. I could see us picking this answer.
C) Hmm. Are much of the data on this weed-killer from around here? If we knew that for sure, then this would make a good strengthener. (The local soil is biased, so if the samples came from here, then the data is biased.) But we don't know that for sure, do we? Feels like a trap.
D) This would weaken the argument, in the exact opposite way that B strengthens it. If this is true, then the weed-killer was tested under a variety of conditions, which is a good thing. For the same reason that B is a strengthener, this one is a weakener.
E) This seems nonsensical to me. Do we know that the data only examined the effects of one form of the molecule? No. Our answer is B. Tough question.

22

## QUESTION 22:

**Principle:** A police officer is eligible for a Mayor's Commendation if the officer has an exemplary record, but not otherwise; an officer eligible for the award who did something this year that exceeded what could be reasonably expected of a police officer should receive the award if the act saved someone's life.

**Conclusion:** Officer Franklin should receive a Mayor's Commendation but Officer Penn should not.

**From which one of the following sets of facts can the conclusion be properly drawn using the principle?**

A) In saving a child from drowning this year, Franklin and Penn both risked their lives beyond what could be reasonably expected of a police officer. Franklin has an exemplary record but Penn does not.

B) Both Franklin and Penn have exemplary records, and each officer saved a child from drowning earlier this year. However, in doing so, Franklin went beyond what could be reasonably expected of a police officer; Penn did not.

C) Neither Franklin nor Penn has an exemplary record. But, in saving the life of an accident victim, Franklin went beyond what could be reasonably expected of a police officer. In the only case in which Penn saved someone's life this year, Penn was merely doing what could be reasonably expected of an officer under the circumstances.

D) At least once this year, Franklin has saved a person's life in such a way as to exceed what could be reasonably expected of a police officer. Penn has not saved anyone's life this year.

E) Both Franklin and Penn have exemplary records. On several occasions this year Franklin has saved people's lives, and on many occasions this year Franklin has exceeded what could be reasonably expected of a police officer. On no occasions this year has Penn saved a person's life or exceeded what could be reasonably expected of an officer.

This argument is bullshit because it makes bold conclusions about both Officer Franklin and Officer Penn, without providing a shred of evidence about either of them. Let's take each in turn:

*Officer Franklin should receive a Mayor's Commendation.* In order for this to make sense, in light of the given principles, Officer Franklin must have an exemplary record. (Otherwise, she would be ineligible for the award.) And we were only given one reason for claiming that anyone "should" get an award—she should have done something this year that exceeded what could reasonably be expected of a police officer and saved someone's life in doing so. So I guess in order to make this argument stand up, Officer Franklin better have saved someone's life while going above and beyond the call of duty. Otherwise, we couldn't possibly know enough about her to say, "She should get it."

*Officer Penn should not get a Mayor's Commendation.* I can see only one way to get here. If Penn has a shitty record, then he's instantly ineligible. Simple as that.

We're asked to identify a set of facts that would lead to the outcome specified in the conclusion: Franklin gets an award and Penn does not. I think we know what we need, so let's tackle the scenarios:

A) That was easy. If this answer is true, then Penn is ineligible for the award and Franklin should get the award. Done deal. Let's read through the other answers though, to protect ourselves from silly mistakes.

B) These facts would definitely prove that Franklin should get the award. But the answer fails to prove that Penn should not get the award. This is because it ignores the possibility that Penn might have done lots of *other* stuff during the year that was also life-saving and beyond the call of duty. Or, similarly, there might be lots of *other reasons* to deserve an award besides doing something life-saving and beyond the call. Just because those aren't mentioned doesn't mean they don't exist. For example, maybe writing the most traffic tickets for the year would also justify an award. We weren't told. A was better.

C) No way. If Franklin doesn't have an exemplary record, then she can't get the award. That's enough to eliminate this answer immediately.

D) Nothing here about the record of either officer. That's not going to get it done—this just isn't even close.

E) Same explanation as B. These facts would prove that Franklin should get the award, but fail to disqualify Penn.

Our answer is A.

## QUESTION 23:

*23*

**Essayist: It is much less difficult to live an enjoyable life if one is able to make lifestyle choices that accord with one's personal beliefs and then see those choices accepted by others. It is possible for people to find this kind of acceptance by choosing friends and associates who share many of their personal beliefs. Thus, no one should be denied the freedom to choose the people with whom he or she will associate.**

**Which one of the following principles, if valid, most helps to justify the essayist's argument?**

A) **No one should be denied the freedom to make lifestyle choices that accord with his or her personal beliefs.**

B) **One should associate with at least some people who share many of one's personal beliefs.**

C) **If having a given freedom could make it less difficult for someone to live an enjoyable life, then no one should be denied that freedom.**

D) **No one whose enjoyment of life depends, at least in part, on friends and associates who share many of the same personal beliefs should be deliberately prevented from having such friends and associates.**

E) **One may choose for oneself the people with whom one will associate, if doing so could make it easier to live an enjoyable life.**

This argument is incomplete. It concludes that something *should* happen, without telling us why we should care. It's not enough for my doctor to tell me the bad things about being overweight, and that I should lose some weight. The doctor needs to connect the two. The doctor has to say, "Being overweight causes early death. *Do you want to die early? No? OK, if you don't want to die early*, you should lose weight." Getting my buy-in is a big part of getting me to adopt the recommendation.

The italicized part of the doctor's argument is what's missing in the essayist's case. We're told there are good things about freedom of association (it will be less difficult to live an enjoyable life), and we hear the essayist's conclusion that we *should*, therefore, allow freedom of association. What's missing is the bridge between those two things. We must find a principle that justifies the essayist's argument. It needs to say, "Do you want people to be able to more easily live enjoyable lives? OK, if you agree with that, then we *should* allow freedom of association."

A) Close, but no cigar. The argument was that happiness comes from *seeing our choices accepted by others.* Our choice to behave as we wish is not at issue here.

B) No, the point isn't, "We should associate with people like us." The point is "We should *have the freedom to choose* the people we associate with." I'm still hoping for an answer that will match our prediction.

C) This will do it. Our prediction was "We want enjoyable lives." This answer says, "We shouldn't prevent enjoyable lives," essentially the same thing. I like it because if you add C to the existing facts, it leads inevitably to the given conclusion.

D) This answer confuses a sufficient condition with a necessary condition. The facts say that freedom of association is sufficient to make living an enjoyable life easier. The facts do *not* say that freedom of association is necessary. When this answer says "depends on," it is indicating a necessary condition. So even if this answer choice were true, it wouldn't complete the argument.

E) There's nothing here about what should or should not happen. Yes, we know individuals "may" choose to make themselves happier... the point is whether or not we, as a society, are going to let them.

Our answer is C.

# 24

## QUESTION 24:

Physician: The rise in blood pressure that commonly accompanies aging often results from a calcium deficiency. This deficiency is frequently caused by a deficiency in the active form of vitamin D needed in order for the body to absorb calcium. Since the calcium in one glass of milk per day can easily make up for any underlying calcium deficiency, some older people can lower their blood pressure by drinking milk.

The physician's conclusion is properly drawn if which one of the following is assumed?

A) There is in milk, in a form that older people can generally utilize, enough of the active form of vitamin D and any other substances needed in order for the body to absorb the calcium in that milk.
B) Milk does not contain any substance that is likely to cause increased blood pressure in older people.
C) Older people's drinking one glass of milk per day does not contribute to a deficiency in the active form of vitamin D needed in order for the body to absorb the calcium in that milk.
D) People who consume high quantities of calcium together with the active form of vitamin D and any other substances needed in order for the body to absorb calcium have normal blood pressure.
E) Anyone who has a deficiency in the active form of vitamin D also has a calcium deficiency.

Wait, what? The argument goes like this: Rising blood pressure can be caused by calcium deficiency. And calcium deficiency can be caused by a vitamin D deficiency, which impairs the body's ability to absorb calcium. So drinking milk can fix blood pressure problems. Um... excuse me but... didn't you *just fucking say* that the problem isn't a lack of calcium in the diet, but a problem with the body's ability to absorb calcium? If that's the case, then wouldn't a glass of milk just go right through a person without its calcium being absorbed?

This is a fairly common phenomenon on the LSAT: The argument that contains its own poison pill. To succeed on the LSAT, you simply *must* train yourself to catch this sort of thing. If you didn't see it while reading the argument, you're going to have a hell of a time wading through the professionally written traps and time-wasters that are sure to be found in the answer choices. The answer choices are not your friend.

But since we articulated why the argument is bullshit before looking at the answer choices—*wouldn't the glass of milk go right through the person who has the vitamin D deficiency?*—we have already won. Now let's figure out what the question is asking, and proceed confidently to the correct answer.

We're asked to find an additional fact that, if true, will allow the conclusion of the argument to be "properly drawn," *i.e.*, proven. So we've got to plug the obvious hole we've identified. Something like "a glass of milk will correct the body's calcium deficiency despite the calcium absorption problem caused by a vitamin D deficiency" would do it. Or maybe "the vitamin D-related calcium absorption problem does not affect all calcium-related high blood pressure sufferers." Either of those, if true, would allow a glass of milk to correct the calcium-related high blood pressure problem of at least some sufferers. And all we need to prove is that *one* sufferer will be cured, since the conclusion of the argument said "some" older people. Some means "one or more."

A) Sure, that would do it. This answer basically says, "Milk has the calcium *and* the vitamin D required to absorb that calcium." This matches our prediction. And if this is true, then some older people *will* fix their high blood pressure with a glass of milk. Cool.

B) This would be great for old folks who want to drink milk, but it's terrible as an answer choice: it does absolutely nothing to prove that milk will cure anyone's high blood pressure. It simply doesn't connect the argument's evidence to its conclusion.

C) This is kind of the same thing as B. The point isn't whether milk will make something *worse*... the point is whether milk will make high blood pressure *better*. If this answer were true, then milk wouldn't exacerbate high blood pressure. But if everyone already has the vitamin D deficiency, then milk isn't going to fix anybody's high blood pressure either. So this doesn't prove the argument's conclusion.

D) This doesn't connect milk to fixing high blood pressure. It doesn't say the word "milk" anywhere. Please don't assume that milk has calcium and vitamin D—you might know this to be true in real life, but we needed a piece of evidence, on the page, that proves it. That's what A did, so A was better.

E) Nah, this doesn't plug the hole we've been looking to plug.

Our answer is A. I gotta be straight with you here: If you didn't find the argument's major flaw *while reading the argument*, you were in big trouble here... you'd be almost randomly guessing between the five answer choices. Most students don't spend enough time carefully reading the argument, and way too much time bouncing back and forth between the answer choices. Experts invest plenty of time comprehending and critiquing *the arguments themselves*. The answers lie within.

## QUESTION 25:

Political philosopher: A just system of taxation would require each person's contribution to correspond directly to the amount the society as a whole contributes to serve that person's interests. For purposes of taxation, wealth is the most objective way to determine how well the society has served the interest of any individual. Therefore, each person should be taxed solely in proportion to her or his income.

The flawed reasoning in the political philosopher's argument is most similar to that in which one of the following?

A) Cars should be taxed in proportion to the danger that they pose. The most reliable measure of this danger is the speed at which a car can travel. Therefore, cars should be taxed only in proportion to their ability to accelerate quickly.

B) People should be granted autonomy in proportion to their maturity. A certain psychological test was designed to provide an objective measure of maturity. Therefore, those scoring above high school level on the test should be granted complete autonomy.

C) Everyone should pay taxes solely in proportion to the benefits they receive from government. Many government programs provide subsidies for large corporations. Therefore, a just tax would require corporations to pay a greater share of their income in taxes than individual citizens pay.

D) Individuals who confer large material benefits upon society should receive high incomes. Those with high incomes should pay correspondingly high taxes. Therefore, we as a society should place high taxes on activities that confer large benefits upon society.

E) Justice requires that health care be given in proportion to each individual's need. Therefore, we need to ensure that the most seriously ill hospital patients are given the highest priority for receiving care.

Wait, what? The second sentence says *wealth* is the most objective way to determine how well society has served an individual. And then the conclusion says we should tax *income*. Are those two things identical? No, no, they are most certainly not. Wealth is how much you *have*—income is how much you *get*. It's possible to be incredibly wealthy and have negligible talent or income (Paris Hilton). It's also possible to have an enormous income and have zero wealth (the lawyer who makes five hundred grand per year but keeps himself in debt slavery with his expensive douchebag lifestyle). My point here isn't that Paris Hilton is worthless or the lawyer is stupid; my point is that the argument is fucked up. Wealth and income are not the same thing.

We're asked to find a similarly-flawed argument. So let's see if we can find another argument that confuses two related, but far from identical, concepts.

A) Boom. Speed and acceleration are certainly related, but not identical. It's possible to accelerate very slowly to an extremely high speed; it's also possible to accelerate very quickly but max out at a relatively low speed. I bet this is the answer.

B) There are a couple of flaws here (just because the study was designed to test maturity doesn't mean it actually works; does high school level maturity justify "complete" autonomy?) but neither of those is the flaw we're looking for. Unlike A, there are no two similar terms being conflated here. This can't be the answer.

C) Again, this is flawed (are corporations people? Does the existence of government subsidies for corporations prove that individuals don't also get benefits from the government?) but not in the way we're looking for. It's a lot easier to get past this answer having already seen a good option in A.

D) The conclusion talks about taxing activities themselves, when the facts say we should tax the individuals who perform those activities. That's a flaw, but it's not the flaw we were looking for.

E) I'm not sure there's any flaw here at all.

Our answer is A, because it contained an identical flaw to the flaw in the philosopher's argument.

# QUESTION 26:

A recent poll showed that almost half of the city's residents believe that Mayor Walker is guilty of ethics violations. Surprisingly, however, 52 percent of those surveyed judged Walker's performance as mayor to be good or excellent, which is no lower than it was before anyone accused him of ethics violations.

Which one of the following, if true, most helps to explain the surprising fact stated above?

A) Almost all of the people who believe that Walker is guilty of ethics violations had thought, even before he was accused of those violations, that his performance as mayor was poor.

B) In the time since Walker was accused of ethics violations, there has been an increase in the percentage of city residents who judge the performance of Walker's political opponents to be good or excellent.

C) About a fifth of those polled did not know that Walker had been accused of ethics violations.

D) Walker is currently up for reelection, and anticorruption groups in the city have expressed support for Walker's opponent.

E) Walker has defended himself against the accusations by arguing that the alleged ethics violations were the result of honest mistakes by his staff members.

The June 2011 LSAT wraps up with a supposed mystery: How is it possible that "almost half" of residents polled believe that Walker is guilty of ethics violations, but "52 percent" of the same survey respondents thought Walker's performance was good or excellent?

Um... is this really a surprise? I'm sure the same can be said about President Obama in 2012. "Almost half" of the country (Republicans) thinks he is trying his hardest to turn the USA into a Communist country (and was born in Kenya), while "52 percent" of the exact same country (Democrats) thinks he is doing just about as well as could be expected given how fucked-up Washington is. In other words, "almost half" and "52 percent" adds up to 100 percent. It's not surprising after all. Let's see if that's basically the answer.

A) This isn't exactly what we were looking for, but I can see a case for it. I'll return to it if need be.

B) This would probably be true, but doesn't explain the current state of public opinion *on Walker*. What do Walker's opponents have to do with anything?

C) Nah. One new fact about a small proportion of the survey respondents doesn't explain the survey's results.

D) No. Same explanation as B.

E) This sounds like a good play for Walker, but does nothing to explain the survey results.

I don't love any of the answers here, but I can make a case for A. If it's true that the people who now believe Walker is a scumbag also previously thought his performance was poor, then this would fit the partisan scenario I laid out initially: The only people smoking the current anti-Walker dope were already against him in the first place. Both sides are preaching to their own choirs, nobody is learning anything, and nothing is getting done. This answer sounds just like Washington, which sounds like our prediction. So our answer is A.

# Epilogue

Whether you think the LSAT is easy or hard, you're right. Mindset is at least half the battle. What I do for a living is convince students like you that the test is actually quite a bit easier than they initially thought. Really, there are just three types of questions:

1) **Questions that are basically easy.** Example: The correlation-equals-causation flaw. Maybe you get these right away, or maybe they trip you up a few times, but after you've done a moderate amount of practice you'll see these questions coming a mile away. This level of difficulty probably makes up a quarter of the test.

2) **Questions that look hard on the surface, but eventually become very easy.** Example: Logic games that require you to understand complex rules and link them together. These will take a lot of practice, but you can become expert at them. This is probably half the test. If you master types one and two, you can score in the 160s.

3) **Questions that are actually hard.** Example: Very long match-the-pattern-of-reasoning questions. These questions are difficult even for experts, and they generally appear toward the end of each section. You can make them incredibly easy by skipping them outright and filling in an answer bubble at random. Or, you can get very good at types one and two so that you have plenty of extra time to devote to these questions. This is probably a quarter of the test. It's not the difference between going to law school and not going to law school, but it does impact what kinds of offers you'll receive.

Start with types one and two. Do a little bit every day. I've never met anyone who couldn't improve his or her LSAT score dramatically by following this simple plan. And as always, let me know if I can help: nathan@foxlsat.com.

# APPENDIX:
# Logical Reasoning Question Types

What you need to do first, foremost, and always is *argue with the speaker,* and you'll be fine no matter what type of question you're looking at.

But certain question types *do* prefer certain types of answers, so after you've already done your best to understand the argument, it's definitely useful to think about what type of question you're dealing with. Here are some of the common question types, and here's how I like to break them down:

### Strategy of Argumentation: (Example: "Mal's response to Zoe proceeds by ... ")

Some questions of this type simply ask you to identify the type of reasoning used by an argument. In this case, you must find the answer choice that best describes the logic of the argument as a whole. Note that the correct answer will probably not contain any of the specific details from the argument. Instead, the answer will contain an abstract, or general, description of the method of argumentation used. Since there are frequently several different ways to abstractly describe an argument, it's difficult to predict the correct answer before looking at the answer choices.

A common variation on this type is a question that asks you to identify the role played in an argument by a particular phrase or sentence. **(Example: "Jayne's assertion that Vera is his most favorite gun plays which one of the roles in his argument?")** On these questions, I always ask myself, "Is it the main conclusion of the argument?" If the answer is no, then I ask a follow-up question: "Does it support the main conclusion of the argument?" Sometimes, you will be able to exactly predict the correct answer in advance. If not, then you will almost certainly be able to narrow down the answer choices by simply understanding whether the phrase in question was the conclusion, a premise that supports the conclusion, or something else. Once you've got that down, you're in good shape.

### Main Conclusion (Example: "Which one of the following most accurately expresses the conclusion of Wash's argument?")

Questions that ask you to identify the main conclusion are among the easiest questions on the LSAT, since you should always be looking for the conclusion of an argument anyway. (How can you be arguing with the speaker if you don't understand their main point?) On this type of question, you absolutely should predict the correct answer before looking at the answer choices. If you're having any trouble, try asking the speaker, "Why are you wasting my time with this?" to see if it helps you zero in on the speaker's main point.

### Must Be True (Example: "Which one of the following must be true, if Kaylee's statements above are correct?")

This question type can be tricky when you first start studying for the LSAT, because you might be inclined to pass up answer choices that seem "too obvious." Don't do that! Be open to the possibility that you're actually plenty smart enough to punch this test in the face. On a question of this type, all you're looking for is the one answer that has been *proven* by the speaker's statements (and nothing more than the speaker's statements ... outside information is not allowed.) The correct answer does not have to be the speaker's main point, nor does the speaker's entire statement have to be related to the correct answer. If any part of the speaker's statement *proves* that an answer choice has to be true, then that's your answer. This question type is pretty easy once you get the hang of it.

A common variation on this type of question is the slightly more fluid, and therefore slightly trickier, question that asks you to find something that might not *necessarily* be true based on the given statement, but is at least partially supported by the statement. **(Example: "Which one of the**

**following is most strongly supported by Kaylee's statements?")** The general idea is the same, and this is still a pretty manageable type of question. Pick the answer that is best supported by Kaylee's statement—and no more than Kaylee's statement. (Again, outside information is not allowed.) The correct answer here might not be *proven* true by what Kaylee has said, but ideally it will be pretty damn close to proven.

### Agree/Disagree (Example: "Simon and River have committed to disagreeing on which of the following?")

This is another very manageable question type once you know what to look for. (Sensing a theme here? Practice, practice, practice and you'll be in good shape.) Here, we are asked to identify the answer that Simon and River have *actually, already, in their statements*, disagreed upon. Easily dismissed incorrect answer choices might give a statement that Simon and River agree on—there are usually one or two of these. But trickier incorrect answers will frequently be something that Simon and River *probably* disagree on. One common trap on this type of question is an answer choice that the second speaker clearly takes a position on, and which might seem contrary to the first speaker's position, but the first speaker didn't actually address. Don't fall for that crap! You should be able to show me, in Simon's statement, where he said "yes" to a particular answer choice, and then show me, in River's statement, where she said "no" to that same statement. Or vice versa.

A common variation on this type of question is a question that asks you to identify a statement that the two speakers *agree* on. This is easy, as long as you don't make the tragic mistake of reading too fast and thinking you're supposed to be looking for a point of disagreement. It's devastating when that happens.

### Weaken (Example: "Which one of the following, if true, most weakens Shepherd Book's argument?")

My primary piece of advice on the Logical Reasoning is "always be attacking," no matter what type of question you're looking at. So a question that asks you to undermine an argument's reasoning shouldn't be too much of a problem. As you read each question, you should always be coming up with weakeners. For me, this takes the form of "Oh yeah, well you're full of shit, because what about this? Or what about that? Or what about this other thing?" I'm constantly barraging the speaker with skepticism. Ideally, by the time the speaker comes around to his conclusion, I'm armed with at least a couple potential holes in the argument. The answer might very well be exactly one of these predictions, or it might be something similar. Even if it's not something I've already thought of, being in that skeptical state of mind helps me spot a kindred argument.

If you're having trouble on weaken questions, you probably aren't quite clear about what it means to "weaken" an argument on the LSAT. Here it is: You weaken an argument by showing that its evidence doesn't justify its conclusion. There are many ways to do this, but at a minimum you *must* know what the conclusion is, and you also must know what evidence was used to reach that conclusion.

Once you understand the argument, there are countless ways to attack it. Maybe Shepherd Book's premises simply don't add up to his conclusion, leaving a big hole in the argument. Or maybe Shepherd Book's conclusion and his evidence can't simultaneously be true. Or maybe he made a sufficient vs. necessary error. (More on that ahead.) Or maybe he made a correlation-equals-causation error. Pick the answer that, if true, causes the argument to be faulty, nonsensical, or just plain stupid. Ask yourself: "Which one of these facts, if I were an attorney arguing *against* Shepherd Book, would I most like to be true?"

Incorrect answer choices on Weaken questions will either strengthen the argument, or, more commonly, simply be irrelevant. One trap to look out for is an answer choice that seems to go against Shepherd Book's position, but doesn't really address his argument. (For example, if Shepherd's argument was about one particular group of people, and the answer choice talks about a different group of people.)

Unlike Must Be True questions, it's totally acceptable to use outside information to answer a Weaken question.

## Strengthen (Example: "Which one of the following, if true, most strengthens Shepherd Book's argument?")

Arguments can be strengthened in just as many ways as they can be weakened. You're really just doing the reverse of the process described above. Pick the answer that strengthens the connection between the premises and the conclusion. If there is a big hole in the argument, then fill that gap as best you can. The correct answer on this type of question won't always prove that the conclusion is true, but you should pick the one that gets you the furthest toward that goal. Ask yourself: "Which one of these facts, if I were an attorney *for* Shepherd Book, would I most like to be true?" Again, outside information is fully acceptable here.

## Which Fact Would be Most Useful (Example: "Which one of the following would be most useful in determining the validity of Shepherd Book's claim?")

This isn't a very common type of question—it appears maybe once, on average, on each test. Each answer choice is itself a question, and you are asked to pick the one that has the most bearing on the argument. I find that if I read the argument to weaken (which I always do) then I can do a pretty good job of predicting what the missing information is. Ask yourself: "If I were a police officer evaluating Shepherd Book's story, which one of these questions would I ask?" Pick the question that, if answered one way, makes Shepherd guilty, but if answered another way, makes Shepherd innocent.

## Necessary Assumptions (Example: "Which one of the following is an assumption on which Inara's argument depends?")

Note the subtle, but very important, distinction between this question type (Necessary Assumption) and the one that follows (Sufficient Assumption). The Necessary Assumption question means, "Which one of the following *must be true in order for Inara's argument to make sense*?" Pick the answer that, if untrue, would make Inara's argument ridiculous. Another way of thinking about this is "Which one of the following is an assumption that Inara actually made?" Avoid answers that are stronger, or more absolute, than the minimum required for Inara's conclusion to make sense. If Badger is on the planet Persephone, and Inara concludes that Badger is a dick, then she has necessarily assumed that at least one person on Persephone *is* a dick. She has *not* assumed that everyone on Persephone is a dick.

## Sufficient Assumptions (Example: "Which one of the following, if assumed, would allow Inara's conclusion to be properly drawn?")

This question means, "Which one of the following, *if true, would prove Inara's conclusion*? Pick the answer that, if true, would force Inara's conclusion to be true. Here, unlike a Necessary Assumption question, there is no limit on the strength or absoluteness of the correct answer. In fact, the bigger the better. If Inara had concluded that Badger is a dick, the correct answer might be something extreme like "Everyone on Persephone is a dick" (if Badger is on Persephone) or even simply "everyone is a dick." If either of these statements were true, then Inara's conclusion would be proven. It might be useful to think of Sufficient Assumption questions as "Super-Strengthen" questions. Conversely, Necessary Assumption questions might be considered more closely related to Weaken questions, because you're picking the answer that, if false, would destroy the argument.

## Applying a Principle that is Given (Example: "Which one of the following would be a proper application of the principle stated by Niska?")

Here, all you have to do is 1) understand the principle and 2) pick the answer that conforms to the principle. Suppose Niska's principle is "I never let anyone damage my reputation without getting revenge." Incorrect answers might include people damaging Niska's reputation without Niska getting revenge, or Niska getting revenge on people who did not damage his reputation. The correct answer would most likely include someone doing something damaging to Niska's reputation, and Niska then exacting his revenge.

## Identifying a Guiding Principle (Example: "Which one of the following principles best justifies Niska's actions?")

This is the reverse of the "Applying a Principle" question discussed above. The prompt would include a story, and you would be asked to identify a principle that would "justify" or "make acceptable" Niska's actions. For example, the story might include someone damaging Niska's reputation, and Niska then getting revenge. The correct answer would say something like "It is always acceptable to get revenge if someone damages your reputation."

### Flaw (Example: "Which one of the following illustrates a flaw in Saffron's reasoning?")

With enough practice, you should get really good at these questions. They are similar to Weaken questions, in that you're asked to identify a problem with the argument. Flaw questions make actual errors of logic. Suppose Saffron had attacked the character of a speaker, rather than addressing the speaker's facts and reasoning. This is the "source attack," or "ad hominem" flaw. The same flaws appear over and over and over on the LSAT, and with practice you will start to see them coming a mile away. (You're not going to fall for the same bad logic more than two or three times, right?) There are way too many flaws to fit in this appendix, but Wikipedia's "fallacy" page is a great resource if you feel like doing some reading.

### Matching Pattern (Example: "Which one of the following arguments is most similar to the reasoning in Patience's argument above?")

These are among the most time-consuming and difficult questions on the LSAT. Most students (let's say, roughly, anyone regularly scoring 160 or below on their practice tests) should be skipping these questions and coming back to them at the end of the section if there's time. This is especially true on the extremely long Matching Pattern questions. Why would we waste our time on a question that takes up its own column on the page, when we could answer two other questions in the same amount of time? Make sure you've harvested all the low-hanging fruit before you break out the 40-foot ladder.

Because Matching Pattern questions are so tough to nail and are often time-consuming, I end up trusting my gut more than anything else. First, I read the argument carefully and see if I can get a feel for the general pattern of reasoning. Then, I ask myself if the logic in the argument is generally good or generally bad. If the logic in the argument is good, then the logic in the correct answer should also be good. If the logic is generally bad, then the logic in the correct answer should also be bad—and bad in the exact same way. If the beginning of an answer choice is wrong, I won't even bother reading the rest of it. (Example: The given argument says nothing about cause and effect, and an answer choice starts out with something about causation.) Sometimes it's impossible to be 100 percent sure that I have chosen the correct answer on a Matching Pattern question. I'm OK with that. But that's also why they're good candidates to skip.

### Matching Flaw (Example: "Which one of the following arguments is most similar to the flawed pattern of reasoning used by Patience?")

This is a slightly easier variation on the Matching Pattern question, because there is something specifically *wrong* with the argument. The correct answer will have the exact same flaw. Make sure you identify the flaw before you look at the answer choices.

### Explanation (Example: "Which of the following, if true, contributes most to an explanation of the puzzling situation described above?")

These questions are fun, because they set up a mystery and then ask you to explain that mystery. For example, the argument might go something like "*Firefly* was a bitchin' space western TV series on Fox. The show had great characters, fun stories, and a rabid fan base. Fox canceled the show after one season." Make sure you understand the mystery before looking at the answer choices. Why the hell would Fox cancel a show with so much going for it? That's the mystery.

The correct answer on an Explanation question should, obviously, *explain* that mystery. The correct answer should, ideally, make you say "Aha!" One type of common incorrect answer for an Explanation question is something simply irrelevant, like "Fox is owned by Rupert Murdoch." That's true, but it doesn't explain anything. Another type of common incorrect answer on an Explanation question will actually make the mystery even harder to understand, like "Fox executives claim to want to produce great shows." Here, the correct answer could be something like "Fox executives don't like shows with great characters." Or "Fox executives don't like fans." Or something broader, like "Fox executives are just plain stupid."

# About the Author

Nathan Fox didn't figure out what he wanted to be when he grew up until he was well past grown. He has been an undergrad economics student, a stockbroker, a half-assed computer programmer, a pro*ject* manager, a pro*duct* manager (and he can't really tell you the difference between the two), a graduate journalism student, an editor, a graduate business student, a law student, and finally an LSAT teacher. He still has nightmares about the first nine things, and loves the last thing so much that he can't believe he gets paid to do it.

He encourages you to keep searching until you find the thing that 1) you are good at, 2) you enjoy doing, and 3) you can get paid to do. There is no reason to settle for less.

# Acknowledgment

My mom, Darlene Fox, was raised in the tiny farm town of Ripon, California. She married my father the day after her 19th birthday. She had her firstborn child (yours truly) shortly after turning 21. She had her second child, my sister Melanie, shortly after turning 24. Like most girls from her place and time, my mom didn't go to college. Neither did my dad. They worked hard, they bought a home, and they poured themselves into their kids. They still live about a mile from where they first met, in kindergarten, in 1959.

But my mom has always had something special burning inside her. The best way I can put it is that she just doesn't half-ass anything. Example: When I was a kid she wanted to remodel our house on Baker Drive, so she bought a do-it-yourself planning kit with sticky walls, doors, and toilets, and she hacked together a floorplan herself. She had no training, but she did the floorplan so well that when she gave it to a draftsman to create the real blueprint, she ended up getting hired as his drafting assistant. Then, when her apprenticeship was over, she started her own drafting business, and was successful at that too.

Another example: As hand-drawing moved to computers, my mom fell out of love with drafting and decided to become a nurse. She didn't have any science background, so she had to start from square one. So when I was in high school, my mom was at Modesto Junior College taking anatomy, physiology, and chemistry with kids half her age. I slacked my way to B's, but my mom never got anything but straight A's.

She still works a few days here and there at the hospital, but she's a grandmother now. She keeps a garden, and that garden is goddamned beautiful. She keeps house, and the house is beautiful too. Her Roomba has a name, Ruby, and she watches over Ruby to make sure that the robot is doing her job properly. My mom's most important project these days is her granddaughter, Hailey Rose. Due in no small part to the influence of her Nana, Hailey is the sharpest and best-behaved 5-year-old you'd ever hope to meet.

Play a game with my mom and it'll drive you crazy. When it's her turn, she'll analyze the board as long as you'll let her, intending to make the perfect—not just good—move. Come over for Thanksgiving, and you'll help her rearrange the tables five times before the other guests arrive to make sure they're perfect. Darlene simply does not fuck around.

The fact that I was reading novels before my first day of kindergarten is my mom's doing, not my own. She read to me every day and, overall, kicked *ass* as a mom, just like she kicks ass at everything else. She's a perfectionist, and I can only hope to bring half of that intensity to my books and classes. The reason it seems like I can write a little bit is not due to talent, it's due to the fact that I can't help but check each sentence ten times to make sure it's doing its job, like my mom watching carefully over Ruby. My mom wouldn't have half-assed this book, and I hope I didn't either. I love you Mom.

# NEED A LITTLE HELP?
## Call me.

### I'M HERE TO HELP

Stop banging your head against the wall! The LSAT and law school admissions aren't as mind-boggling as you might think. If there's a type of LSAT question that's bothering you, or you're really confused by the whole "sufficient vs. necessary" thing, or you want to know how to negotiate for law school scholarships... please let me help! I'm a nerd about this stuff, and I love to show students how easy it can be. Email me any time at **nathan@foxlsat.com**, or just pick up the phone. I'm generally available to talk between 9 am and 7 pm PST.

### ONLINE LSAT COURSE

If you like my books, I think you'll love my online LSAT class. It includes the exact same tests, quizzes, and lectures as my 12-week "Extended-Length" Class in San Francisco. Students pay $1495 for the 12-week classroom experience, but the class video is yours to watch and rewatch at your own pace from anywhere in the world for just $595. All materials included. And you're always encouraged to call or email me directly if you have any questions during the course. Like I said, I'm a nerd.

**www.foxlsat.com/online-lsat-course**

*No confusing jargon, no pulled punches, no bullshit.*
LSAT made simple.

@nfox
facebook.com/FoxTestPrep
foxlsat.com/lsat-blog
linkedin.com/in/foxlsat

## CALL NATHAN TODAY
# 415-518-0630